TRIBAL RELIGION

TRIBAL RELIGION

Religious Beliefs and Practices among the Santals

J. TROISI

Foreword by
ANDRE BETEILLE

MANOHAR
2026

First published 1979
Reprinted 2000, 2020, 2021, 2022, 2023, 2024, 2025, 2026

ISBN 978-81-7304-340-6

Published by
Ajay Kumar Jain *for*
Manohar Publishers & Distributors
4753/23 Ansari Road, Daryaganj
New Delhi 110 002

Printed at
Replika Press Pvt. Ltd.

for

RICHARD AND GEORGINA TROISI
MY PARENTS
AND MY BROTHER TONY

Preface

This book has developed from a Ph. D. dissertation which was carried out in the Department of Sociology, Centre of Advanced Study in Sociology, Delhi School of Economics and submitted to the University of Delhi in 1977. I take this opportunity to express my thanks to those who have helped me in the preparation of thir work. I am deeply grateful to Professor Andre Beteille for his insightful guidance and constant encouragement in carrying out this work. If this book makes any contribution to the sociological study of religion, it is because of Professor Beteille's scholarly concern for methodological rigour and systematic analysis of the relationship between religion and the processes of social and cultural change in tribal society and, in particular, that of the Santals.

I am also particularly indebted to Dr Alfred de Souza, Director of Research and Publication at the Indian Social Institute for his valued suggestions and criticisms both in the initial stages and also in the final editing of this study. I recall with deep gratitude the hospitality and generous cooperation extended to me by the people of Pangro, especially by Smt. Dulari Marandi, whose house was a second home for me. During the period I lived with them I experienced their warm friendship and their readiness to help me to understand them. Had they not enlightened me, I would have missed the significance of many aspects of their religion, culture and social organisation.

I acknowledge the financial support which I received as Research Fellow from the University Grants Commission during the course of my research. Finally, I am also grateful to the Director and staff of the Indian Social Institute for their interest and support, and to Mr. Roshan Lal Kalra and Mrs. Mini Mull for efficient secreterial assistance.

Indian Social Institute
15 October 1978

Joseph Troisi

Foreword

India's tribal population provides an important and interesting component to its many-faceted society and culture. Though the tribal people comprise less than 7 per cent of the population of the country, with a strength of over 40 million persons, they are numerically as well as culturally a significant category. How far India will succeed in integrating its tribal people into its wider society and culture without requiring them to abandon their distinctive ways of life, only time can tell; but the outcome of this venture will be as good a measure as any of the new India's success in preserving the best that was in the old.

India's tribal population is not only very large, it is also very diverse. There are more than four hundred tribes, located in different geographical areas, speaking a variety of languages and engaged in several types of productive activity. The diversity of tribal India reflects in a way the diversity of the country as a whole. Conversely, the four hundred or more tribes inhabiting the different parts of the country constitute some kind of a unity only in so far as India itself constitutes a unity. The Mundas, the Juangs and the Bhils are not merely tribal people: they are tribal people who have been associated with a particular historical tradition and now co-exist in the context of a particular political economy.

The Santals occupy a pre-eminent position among the tribal people of India. They are the largest of the Indian tribes, with a population of over three and a half million people. Although their homeland is in and around the Santal Parganas district of Bihar, they have moved far and wide, and there are now over a million Santals in the state of West Bengal. They have also a colourful history, and the Santal Rebellion of 1855-57 has become a legend, a legend that is treasured by tribal as well as non-tribal people.

The tribes of eastern India were among the first to attract the attention of social anthropologists, both Indian and foreign, when the subject became established as an academic discipline in the country more than fifty years ago. Since then social anthropologists have extended their interests to other sections of Indian society, and in recent years tribal studies have, if anything, suffered a certain neglect. This study of Santal religion by Dr Troisi places itself squarely within the tradition of research established by scholars like S.C. Roy and J.H. Hutton, and will be welcomed by everyone as a significant addition to the literature on tribal India.

If fieldwork is the hallmark of social anthropological research, then the fieldwork on which this study is based is exemplary. The author spent a period of over sixteen months in the area in which he did his fieldwork, living with the Santals as one among them. He learnt their language, and participated not only in every major religious ceremony but also in the ordinary round of everyday activities. It was only by identifying himself closely with the Santal way of life—by transforming himself from Joe Troisi to Joe Marandi—that he was able to amass the wealth of material on which this study is based.

Nor is the study based solely on data collected by the author himself in the field. The Santals are not an unknown people inhabiting a remote corner of the earth. A long line of missionaries, administrators and scholars have lived among the Santals and written about them. Dr Troisi has made extensive use of the published material, in more than one language, on the people he has investigated in the field. Since the earliest published material on the Santals goes back a century in time, the author has been able to draw attention to some of the changes that have taken place between then and now. Also, he has used this published material critically, pointing to inadequacies and inconsistencies in it.

Perhaps even more important than Dr Troisi's detailed

knowledge of the people he has studied is his deep sympathy for them. Himself a Roman Catholic, he is well aware of the difference in orientation between his religion and theirs. But he has not allowed his faith to obscure his appreciation of the Santal way of life. Rather, he has put his own religious sensibilities to use in exploring the inner recesses of Santal religion and in explaining its nature and significance to his readers.

Dr Troisi, in my view, wisely avoids giving a label to Santal religion. He considers labels such as "animism" and "bongaism" proposed by earlier writers, and finds them to be unsatisfactory, Far too many people have dealt with tribal religions with the main objective of fitting them into this or that theoretical scheme. In this sense Dr Troisi does not have any theoretical axe to grind. Rather, he has tried to understand Santal religion on its own terms, and in its relations with other religions, particularly Hinduism. A notable feature of the study is that where similar religious traits are found among the Santals and the Hindus, the author does not automatically conclude that the former have borrowed them from the latter; it is at least plausible that the flow might sometimes have been in the opposite direction.

Although the focus of this study is on religion, it is based on an understanding of Santal life as a whole. Dr. Troisi spent most of his time with the Santals in a single village, observing and participating in the religious activities of the people in their various spheres of life. Thus we get from this study a fair idea of the major groups and categories of Santal society, and of the economic and other institutions that hold them together. This way of looking at Santal religion reveals the extent to which it is a living thing. Dr Troisi is to be congratulated for using his scholarship and his sympathies in bringing to life an important segment of Indian society and culture.

Cambridge, Andre Beteille
30 October 1978

Contents

Tables

Maps

Diagram

Chapter I

Introduction

Religion is the term generally used to describe man's relation to the supernatural powers and the various organised systems of belief and worship in which these relations have been expressed. There are no peoples, however primitive, who are without religion. Religion interacts significantly with other cultural institutions to such an extent that no social phenomenon presents a larger range of expression and implication.

The phenomenon of religion is so complex and yet so intriguing that it has been studied by scholars from various disciplines. Philosophers have studied its meaning and have tried to relate it to human nature and the ultimate cause of everything. Psychologists have tried to find why man is religious. Historians have studied its origin, growth and change. Anthropologists and sociologists were particularly interested in the study of religion, realising that it fulfils an important role in every society. I shall now give a brief historical perspective of the various sociological studies or religion in primitive societies, pointing out their salient features.

Many sociologists and social anthropologists of the nineteenth and early twentieth century made the study of religion the central focus of interest in their more general conceptions of social and cultural life. Evans-Pritchard classifies the various theories of primitive religion into two major groups, psychological and sociological, though he points out that 'some writers fall between these headings or come under more than one of them' (1965:4). From another point of view, studies in the sociology of primitive religion from the nineteenth century onwards reveal two major trends, evolutionism and functionalism. The evolutionist tendency dominated largely the nineteenth century and the functionalist the first part of the twentieth. It must be admitted, however, that these tendencies are not mutually exclusive. For example, though Spencer propounded the theory of social evolution, it also included elements which were later associated with the theory of functionalism. On the other hand, Durkheim, though primarily concerned with functionalism, did not completely exclude the evolutionistic and historical assumptions. It should also be noted that even among the exponents of the functionalist theory, there are differences of approach.

The social anthropologists and sociologists who had adopted evolutionist perspectives tried to account for religious phenomena primarily in terms of religious belief. This gave rise to a number of theories regarding the origin of religion. Broadly speaking, two lines of argument were put forward, one stressing the intellectual aspect and the other, the emotional. Following Evans-Pritchard (1965:4), we shall use Wilhelm Schmidt's terminology in describing the first approach as intellectualist and the second as emotionalist.

The main proponents of the intellectualist approach were Spencer and Tylor. They explained religious beliefs in primitive societies as an intellectual attempt on the part of primitive man to understand natural phenomena and biological events.[1] Both Spencer's theory of 'manism' or ancestor worship and Tylor's theory of animism 'might be regarded as two versions of a dream theory of the origin of religion' (Evans-Pritchard, 1965:25). Primitive man, according to them, as a result of his reflection on various natural phenomena and on biological

[1]See Herbert Spencer, *The Principles of Sociology* 3 vols, London: William and Norgate, 1876-1896; E.B. Tylor, *Primitive Culture*, Vol. 1, New York: G.B. Putnam's Sons, 1920, 6th edition. According to both these authors, primitive men essentially thought out certain notions, came to certain conclusions and instituted practices based on what they had thought out. In this manner, beliefs are primary. Action or ritual only followed on belief.

facts such as sleep, trances, illness and death, on the one hand, and dreams and visions, on the other, deduced the existence of duality in his own nature.

In Tylor's view, since primitive man regarded other things to be like himself, by analogy he posited the existence of a soul not only in living creatures but also in inanimate objects. Man realised that the soul, the principle of life, survives the body and has physical power. After death the ghost-souls become spirits and these in turn are first admired and then worshipped by living men. According to Spencer, the origin of religion is to be found in the belief in ghosts rather than in souls. Death is seen as a temporary absence of the ghost from the body and re-animation, the belief in the return of the ghost to the deceased body, is one of the earliest forms of religion. When it became clear that death was a permanent departure, primitive man concluded that the ghost must inhabit another world. In time, the idea of ancestral ghosts developed into an idea of gods who needed to be propitiated and worshipped. By analogy, animals, plants and material objects were also deemed to have indwelling spirits, and to be the haunts of human ghosts.[2]

The emotionalist approach, on the other hand, rested on the claim that primitive man's belief in spiritual phenomena arose out of feelings of awe, wonder, fear, respect and admiration aroused by such natural entities as mountains and the sun or such natural occurrences as storms. Following this line of thought, Marett posited a pre-animistic stage where a belief in 'mana' prevailed.[3] What was common to most nineteenth century evolutionists was the assumption that primitive religion arose out of ignorance and intellectual inadequacy and, therefore, would not last for ever. Though they emphasised the social usefulness of various religions, they looked at them as bodies of erroneous beliefs and illusory practices.

An alternative approach to the study of religion was

[2]Commenting on Spencer's theorising, Pareto points out that Spencer made 'primitive man like a modern scientist working in a laboratory to frame a theory'. *The Mind and Society*, Vol. 1, New York: Harcourt, Brace, 1935, p. 192.

[3]See R.R. Marett, *The Threshold of Religion*, London: Methuen, 1900.

influenced by what is called the functional theory according to which society is made up of interdependent social institutions in such a way that changes in one affect the others and the whole. The main problem for the functionalists was to explain the contribution which each institution makes towards maintaining the social system in existence. Thus in the field of sociology of religion, the adherents of the Functionalist school like Durkheim, Radcliffe-Brown, Malinowski and Evans-Pritchard attempted to show that religion is functional to social cohesion and solidarity of society.

The main protagonist of functionalism in the sociology of religion was Emile Durkheim. In his attempt to establish a general theory regarding the nature and function of religion in human society he was influenced among others by the ideas of Fustel de Coulanges and Robertson Smith.[4] He started by saying that, in view of its endurance and universality, religion had to be something real that had some social value and was not merely the product of false reasoning or mere fantasy under emotional stress. Emphasising the social meaning of religion, Durkheim sought its origin on the social rather than on the individual psychological or natural level. He proceeded to adopt two criteria which he assumed would coincide: (*i*) the communal organisation of men for the community cult;[5] and (*ii*) the dichotomous relation between the sacred and the profane.[6] Basing himself on writings about various Australian aborigines, especially on the Arunta tribe of Central Australia whose

[4]Fustel de Coulanges claimed that religion was the prime cause of everything that was foremost in the social, political and intellectual life of Ancient Greece and Rome. Having studied the custom of sacrifice among the Semitic and in particular the Hebrew religion, Robertson Smith built up his theory that religion was primarily social in nature having the social function of strengthening group integration.

[5]Contrary to the utilitarian theory that the psychology of the individual could account for the development of society, Durkheim emphasised the necessity of a common commitment to a common set of values—what he called the collective conscience.

[6]According to him, while the profane referred to everyday life experience, the sacred evoked an attitude of awe and reverence. Religion, in turn was the attitude characteristic of this sacred kind of mxperience and was concerned, through beliefs and practices, with eaintaining the radical segregation of the sacred from the profane.

chief cult was that of the clan totem, he showed how this totemic ritual at which the community gathered, gave rise to a collective effervescence.[7] This emotion expressed by the ritual was projected on to the totem which, thereby, became sacred for that group. He thus regarded the expressive crowd as the key to primitive religion and, therefore, saw the object and cause of religion to be society.[8]

The worship of god was seen as the disguised worship of society on which each member depended. From this followed the function of religion in society. He saw religion as a major factor making for social solidarity, cohesion and integration within a given social structure. Through religious ritual, society reaffirmed itself in a symbolic acting-out of its attitudes. By strengthening these commonly-held attitudes, society itself was strengthened.

Durkheim can be seen as a model of the 'circular reaction' functionalist in the sense that according to him religion produced by the collective excitement, in its turn reinfluenced the group in a circular reaction. Thus, religion both derives from social solidarity and strengthens it. This led Durkheim to the generalisation that, in spite of change, no society can fail to generate a religion and no religion can fail to strengthen its specific society. In contrast to this, magic was considered as something antithetical to collective solidarity and, therefore, hostile to society. Though much of Durkheim's theory, especially its explanation of the cause of religion, has been criticised by various scholars, its functional analysis has had enormous influence in terms of general assertions regarding the social significance of religion.[9] Similarly, his emphasis on

[7]Durkheim maintained the religious nature of totemism at a time when most scholars had already discarded the idea of there being any connection between religion and totemism. Furthermore, the information which Durkheim used was considered unreliable. The Arunta tribe studied by Spencer and Gillen and by Strehlow proved atypical.

[8]Unlike Fustel de Coulanges' view that society is determined by religion, Durkheim said religion is the product of society.

[9]One of the criticisms levied against Durkheim is that the division of all things into two categories which are so dichotomously related cannot be held. Fieldwork showed the need of another category—the mundane. It is also difficult to understand how religion can be

religious practice has been important since it diverted attention from the purely ethnographic aspects of religion.

Many post-Durkheimian scholars, while accepting the function of religion proposed by Durkheim, rejected his view that the collective effervescence which ensued on crowd gatherings was the cause of religion. Thus for example, Malinowski, one of the founders of British functionalism, conceived of religion as arising from basic human needs and predicaments. In the light of his in-depth study of the Trobriand Islanders, he argued that both magic and religion arose from emotional stress and anxiety in the face of difficulties and uncertainties.[10] Primitive religion had a survival value, helping, as it did, individuals and groups to meet their biological and psychological needs, the demands of existence, so as to emerge victorious in their struggles on earth, and to face the future after death with confidence. In other words, religion sacralises and guides human beings through their earthly crises. Religious ritual is also a public statement of religious dogma, which in turn contains the value structure, namely, the social values, social rights and obligations, upon which the proper functioning of society depends. Malinowski argued that it is essential, especially in primitive societies, for the society's doctrines to be regularly acted out in order to ensure their preservation and transmission to succeeding generations. He disagreed with Durkheim's view of magic as being necessarily anti-social and though he did not deny the fact that magic can be used in pursuit of conflicting individual interests, he showed that magic, like religion, is socially conservative in its effects. Magic supplements man's practical knowledge and thereby enhances his confidence, especially in times when uncertainty is high and where important social values are involved.

regarded as the social, pure and simple. Several sociologists dismiss Durkheim's theory that the social order is the only referent of symbols. According to them the empirical representatives could be god, mankind, etc. Moreover, a great deal of belief and religious inspiration could be traced back to solitary experiences of man.

[10]Malinowski was of the opinion that a distinction was to be made between social collaboration for the enactment of a belief on the one hand, and the creation of the belief, on the other, (1954: 63).

One of the criticisms levied against Malinowski was that his functionalism was purposive rather than relational. More bent on showing how everything fits together, he failed to distinguish clearly between psychological and social factors. With his attention fixed more on the individual rather than on society, he was concerned only with what actions do than with what they say. Thus, his analysis of society, considered as a structure of relationships, remains superficial.[11]

Radcliffe-Brown, who elaborated many ideas that were implicit in Durkheim, concentrated not only on how religion, as expressed in its rituals, has a useful function in ordering society but emphasised the fact that this function is 'the essential and ultimate reason for their existence' (1959). Following Robertson Smith, Loisy, and various Chinese philosophers, he stressed the view that rituals are the most important aspect of religion, beliefs being secondary. His theory is that religion is an essential part of the constitution of a society enabling its members to live together in an orderly social way.[12] He adopted the working hypothesis that the existence and continuance of an orderly social life depended on the presence of collective sentiments in the minds of the individual members. These in turn regulate the conduct of each individual, in conformity with the needs of society. In a society rituals are the symbolic expressions of these collective sentiments and in this way 'regulate, maintain and transmit from one generation to another sentiments on which the constitution of the society depends' (1959:157). He advocated a close correspondence between the form of religion and the form of the social structure.[13] He was interested in testing the hypothesis regarding the correspondence between religion and the manner in which a society is constituted by a comparative study of various societies. As a

[11]Leach remarks that, 'when Malinowski tells us what is the function of this or that activity, he in fact relies entirely on his own intuition' (1965: Vol. 1, XVII).

[12]'Amongst the fundamental conditions that must be fulfilled if human beings are to live together in society is the existence of this thing that we call religion' (1964: 406).

[13]As societies differ from one another in their structure and constitution, they also have different systems of collective sentiments and, as a result, have different forms of religion.

result of fieldwork among the Andaman Islanders, he thought he had established a close correlation between lineage structure and ancestral worship, admitting that it existed only where lineages operated.

Another important scholar in the analysis of primitive religion is Evans-Pritchard. Like his predecessors, he attacked those theories which explained religion and magic as fantasy or illusion. He showed how many sociologists and social anthropologists who adopted the evolutionist perspective were only armchair anthropologists who applied their own cultural criteria of truth to quite different systems of thought and action. He criticised especially the analysis of belief in isolation from practice, and emphasised the importance of analysing religious facts as a whole and in relation to other institutional systems of society. In his criticism of Durkheim's view that religion is the social, pure and simple, he remarked that 'It was Durkheim and not the savage who made society into a god' (1956:313).

He tried to show the reasonableness of a primitive system of thought by analysing religion among the Nuer and magic and witchcraft among the Azande.[14] The two societies differed in their social structure, economy and magico-religion. Basic to the Nuer religious thinking was the concept of 'spirit' used of God as the creator, unseen, disembodied and universal, and also of a vast range of spirits inhabiting the world. Among the Nuer there was no magical mode of thought operating alongside the 'spirit' mode. The systematising of all experience in terms of 'spirit' seems to have made magical thinking unnecessary. In comparison, among the Azande, though there was a vague belief in a 'Supreme Being' which was never expressed in ritual, magic, as revealed in witchcraft, sorcery and oracular divination, occupied a very important role. The results of these two studies add weight to Evans-Pritchard's emphasis on the need for comparative studies of different societies.

In India, which abounds with innumerable tribal societies, various scholars have studied the religious aspect of these cultures. The pioneers were mostly European travellers,

[14]Evans-Pritchard, E.E., *Witchcraft, Oracles and Magic among the Azande*, Oxford: Clarendon Press, 1937; *Nuer Religion*, Oxford: Clarendon Press, 1956.

missionaries, natural historians and humanistic scholars. These were mainly interested in recording ethnic beliefs and rituals. The various Census Reports also contain a lot of ethnographic records on different tribal religious customs. Perhaps the first monograph on tribal religion is the one by P. Dehon on the religion and customs of the Oraons.[15] S.C. Roy's *Oraon Religion and Customs* (1928) may be considered as the first full-length study of a particular tribal religion. Though his other ethnographic studies on the Mundas (1912), the Birhors (1925)[16] and the Kharia (1937) do not deal exclusively with the religion of these three tribes, they contain a lot of invaluable material on their religious beliefs and customs. In his book, *A Tribe in Transition: A Study in Culture Pattern* (1937), Majumdar coined the term 'Bongaism' to describe the religion of the Hos.[17] In his full-length study of Saora religion (1925), Elwin supports the concept of 'Spiritism' suggested earlier by S.C. Roy (1928) to describe the religion of this tribe of Orissa. Vidyarthi (1963) deals with the Malers' approach to supernaturalism in his book, *The Maler: A Study in Nature-Man-Spirit Complex of a Hill Tribe in Bihar*.

Among the various articles written exclusively on tribal beliefs and customs, there is one by J.K. Bose in which he provides an ethnographic description of the religion of the Aimol Kukis. G. Ray *et al.*, examine various religious beliefs among the Hos. Furer-Haimendorf describes the cult of the clan gods among the Raj Gonds of Hyderabad.[18] In a later article (1953), he analyses various tribal beliefs regarding the nature of after-life. Friend-Pereira studies the nature of

[15]Dehon, P., 'Religion and Customs of the Uraons', *Memoirs of the Asiatic Society of Bengal*, Calcutta, 1, 1906, pp. 121-81.

[16]Roy, Sarat Chandra, *The Birhor: A Little Known Jungle Tribe of Chotanagpur*, Ranchi: Man in India Office, 1925.

[17]He further elaborated this concept in a later work, *The Affairs of a Tribe: A Study in Tribal Dynamics*, Lucknow: Universal Publishers Ltd., 1950.

[18]Bose, J.K., 'The Religion of the Aimol Kukis', *Man in India*, Ranchi, 14(1), Jan.-Mar. 1934, pp. 1-14; Ray, G., Chattopadhyay, G., Banerjee, B., 'Religious beliefs of the Hos', *Man in India*, Ranchi, 34(4), Oct.-Dec. 1954, pp. 288-300; Furer-Haimendorf, Christoph von, 'The Cult of the Clan Gods among the Raj Gonds of Hyderabad', *Man in India*, Ranchi, 15(3), Sept. 1945, pp. 149-86.

totemism among the Khonds, while S.C. Roy describes the same phenomenon among the Oraons and the Asurs.[19] Ferreira studies the evidence of totemism among various tribes of India.[20]

N.K. Bose in his article 'Hindu method of Tribal Absorption' indicates how the acculturation of Hindu religious beliefs and practices by different tribal groups has followed an economic and power gradient.[21] S.L. Kalia (1961) examines the processes of Sanskritisation and Tribalisation among various tribes of Madhya Pradesh. Sahay discusses various trends of Sanskritisation among the Oraons and the Parahiyas of Lolki.[22] According to Sachchidananda, Vaishnavism has had considerable influence over the Mundas and the Oraons. He also discusses the tribe-caste continuum among the Gonds in Bihar.[23]

Christianity has, since the last century, been an important factor in tribal areas. S.C. Roy describes in great detail the

[19]Friend-Pereira, J.E., 'Totemism among the Khonds', *Journal of the Asiatic Society of Bengal*, Calcutta, 73, Pt. 1, 1904, pp. 39-56; Roy, Sarat Chandra, 'Probable Traces of Totem Worship among the Oraons', *Journal of the Bihar and Orissa Research Society*, Patna, 1(1), Sept. 1915, pp. 53-6; 'A Note on Totemism among the Asurs', *Journal of the Bihar and Orissa Research Society*, Patna, 3(4), Dec. 1917, pp. 567-71.

[20]Ferreira, John V., *Totemism in India*, Bombay: Oxford University Press, 1965.

[21]Bose, N.K., 'The Hindu Method of Tribal Absorption', *Science and Culture*, Calcutta, 7(4), Oct. 1941, pp. 188-94.

[22]Sahay, K.N., 'Trends of Sanskritisation among the Oraons', *Bulletin of the Bihar Tribal Research Institute*, Ranchi, 4(2), Sept. 1962; 'A Study in the Process of Transformation from Tribes to Caste: Parahiyas of Lolki: A Case Study', *Journal of Social Research*, Ranchi, 10(1), Mar. 1967, pp. 64-89.

[23]Sachchidananda, *Culture Change in Tribal Bihar*, Calcutta: Bookland (P) Ltd., 1964; 'Tribe-Caste Continuum: A Case Study of the Gond in Bihar', *Anthropos*, Freiburg, 65, 1970, pp. 973-97.

See also Sinha, Surajit, 'The Media and Nature of Hindu-Bhumij Interactions', *Journal of the Asiatic Society (Letters and Science)*, Calcutta, 23, 1957, pp. 23-37; 'Tribe-Caste and Tribe-Peasant Continuum in Central India', *Man in India*, Ranchi, 45(1), Jan.-Mar., 1965, pp. 57-83; Srivastava, S.K., *The Tharus—A Study in Culture Dynamics*, Agra: Agra University Press, 1958; Patnaik, N., 'From Tribe to Caste: The Juangs of Orissa', *Economic and Political Weekly*, Bombay, 15(18), May 4, 1963, pp. 741-2; Berreman, G.D., 'Brahmins and Shamans in Pahari Religions', in E.B., Harper (ed.), *Aspects of Religion in South Asia*, Seattle: Washington University Press, 1964, pp. 53-69.

work done by Christian missionaries among the Mundas. The work of Christian missionaries among some tribes of Assam is described by L.M. Shrikant.[24] K.N. Sahay analyses the impact of Christian missionaries on the Oraons of Ranchi.[25] In a later study he shows how Christianity has been an important factor of cultural change among tribals.[26] Jyoti Sen traces the course of Christianity in her study of community development in Chotanagpur.[27] K.T. Paul, and Mohapatra *et al.*, analyse the implications of tribal conversion to Christianity.[28]

There have been a number of revitalisation movements in tribal India. S.C. Roy describes the Birsa Movement among the Mundas. He also analyses the various Bhagat Movements among the Oraons (1928). The Birsa Movement is also described in depth in a full-length study by K. Suresh Singh.[29] Jay examines various nativistic and reformist movements among the Mundas, Bhumij and Oraons.[30] Fuchs (1965) makes a comprehensive survey of the published literature on the messianic movements among tribal and peasant societies.

Radcliffe-Brown's study on the Andaman Islanders (1922) may be regarded as the first structural-functional approach to the interpretation of the religion of a tribal group in India. Since the last decade, a number of ethnographic monographs describing the relation between different tribal religions and their

[24]Shrikant, L.M., 'Work of Christian Missionaries in Assam Tribes', *Vanyajati*, Delhi, 2(1), Jan. 1954.

[25]Sahay, K.N., 'Christianity and Cultural Processes among the Oraon of Ranchi', in L.P., Vidyarthi, (ed.), *Aspects of Religion in Indian Society*, Meerut: Kedar Nath Ram Nath, 1961, pp. 323-40.

[26]Sahay, K.N.. 'Christianity as an Agency of Tribal Welfare in India', in L.P., Vidyarthi, (ed.), *Applied Anthropology*, Allahabad: Kitab Mahal, 1967.

[27]Sen, Jyoti, *Community Development in Chotanagpur*, Calcutta: Asiatic Society, 1968.

[28]Paul, K.T., 'How Missionaries Denationalise Indians', *International Review of Missions*, Edinburgh, 8(4), Oct. 1919; Mohapatra, Ch. P.K., and J. Swain, 'Conversion to Christianity', *Man in India*, Ranchi, 49(3), Sept. 1969, pp. 253-8. Other studies include Das, A., 'Impact of Christianity on the tribals', *Adibasi*, Orissa, 10(1), April 1968-1969, pp. 87-96; F. de Sa, *Crisis in Chotanagpur*, Bangalore: R.K. Murthy, 1975.

[29]Singh, Kumar Suresh, *Dust Storm and Hanging Mist. Study of Birsa Munda and his Movement*, Calcutta: Firma K.L. Mukhopadhyaya, 1966.

[30]Jay, Edward J., 'Revitalisation Movements in Tribal India', in L.P.,

social structure have been published by the Anthropological Survey of India.[31]

OBJECTIVES OF THE STUDY

The importance of religion in understanding culture and society cannot be overemphasised. It is recognised that religion is a binding force among individual members in a society. This, as Radcliffe-Brown remarks, is perhaps a truism. For a sociologist, however, it is important to show how this is done in a particular society. In this light, the present study is concerned with examining the social function of religion in a particular society, namely, Santal society. On the basis of empirical data it will be shown how Santal religion, as manifested and expressed in its beliefs and practices, contributes to the existence and maintenance of Santal society. In doing this, it is hoped that this empirical study may become part of that 'systematic comparison' of religions of diverse types and in diverse societies which Radcliffe-Brown believed would make it 'possible to establish a general theory of the nature of religions and their role in social development' (1959:169).

The object of observation and analysis is not religion as a body of doctrine or a mere mental force making for a more highly organised attitude of mind, but religion as manifested and expressed in its beliefs and rituals which, in turn, are invariant factors in all religions. Every religion has some supernatural objects of belief, but religions differ on this point in their orientation. This is where particular beliefs and particular rituals become variant factors. In other words, the beliefs and rituals of one society differ from the beliefs and rituals of another society. As expressive actions of behaviour, rituals are symbolic and as such are not arbitrary but appropriate to a

Vidyarthi, (ed.), *Aspects of Religion in Indian Society*, Meerut: Kedar Nath Ram Nath, 1961, pp. 282-315.

[31]Among these monographs we find Banerjee, S., *Ethnographic Study of the Kuvi-Kandha*, Memoir No. 21, Calcutta: Anthropological Survey of India, 1968; Hajra, D., *The Dorlas of Bastar*, Memoir No. 16, Calcutta: Anthropological Survey of India, 1970; Nandi, S., *et al.*, *Life and Culture of the Mala Ulladan*, Memoir No. 26, Calcutta: Anthropological Survey of India, 1971; Guha, Uma, *et al.*, *The Didayi*, Memoir No. 23, Calcutta: Anthropological Survey of India, 1972.

given culture. This study proposes to show how Santal religious beliefs and rituals shape the behaviour of the Santals and their outlook on life. The Santals, in other words, know who they are because their lives are given meanings as they are lived within the context of their social framework.

Although the Santals have had no written records of their own, a great deal has been written about them.[32] The earliest works on this tribe were ethnographic accounts collected by travellers, missionaries and British administrators. The first book on the Santals, published in 1867, was titled *Sonthalia and the Sonthals*. The author, E.G. Man, was an Assistant Commissioner in the newly formed district of Santal Parganas. The works of other administrators such as Carstairs, O'Malley, Hunter and Archer contain very good accounts of the Santals, their land, customs and habits. But it is the Christian missionaries who have left us the greatest body of invaluable data on the Santals. They were the first to take active interest in the Santal language and culture.

It is not possible here to mention the names of all the missionaries whose works have helped in promoting a better understanding of Santal culture. Mention, however, must be made of Lars Olsen Skrefsrud and Paul Olaf Bodding. The former's book on the traditions and institutions of the Santals published in Santali in 1887 is regarded as authoritative and, in fact, is frequently referred to in law courts of the Santal area whenever the Santals' customs are in dispute. In the course of more than thirty years passed in Santal Parganas, Bodding published more than twenty-five works on the Santals, including two grammars and a five-volume dictionary. It is interesting to note that most of the studies by foreign scholars were done before India became independent in August 1947, while most of the studies by Indian scholars were done after independence.[33]

[32]In his classified and annotated bibliography on the Santals, Troisi (1975) lists 487 entries of books, monographs, articles and reports on the Santals written up to 1975.

[33]Thus, prior to August 1947, sixty-two books and eighty-three articles dealing with the Santals either exclusively or in part, were written by foreign scholars, while after August 1947 only thirteen books and twelve articles on the Santals were published by foreign scholars. On the other hand, prior to independence, Indian scholars had published

No less than 283 studies by foreign and Indian scholars have been written exclusively on the Santals. Among these, thirty-five articles deal exclusively with one or the other aspect of Santal religious beliefs and practices, such as witchcraft, magic, festivals, spirits, etc. As can be expected, a number of valuable references can be found to various aspects of Santal religion in the other studies.[34] Thus, in two of his monographs on *The Santals and Disease* (1925) and *Santal Medicine* (1927),[35] Bodding discusses the various beliefs and rituals connected with the origin and cure of disease. Orans (1965) discovered a 'nativistic' movement among the Santal industrial workers at Jamshedpur arising out of their political solidarity drive. In his study, *The Santal: A Study in Culture-Change* (1956), Nabendu Datta-Majumder, who studied four Santal villages near Santiniketan, West Bengal, shows that, though all aspects of Santal life have been affected by contact with alien peoples, the degree of change is least in the religious sphere.

So far, however, no full-length study dealing exclusively and in a systematic way with all the aspects of Santal religion has been made. The present study attempts to fill this gap. Based on empirical data and taking into account the existing literature on the subject, it provides a systematic and comprehensive sociological description of Santal religion as manifested in its beliefs and practices. This study has also the advantage of having been conducted in the *Damin-i-koh,* the heart of the Santal homeland. Hardly any in-depth studies of the Santals have been conducted in this area.[36] It is here, however, that the Santals live in an environment in which they are able to organise their social and cultural life in keeping with the

eleven books and forty-nine articles which studied the Santals either exclusively or in part, and forty-five books and 163 articles after independence.

[34]The Census Reports, District Gazetteers and Census Handbooks, and various books on tribals in general, also contain a certain amount of data on Santal religion and customs. For an exhaustive listing of such studies see Troisi (1976).

[35]Bodding, Paul Olaf, 'Santal Medicine', *Memoirs of the Asiatic Society of Bengal*, Calcutta, 10(2), 1927, pp. 133-426.

[36]Strictly speaking, only two books and eight articles deal exclusively with the Santals of the *Domin-i-koh*. See Troisi (1976).

pristine forms of their religious beliefs and to observe their religious rituals and ceremonies in relative freedom from external constraints. As a result, one is in a better position to observe and study the close correspondence between Santal religion and the manner in which Santal society is constituted.

The sociological study of religion in the context of an Indian village was initiated by M.N. Srinivas in his book *Religion and Society Among the Coorgs of South India* (1952). This was followed by a number of village studies on religion in various parts of India. The studies by Marriott, Mathur, Gumperz and Pocock offer cases in point.[37] The present study is also based on intensive fieldwork conducted in Pangro, a village in the *Damin-i-koh* area of Santal Parganas district of Bihar. Pangro was selected as the focus of this study because I wanted to make detailed observations of all the aspects of Santal religion, especially their rituals and ceremonies in a convenient territorial unit rather than because I was interested in knowing more about this particular village.

As a village study, the present study raises, as the earlier village studies did, the question of the validity of generalising from data on the village level (microcosm) to society at the macro level of which the village forms a part. Srinivas (1952), Marriott, Bailey and Beteille persuasively argued that intensive village studies provide rich insights into processes taking place

[37]Marriott, McKim, *Village India. Studies in the Little Community*, Bombay: Asia Publishing House, 1955; Mathur, R.S., *Caste and Ritual in a Malwa Village*, Bombay: Asia Publishing House, 1964; Gumperz, J.J., 'Religion and Social Communication in villages of North India', in E.B. Harper, (ed.), *Religion in South Asia*, Seattle: University of Washington Press, 1964, pp. 89-97; Pocock, David, *Mind, Body and Wealth*, Oxford: Basil Blackwell, 1973. See also Sinha, Surajit, 'Changes in the Cycle of Festivals in a Bhumij Village', *Journal of Social Research*, Bihar, 1(1), Sept. 1958, pp. 24-49; Opler, Morris E., 'The Place of Religion in a North Indian Village', *Southwestern Journal of Anthropology*, New Mexico Univ., 15(3), Autumn 1959, pp. 219-26; Carstairs, G.M., 'Pattern of Religious Observances in Three Villages of Rajasthan', in L.P. Vidyarthi (ed.), *Aspects of Religion in Indian Society*, Meerut: Kedar Nath Ram Nath, 1961, pp. 59-113; Atal, Yogesh, 'The Cult of Bheru in a Mewar Village and its Vicinage', in L.P. Vidyarthi, op. cit., pp. 140-50; Singh, I.P., 'Religion in Daleke: A Sikh Village' in L.P. Vidyarthi (ed.), op. cit., pp. 191-219.

at the macro level.[38] As Srinivas, while noting the critical importance and significance of intensive village studies, points out:

> to the anthropologist the villages are invaluable observation centres where he can study in detail social processes and problems to be found occurring in many parts of India.[39]

Similarly, Beteille is of the opinion that:

> it is possible to study within the framework of a single village many forms of social relations which are of general occurrence throughout the area.[40]

He goes on to show how the norms and values which govern these social relations enjoy a certain amount of generality.

While every observation of religious beliefs and practices of the Santals of Pangro cannot be generalised, there is a certain uniformity in the religious life of the Santals over a wide geographic spread as an analysis of the studies by various scholars shows. Thus, an in-depth study of the nature and function of Santal religion in Pangro provides valuable insights into the religious norm and values which are shared by most Santals and also shows how these operate in concrete situations.

METHODOLOGY

The intensive fieldwork on which this study is based, extended over a period of sixteen months from April 1972 to January 1974. Prior to this, however, I gained a certain amount of

[38]Srinivas, M.N., 'Village Studies and their Significance', in M.N., Srinivas, *Caste in Modern India and other Essays*, Bombay: Asia Publishing House, 1962, pp. 120-135; Marriott, McKim, op. cit.; Bailey, F.G., *Caste and the Economic Frontier*, Bombay: Oxford University Press, 1958; Beteille, Andre, *Caste, Class and Power. Changing Patterns of Stratification in a Tanjore Village*, Bombay: Oxford University Press, 1966.

[39]Srinivas, M.N., op. cit., p. 134.

[40]Beteille, Andre, op. cit., p. 1.

general familiarity with Santal culture through literature on various aspects of Santal life and by visiting a number of Santal villages in the district of Santal Parganas. I also prepared myself by studying the Santal language. The fieldwork proper was carried out mainly in a village called Pangro which was selected; as mentioned earlier, because of its location in the *Damin-i-koh* area of Santal Parganas and its relative isolation from direct urban influences. The presence, within the village, of Santal Christians and, in the neighbouring villages, of a variety of Scheduled Tribes, Scheduled Castes and Muslims, permitted a comparative approach to the analysis of Santal religious and social interaction.

In his book on *Nuer Religion* (1956), Evans-Pritchard points out that a very close acquaintance with the people and their language is necessary before the anthropologist can say what the system of religious and magical thinking is. In my attempt to integrate myself in the village, I lived in a Santal household leading a life as close as possible to that of the villagers, eating and dressing in the same way they do and even working in the fields and participating in the daily routine of household jobs. My acceptance by the villagers was further facilitated by my knowledge of the language, my ability to sing a number of Santali tunes and to play the *tamak* (dancing drum) on festive occasions, and my undergoing an adapted initiation ceremony, taking the name of Joe Marandi.

For the Santals a knowledge of their language forms a basis for intimacy, and the fact that I did not make use of any interpreters proved to be a very important research tool. Dancing and singing occupy a very important role at all Santal festive occasions. As a result of their social character, dancing and singing act as an effective means of strengthening village solidarity. In this manner, my ability to take part in the singing and dancing further complemented my 'incorporation' into the life of the village. Among the Santals it is not proper to address anyone by name. Assumed kinship relations (*ato sagai*) operate and guide inter-personal behaviour in the village. For all practical and social purposes, I was considered to be the nephew of the widow with whom I was staying. On the basis of this assumed relationship, I acquired assumed kinship ties with all the villagers.

In describing the purpose of my stay and my role to the village officials and later on to the people, I described myself as a university research student come to Pangro to gather data on the Santal way of life in order to write a book. This was a fully comprehensible and readily accepted role. The people, in fact, felt rather proud that I had chosen their particular village for study and to write about their customs and traditions. This could be seen from their eagerness to explain and to show me various things associated with their way of life.

The broad purpose of my fieldwork was to collect data on Santal religious beliefs and practices. On my first field trip, however, I was not selective but collected virtually everything I could get hold of. During my second and third field trips I was more selective becoming increasingly aware of the close and constant interaction between the Santal religious beliefs and practices, and their social system.

Various research procedures were employed. In the first month, I undertook a census of the whole village after which I traced the genealogy of every household. This helped me to become more familiar with all the villagers, to gain access to their houses, and to become cognisant of the various social units—clan, subclan and household. After this, and throughout my stay in the village, much time was spent in both formal and informal interviewing of the villagers. Often, it proved virtually impossible to interview the villagers individually, owing to the fact that other villagers soon gathered around. This, however, proved to be a blessing in disguise since in a group, aided by the sharing of *thamakur* (tobacco) mixed with lime (*cun*), the villagers felt freer to speak and were more candid. It was also easier to identify the areas of agreement and patterns of reaction. In this manner additional information and valuable insights were more often than not provided.

The bulk of my time, however, was actually spent in participant-observation. In working with the villagers I not only succeeded in coming to know various things about them, their way of life and the various spheres of their culture, but came to know the people from within. I attended virtually every public event—the annual cycle of festivals, the rites and ceremonies which accompany an individual's life-cycle, and village disputes—within and outside the village. I also accompanied the villagers whenever they attended any festival or ceremony outside the village and whenever they went to the market place on Sundays. Though my marksmanship was never something I could boast of, I took part in two annual hunts or *disom sendras*. Having gained access to the villagers' houses, I was given the rare opportunity of witnessing the rituals and ceremonies which accompany the worship of *abge, orak and hapram bongas* (subclan, household and ancestral spirits). I considered this an honour since only a small group of close relatives take part in these ritual celebrations. As a result of my friendly relations with Bharat Soren, one of the *ojhas* or medicine-men of Pangro, I was invited to observe him at work whenever his services were called upon. My knowledge of Santal magic increased considerably after taking part in a month's instruction in *ojhaism*.

In many of the interviews and on other occasions, handwritten notes were taken on the spot. The people of Pangro were so co-operative in that they not only did not mind my jotting down notes during a religious or social celebration, but actually made sure that I got a good view. Whenever note-taking was not possible, as for example when I was working, I wrote notes later at home. Every two days, these were indexed according to different topics. Three prolonged visits to the field enabled me to cover all the major events and festivals associated with the seasonal cycle. Moreover, as I witnessed a number of public events more than once during my fieldwork, I had the opportunity to compare the notes taken during each event.

A danger which the sociologist of religion faces, is the fact that in studying a primitive or tribal religion, his religious and cultural background may come in the way, in the sense that he may interpret the people's beliefs not by a reference to their own mental life but by reference to his own. In my attempt to overcome this difficulty and to reach a relative degree of objectivity in describing and analysing Santal religious beliefs and practices, I did not rely merely on my own observations but always took into account the explanations given by the people themselves. To gain a wider view I questioned a number of individuals on the same interpretation given. Had the people not enlightened me, I would have missed the significance of many aspects of their religious beliefs and practices. Moreover, I followed Radcliffe-Brown's two rules of interpretation: (*i*) that 'when the same or a similar custom is practised on different occasions, it has the same or a similar meaning in all occasions'; (*ii*) On the other hand 'when different customs are practised together on one and the same occasion there is a common element in the customs' (1964:235).

PLAN OF PRESENTATION

This study of Santal religious beliefs and practices seeks to make a systematic presentation of empirical data and, at the same time, develop their theoretical implications for the sociology of religion. As already mentioned, as a social phenomenon, religion is an integral part of the social structure of a society. This is all the more true of tribal societies in which, as a result of their relatively simple technology and the low degree of differentiation in their social structure, there is a greater involvement in the religious sphere, giving religion a more important role.[41] As a result of this intimate inter-relationship between religion and the social structure of a society, neither can be fully understood unless their functions, their interdependence and their organic relations are studied and explained. To be able to understand better the role of religion in Santal social life and how it interacts with other aspects of the total social system, Chapter II presents a detailed description of the structure of Santal society and its social institutions and shows their relevance in the context of Pangro, the village selected for intensive study. The first part of Chapter II provides basic information on the Santal

[41]Primitive societies are characterised by what Durkheim called 'Mechanical solidarity' which is upheld by the sacred things of the society. Here the members share the same knowledge and experience and, therefore, accept the same rules, values and authority. See Gluckman, Max (ed.), *Essays on the Ritual of Social Relations*, Manchester: University Press, 1962; Junod, Henri A., *The Life of a South African Tribe*, New York: New Hyde Park, 1962.

tribe, their demographic characteristics, social organisation and the process of settlement in the *Damin-i-koh*. The latter part of the chapter describes the social, economic and political organisation of Santal society in Pangro. Also considered is the interaction of this village with the external economic, social and administrative elements of the wider regional culture.

Peter Berger (1969:100) notes that 'In all its manifestations, religion constitutes an inner projection of human meanings into the empty vastness of the universe'. The Santals are aware that despite their experimental knowledge and physical efforts, the course of nature is at times affected by agencies outside their sphere of control. To cope with the mysterious supernatural world, the Santals, like other tribes at the same level of culture, have evolved a system of beliefs and practices. According to them, the supernatural world is peopled with a large number of supernatural spirits called *bongas* and with a large number of impersonal supernatural powers. They are believed to shape the course of nature and of human events. Chapter III discusses the nature of these supernatural agencies and the function they have in Santal society. This chapter also examines the view of scholars and missionaries that Santal religion is a religion of terror and that all spirits are malevolent and the enemies of man.

It is only by considering religion as a mode of action as well as a system of belief that the vital meaning of ritual and belief becomes apparent. Ritual activities are the best expressions of the religious life of human groups These symbolic actions help men to enter into and reassert their social relationships with the supernatural world.[42] Similarly, the intimate relationship between the Santals and their *bongas* is correctly manifested in their various rites and ceremonies. Chapter IV describes the seasonal rites and festivals which manifest the Santals' dependence on, and fellowship with, their *bongas*. They also serve to strengthen and express the village solidarity. Since Santal religion is so intimately related to agriculture, their chief source of livelihood, special emphasis

[42]Goode, William J., *Religion among the Primitives*, London: The Free Press of Glencoe, Collier-Macmillan Ltd., 1964, p. 49.

is given to those rituals and festivals which mark every important stage in the Santal agricultural cycle.

Chapter V discusses the nature and function of the various rituals and ceremonies which, in Santal society, mark the different turning points in an individual's life-cycle—birth, initiation, marriage and death. This chapter shows how these rites and ceremonies aim at securing the active help of the benevolent spirits to ensure the safety and well-being of the individual. They are also public and collective occasions which emphasise the relations of mutual harmony between an individual and the village community.

This study would be incomplete if we were to by-pass the problem of magic which, like religion, pervades the life of the Santals. Chapter VI examines the nature and function of Santal magical beliefs and practices and discusses the actual relationship between magic and religion as perceived by the Santals. In the light of these data, certain theories regarding the relationship between magic and religion are evaluated.

On the basis of empirical data discussed in the earlier chapters, the conclusion (Chapter VII) examines the validity of classifying Santal religion as *Animism* or. *Bongaism* In addition, the problem of continuity and change of Santal religion is examined in terms of its interaction with the two major religious traditions of Hinduism and Christianity.

A select bibliography has been included. Those who wish to have a comprehensive bibliography on the Santals can refer to Troisi, J., *The Santals: A Classified and Annotated Bibliography*, Delhi: Manohar Publications, 1976.

A Santal *kulhi*-village street

The *Jaherthan* or Sacred Grove, the abode of the Santals' 'national' spirits.

The *Manjhithan*, the abode in honour of *Manjhi Haram*.

A Santal household.

Chapter II

The Setting

Since pre-historic times, India has been the homeland of a large number of ethnic groups and cultures. These communities, believed to be the earliest inhabitants of the country, are known by various names, the most extensively known term being Adivasi.[1] Many of these communities have more or less retained their separate social identity as far as their customs and regulations are concerned. Since 1891, these communities have been enumerated variously in different Census Reports. Thus we see them enumerated as people having a tribal form of religion (1891), animists (1901), tribal animists or tribal religion (1911), hill and forest tribe (1921), primitive tribe (1931), tribe (1941) and Scheduled Tribe (1951, 1961, 1971).

Not all the tribal communities in India are considered as Scheduled Tribes. This is evident from Article 342 of the Constitution of India which:

> provides for specification of tribes or tribal communities or parts of or groups within tribes or tribal communities which are to be deemed for the purposes of the Constitution

[1]Among the other popular names used to designate these communities we find the following: Vanyajati (castes of forest), Vanvasi (inhabitants of forest), Paharia (hill-dwellers), Adimjati (original communities) and Janjati (folk people).

to be Scheduled Tribes in relation to the various States and Union Territories.[2]

According to the 1951 Census, the Scheduled Tribes' population of India was 22,511,854 or 6.25 per cent of the country's total population. As a result of four Presidential Orders (1956i, 1956ii, 1959 and 1960), they numbered 29,879,249 or 6.87 per cent of the total population (Census 1961). Later, five more Presidential Orders (1961, 1966, 1967, 1968 and 1970) were issued which further added to their population. Thus, according to the 1971 Census, the Scheduled Tribes' population in India was 38,015,162 or 6.9 per cent of the total population.

DEMOGRAPHIC CHARACTERISTICS

The Santals are the largest homogeneous Scheduled Tribe in the country.[3] According to the 1971 Census they numbered 3,633,459 or 9.55 per cent of the country's Scheduled Tribes' population. This figure, however, must be accepted with some reservations. It does not include fairly large numbers of Santals to be found in certain States like Assam and Meghalaya where they are not listed as Scheduled Tribes.[4] As can be seen

[2]*The Report of the Advisory Committee on the Revision of The Lists of Scheduled Castes and Scheduled Tribes*, Government of India, Department of Social Security, 1967, p. 1. The Constitution has not expressly prescribed any principles or policy for drawing up lists of Scheduled Tribes. However, there are indications in the Constitution that extreme social, educational and economic backwardness would qualify a tribe to be included in these lists. In revising the list of Scheduled Tribes, the Advisory Committee remarked 'we have looked for the indications of primitive traits, distinctive culture, geographical isolation, shyness of contact with the community at large, and backwardness; we have considered that tribes whose members have by and large mixed up with the general population are not eligible to be in the list of Scheduled Tribes' (1967:7).

[3]Numerically, the Gonds and Bhils are larger. They are, however, very heterogeneous and, in fact, are considered to be the constituents of a group of tribes designated by a common name.

[4]Thus, although according to the *Centenary Monograph No. 10, Language Handbook of Mother Tongues, Census of India*, 1971, p. 220, there are 67,262 persons in Assam who have Santali as their mother

from the following Table, the Santals are mostly to be found in Bihar and West Bengal. They are in fact, the largest of the Scheduled Tribes of these two States, constituting 36.51 and 54.36 per cent of these States' Scheduled Tribes' population.

TABLE 2.1: STATEWISE DISTRIBUTION OF SANTAL POPULATION SHOWING THEIR PROPORTION TO THE TOTAL SCHEDULED TRIBES' POPULATION IN EACH STATE

	Total Population	*All Scheduled Tribes*	*Santals*
India	547,949,809	38,015,162	3,633,459 (9.55)*
Bihar	56,353,369	4,932,767	1,801,304 (36.51)
Orissa	21,944,615	5,071,937	452,953 (8.93)
Tripura	1,556,342	450,544	2,222 (0.4)
West Bengal	44,312,011	2,532,069	1,376,980 (54.36)

Source: *Census of India 1971*, Series 1, Paper I of 1975, 'Scheduled Castes and Scheduled Tribes', pp. 141-61.
Census of India 1971, Series 1, Paper II-A(1) 'General Population Tables', pp. 56-70.

*The figures in parenthesis indicate the percentage of the Santals to the total population in the State.

In Bihar, the Santals are mainly concentrated in the districts of Santal Parganas, Singhbhum, Hazaribagh, Dhanbad, and Purnea, (see Appendix I). In West Bengal, they are mainly to be found in the districts of Midnapore, Purulia, Burdwan, Bankura, West Dinajpur, Birbhum and Malda (see Appendix II).

tongue, they are not enumerated in the list of Scheduled Tribes in the State. The reason for this omission is given by the Advisory Committee for the revision of the lists of Scheduled Castes and Scheduled Tribes according to whom, the tea plantation tribal labourers were not to be treated as Scheduled Tribes (1967:18). Fairly large numbers of Santals are also to be found in Bangladesh and Nepal.

The name Santal, according to Skrefsrud (1968), is a corruption of Saontar. This was adopted by the Santals when they lived in the area around Saont now identified with Silda Pargana in Midnapore district of West Bengal. W.B. Oldham was of the opinion that 'Santal' is an abbreviation of 'Samantawala'. According to this author 'Samanta' is another name given to the country around Saont.[5] According to O'Malley (1910:99) 'Santal' 'is an English form adopted from Hindi which corresponds with the form "Saontar" used by the Bengali speaking peoples'. It is interesting to note that Sir John Shore, in the earliest mention of the Santals ever recorded, designated them as 'Soontars' while McPherson spelled the name as 'Saungtars'.[6] Despite this variety of names, most anthropologists agree that 'Santal' is a name given to this tribe by non-Santals. In fact, the Santals among themselves use the term *Hor* meaning man. Some, especially those living in West Bengal, use the term *Manjhi* to designate their identity.

The Santals speak an independent language known as Santali. It belongs to the Munda family of languages which Pater W. Schmidt classified as belonging to the Austro-Asiatic language group.[7] Numerically, Santali is the most important of all the Munda group of languages. It is also one of the oldest tongues of India and according to Campbell, 'has reached a much higher stage of development than any other sister language'.[8] Though many of the Santals, especially those in West Bengal, are bilingual, they are the largest tribe in India to retain an aboriginal language to the present day. They have managed to keep their language, insofar as their grammar or the agglutinating principle is concerned, astonishingly free from foreign influence. Their vocabulary, however, has met with a

[5] *Some Historical and Ethnical Aspects of Burdwan District*, Calcutta: Bengal Secretariat Press, 1894.

[6] Shore, John, 'On Some Extraordinary Facts, Customs and Practices of the Hindus', *Asiatic Researches*, Calcutta, 4, 1975, pp. 331-50; Mcpherson, H., *Note on Aboriginal Races of the Sonthal Parganas*, 1908.

[7] Schmidt, W., *Die Mon Khmer Volker, ein Bindeglied Zwischen Volkern Żentralasiens und Austronesiens*, Braunschweig, 1906.

[8] Campbell, G., *Specimens of Languages of India including those of the Aboriginal Tribes of Bengal, the Central Provinces and the Eastern Frontier*, Calcutta: Bengal Secretariat Press, 1874.

different fate. A lot of words from other languages have been adopted and adapted to Santal ideas and linguistic rules. Since the Santals have no alphabet of their own, they have adopted the Roman script, using certain diacritical marks to denote sounds differing from those which these letters have in English. This was done under the influence of Christian missionaries who were the first to take an active interest in the study of the Santal language. In fact, as early as 1852, Rev. Jeremiah Phillips, a Baptist missionary living in Orissa published in Santali *An Introduction to the Santali language*, using the Bengali script. In some parts of Orissa, the Oriya script has also been used.

Physically, the Santals are characterised by short to medium stature, dark skin, scanty beard, large mouth provided with thick lips, a broad flat nose and wavy to curly hair. Like other Mundari speaking tribes, the Santals have been designated by anthropologists as pre-Dravidians, Kolarians, Dravidians, Proto-Australoids, Nishadics and Austrics. Risley's classification of the Santals as typical examples of the pure Dravidian stock is considered by many as outdated. Various scholars have shown that the Santals differ racially from the Dravidian-speaking tribes. Pater W. Schmidt classified the Santals as Austro-Asiatics. Haddon grouped them with the pre-Dravidians. E.von Eickstedt (1935, Vol. I:38) grouped the Mundas, Hos and Santals as Austro-Asiatics. In his classification of the races which inhabit India into six main types, Guha grouped the Santals with the Proto-Australoid group since, according to him, there is a racial similarity with the aborigines of Australia. A. Von Heine-Geldern held that the Santals are a Mongoloid people. S.S. Sarkar was of the opinion that the Santals appear to possess a strong Australoid strain in addition to a Mongoloid element.[9] Though certain Mongoloid traits have been observed

[9]Haddon, A.C., *Races of Man and their Distribution*, New York: Gordon Press Publications, 1919; Guha, B.S., *An Outline of the Racial Ethnology of India*, Calcutta, 1937; Heine-Geldern, R. Von, 'Urheimat und Fruheste Wanderung Austronesier', *Anthropos*, Freiburg, 27, 1932, pp. 558-619; Sarkar, S.S., 'The Racial Affinities of the Santal', *Silver Jubilee Session of the Indian Science Congress*, Calcutta, Jan. 1938.

among the Santals, Risley and Bodding have denied the hypothesis of the Santals' Mongoloid descent.[10]

SOCIAL ORGANISATION

The Santals have a patrilineal exogamous clan organisation. The Santal myth of the origin of man and of how the twelve clans came about has been recorded, in slightly varying form, by different authors. The fullest account is the one told by Kolean and recorded by Skrefsrud (1887). Bodding (1942:3-14) translated it into English. The following account which brings out the essential features of the story, is a paraphrased version of the previously published ones.

In the beginning, a waste of waters covered the earth and there was no land. Then *Thakur*, the Supreme Being, created the beings that live in water, after which he decided to create man. He made two people of mud but the Day-horse came and trampled them to pieces. *Thakur*, then, made a goose and a gander pulling the material off from his chest. He breathed on them and they came to life.

After some time the two birds made their nest and laid two eggs in a clump of thatching grass at Hihiri Pipiri. From those two eggs two human beings, a boy and girl were born. Their names were *Pilcu Haram* and *Pilcu Budhi* which literally mean 'First Old Man' and 'First Old Woman'. One day *Maran Buru*, disguised as *Lita*, came to visit them. He showed them how to brew rice-beer. They drank till they were both drunk and then had sexual intercourse. As time passed, they had seven boys and seven girls. The father used to take the boys with him to hunt while the girls used to help their mother gather vegetables and leaves. One day, the girls went to the forest alone and finishing their work early they began playing and singing near a banyan tree. On returning from the hunt, the boys, who also were alone, were attracted by the girls' singing. They

[10]Bodding, P.O., 'Mongolian Race Marks among the Santals', *Journal of the Asiatic Society of Bengal*, Calcutta, 73(2), Pt. 3, 1904, p. 26. These different opinions have been summarised and examined by Fuchs and Ferreira who in turn classified the Santals along with the Mundas and the Hos as Austro-Asiatics (1973:29).

danced together the eldest boy choosing the eldest girl, the youngest boy the youngest girl. They paired off. Seeing this, their mother and father married them and all got children. To avoid incest, *Pilcu Haram* and *Pilcu Budhi* divided them into seven exogamous clans, so that 'a brother may not marry a sister'. The clans were Hasdak, Murmu, Kisku, Hembrom, Marandi, Soren and Tudu.

Then they went to Khoj Kaman[11] where they became very bad—'Kada bitkil lekaenako'—acting sexually like buffaloes and buffalo cows. Seeing this, *Thakur* became very angry and told them that he would destroy mankind if they did not change their ways of living. But they did not heed him and *Thakur* rained down fire for seven days and nights destroying all mankind except a couple whom he had chosen and sent to a cave at Harata mountain. Here the Santals once again increased and multiplied. Then they migrated to Sasanbeda where they stayed for a long time and where, once more, they were divided into clans. Besides the original seven clans, five more were formed: the Baske, Besra, Pauria, Core and Bedea, the last of which disappeared long ago.[12] From here they moved from one country to another till they finally reached the Campa land. Here they stayed for a long time and 'we were a great people . . . not subordinate to anyone' (Bodding 1942:10). To defend themselves against their enemies they built forts, each clan having its own fort and password.

In Campa, it is said, each clan was occupational and there were social distinctions or divisions between them.

> The Kiskus became the royal tribe under the cognomen of Kisku Raj. The Murmus became the princely tribe and were named Murmu Thakur. Hembrom was ennobled and known as Hembrom Kuar. The Soren became the soldier tribe and were named Soren Sipahi. The Marndis were

[11]Certain stories mention a number of different countries where the Santals stayed prior to their reaching Khoj Kaman.

[12]Various accounts have been written regarding the origin of the last five clans. See Bodding, P.O., *A Santal Dictionary*, Vol. 1, Oslo: A.W. Broggers Boktrykkeri, 1932, p. 209; Campbell, A., 'The Traditions of the Santals', *Journal of the Bihar and Orissa Research Society*, Patna, 2(1), March 1916, pp. 15-29.

> appointed the king's treasurers and stewards and named Marandi Kipisar. The Tudus took to music and received the title of Tudu Mandariya. There is no record of the offices conferred upon the others.[13]

These occupational distinctions, however, rapidly disappeared. At present, though certain clan members still bear the occupational appellation, there is no trace of occupational specialisation. Formerly, the members of other clans avoided marriage with the members of the Besra and the Core clans since these were regarded as somewhat inferior. Nowadays, however, all the clans enjoy the same social status. They are scattered all over the Santal territory, and every Santal village includes members of different clans.

These clans are further subdivided into a number of subclans (*khuts*), the number of which varies from clan to clan. Gausdal (1960) mentions 405 subclans. The following list, showing the number of *khuts* in each *paris* (clan), has been tabulated from Gausdal's study.

Paris		*Khut*
Hasdak		41
Murmu		65
Kisku		32
Hembrom		32
Marndi		49
Soren		46
Tudu		48
Baske		31
Besra		27
Core		18
Pauria		16
	Total	405

[13]According to Culshaw, this division on occupational basis is 'probably of comparatively recent date and may have arisen out of the need to compensate the Santals or at least certain of the clans, for their low social status in the eyes of their castes Hindu neighbours' (1949:70).

Each of these subclans has a distinctive myth regarding its origin. Some also have customs that differentiate them from the others. Thus, for example, the Sada subclans do not apply vermilion at the time of marriage nor during any sacrificial offering. Some of the Murmu subclans—the Jaher Murmus, the Nij Murmus, the Manjhi khil Murmus, the Naeke khil Murmus and the Sada Murmus—cannot build houses with four cornered roofs.[14]

The main function of the clan organisation is to regulate marriage relationships within the tribe. A Santal cannot marry a member of his own clan. If he does so, then he is an outcaste (*Bitlaha*). The prohibition was formerly more rigid in the case of intra-subclan marriage. A Santal was prohibited from marrying a girl belonging to his mother's sub-clan. The various subclans are also linked up with the worship of the *abge bongas* or subclan *bongas*. This is expressed in the Santal saying, 'Mit khutren kanale, mit khondrele', meaning 'we are of one stock, we perform sacrifices in the same circle'.[15]

MIGRATION AND SETTLEMENT

The Santals have no recorded history and as one of them told me, 'the mouth is our printed book'. Like other human beings, they have tried to explain the mysteries of creation, history and life by means of myths and legends. The needs which Santal folktales, like other folklore, serve are very important and far-reaching. They preserve tribal knowledge and give sanction to tribal customs. They emphasise standards and assert values and above all, they create solidarity and inspire confidence.

The traditions of the Santals represent them as a race wandering from one land to another. We can, in fact, summarise the first part of Santal history in four lines.

[14]For a further study of the distinguishing customs of the Santal *khuts* see Gausdal (1960); Campbell, A., 'The Traditions of the Santals', op. cit., pp. 22-23.

[15]Bodding, P.O., *A Santal Dictionary*, Vol. III, Oslo: A.W. Broggers Boktrykheri, 1935, p. 750.

Hihiri Pipiri rebon janam len
Khoj Kaman rebon khoj len
Harat rebon hara len
Sasan Beda rebon jatena ho.

We were born in Hihiri Pipiri
We were called to the Promised Kaman
We grew and multiplied at Harata
We were divided into clans at Sasan Beda.

To reach Sasan Beda, the Santals, according to their traditions, had to pass through several countries. Then, from Sasan Beda they went to Campa from where, after a long sojourn, they had to flee out of fear of having their daughters ravished by the powerful tyrant Mando Sin.

On the basis of the Santal traditions, several theories have been advanced regarding their origin. Efforts have also been made by different scholars to identify the countries, rivers, forests, etc., mentioned. In many instances, localities have been found bearing the traditional names and it has been inferred that it was here that the Santal institutions had their origin. Since, however, there is no supporting evidence from other sources, it has not been possible to offer any definite explanation.[16] Whatever their original habitat might have been, there is no doubt that by about the middle of the eighteenth century, at the beginning of British rule in India, large numbers of Santals were to be found in Chotanagpur, especially in the districts of Hazaribagh, Palamau and Singhbhum and in the neighbouring districts of Midnapore and Birbhum. There are authentic records to prove this. Thus as early as 1795, Sir John Shore spoke of the Santals in Ramgarh in Birbhum district.[17] Toward

[16]For a study of these different hypotheses see Campbell, A., 'Traditional Migration of the Santal Tribes', *The Indian Antiquary*, Bombay, 23, April 1894, pp. 103-4; Chattopadhyay, K.P., 'Santal Migration', *Proceedings of the 31st Indian Science Congress*, Delhi, Part 3, Abstracts 1944, p. 101; Waddel, L.A., 'The Traditional Migration of the Santal Tribe', *The Indian Antiquary*, Bombay, 22, Oct. 1893, pp. 294-6; O'Malley (1910); Skrefsrud (1873).

[17]Further information about the Santals at this early time is found in Sutherland, H.C., *Report on the Management of the Rajmahal Hills*, dated 8th June 1819, Dumka: Deputy Commissioner's Record Room,

the end of the eighteenth century, the Santals who were 'very expert in clearing forests and bringing them into cultivation', began to migrate to the Rajmahal Hills situated on the north-eastern side of the Chotanagpur plateau.[18]

Two reasons are given for this migration. Towards the end of the eighteenth century, many of the Chotanagpur jungles had been cleared and there was a considerable influx of population from the infertile uplands which could not support them. Second, the introduction of the Permanent Zamindari Settlement by the East India Company in 1793 'resulted in a general extension of tillage' and in the creation of a new set of landlords. These landlords began hiring Santal labourers to clear the virgin forests in the Rajmahal Hills' area so as to bring more land under cultivation. They enticed them by promising them high wages and rent-free farms. This area had been the homeland of the Mal Paharias and the Sauria Paharias, notorious robbers and cattle lifters who often raided the villages in the plains.[19] Their villages were, and still are, situated on the hill-tops. Various efforts were made by the British Government to win over these tribals and to bring them under control. For a time, the situation seemed to be in hand, but after some time the same old trouble started again.

In 1833, the Government demarcated an area surrounding the Rajmahal Hills comprising 1,366 square miles. It came to be known as the *Damin-i-koh* which literally means 'the skirts of the hills'. The idea behind this move was to declare this hill tract occupied by tribals the property of the Government.

1819; Montgomery, Martin, *Eastern India*, London, 1832; Sherwill, Walter S., 'Notes upon a Tour through the Rajmahal Hills', *Journal of the Asiatic Society of Bengal*, Calcutta, 20(7), 1851, pp. 544-606; Man (1867); Mitchell, Murray, *A Missionary's wife among the Wild Tribes of South Bengal. Extracts from the Journal of Mrs. Murray Mitchell*, London: James Nisbet, 1871, McPherson, H., '*Note on the Aboriginal Races of the Sonthal Parganas*, 1908.

[18]The Rajmahal Hill range occupies the north-eastern portion of the Santal Parganas. To the southwest it continues, more or less, along with the same range to Mandar Hill which lies thirty-two miles west of Bhagalpur. This hilly tract extends to the Ramgarh Hills in the district of Birbhum in West Bengal.

[19]Bradley Birt, F.B., *The Story of an Indian Upland*, London: Smith, Elder & Co., 1905.

The Santals were now encouraged to settle in the area. During the next fifteen years, they moved to this region in such great numbers that the population of the area increased by more than twenty-six times. Captain Walter S. Sherwill who was employed in the Government Revenue Survey of the Bihar Province, noted that while in 1838 there were about forty Santal villages in the area with a population of about 3,000, by 1851 the Santal population in the area had increased to 82,795, inhabiting 1,473 villages.[20] The *Damin-i-koh* soon became the centre of Santal life. Little did the Government think, however, that these Santals were to revolt twenty years later.

The single most important event in the history of the Santals, the rebellion of 1855-57, has become part and parcel of their consciousness. This can be seen from the number of dramas and songs celebrating this event and mythologising its leaders. The Santal rebellion was not 'a mere spasmodic outburst of the crude instincts of the semi-savage Santals', but the outcome of a 'long course of oppression silently and patiently submitted to by these unsophisticated people unaccustomed to fight for their own rights in the legitimate ways of their neighbours' (Datta: 1940:5). The rebellion came at a time when the destitution and sufferings of the Santals had reached an extremely high level because of the oppression and merciless exploitation of the money-lenders and merchants.

Writing in 1867, twelve years after the outbreak of the rebellion, E.G. Man (1867:110) concluded that four Santal grievances were chiefly responsible for the rebellion: (*i*) The rapacity of the money-lenders in their transactions with the tribals; (*ii*) the increasing misery caused by the iniquitous system of allowing personal and hereditary bondage for debt; (*iii*) unparalleled corruption and extortion of the police in aiding and abetting the *mahajans* (money-lenders); (*iv*) the impossibility for the Santals to obtain redress from the courts. There is abundant evidence, as we shall see, that Man's understanding of the rebellion was substantially correct.

We have already noted that the Santals were induced to migrate to the *Damin-i-koh* with promises which were never

[20]Sherwill, Walter S., 'Notes upon a Tour through the Rajmahal Hills', *Journal of the Asiatic Society of Bengal*, Calcutta, 20(7), 1851, pp. 544-606.

honoured. At the same time as they began occupying the *Damin*, Hindu traders and money-lenders began to infiltrate the area and when the Santals took loans, they found themselves trapped in a vicious circle of extortion from which they could not escape during their life-time.[21]

One of the devices used to exploit the Santals was the execution of bonds. There were two kinds of bondage systems—the *kamiotee* and the *harwahee*. According to the former, a man borrowed money and bound himself to work without pay for the money-lender whenever required till the loan was repaid. Under the *harwahee* system, the borrower had, in addition to personal service, to plough the money-lender's fields whenever required till the loan was repaid. It was thus practically impossible for the borrower to repay the loan because his services were required during the harvest and the other busy seasons of the year, and thus he did not have enough time to plough his own fields or work for wages. As interest was taken in advance, the debtor could never work off his debt. The debtor's children and near relatives were considered liable in the case of his death.[22] As *The Calcutta Review* reported in 1860 (pp. 510-51), the Santal thus 'saw his crops, his cattle, even himself and family appropriated for a debt which ten times paid remained an incubus upon him still'.

The Santals had made many attempts to present their grievances to the Government but were repeatedly rebuffed.[23] The courts of law gave more security to the propertied classes and, as far as the Santals were concerned, legalised the rapacity of the money-lenders. The administration in the *Damin-i-koh* area was riddled with abuses. For the puspose of revenue administration, it was under the Superintendent assisted by four *naib suzawala* who used to visit the area in order to collect

[21]Datta (1940:5).

[22]William Le Fleming Robinson who worked for the abolition of this form of slavery in Santal Parganas, reports the case of a Santal who worked the whole of his life to repay the twenty-five rupees he had borrowed. On his death, his son, and later his grandson, did the same. See George Yule, 'Report on the Santal Pergunnahs for 1858', in E.G. Man, (1867:22-7).

[23]According to *The Calcutta Review*, 'The Santals harassed by their landlords and exploited by usurers beyond endurance, could not get redress in the British courts' (1856:223-64).

rent and settle land disputes. They were notoriously corrupt. For civil and criminal cases, the Santals had to go to the courts at Deoghar or Bhagalpur. Regular access to these courts by the aggrieved Santals was extremely difficult not only because of the inconvenience of the long journey but also because of the corruption of the *amlahs* (clerks), *mukhtears* (pleaders) and peons attached to these courts. Since the Santals did not know any language other than Santali, they were forced to make use of interpreters and pleaders who were in the pay of their oppressors. In this manner while the Santal:

> found justice in the shape of the Magistrate so far off and so terribly difficult of access, he found justice nearer home in the shape of *Darogahs* and Thana Police, the authorised agents of the District Magistrate, but found it only to find it his bane (Roy Chaudhury, 1965:76).

Thus, the situation in the *Damin-i-koh* prior to the rebellion was one in which the *zamindars*, the police, the revenue and court clerks managed a combined system of extortion, and subjected the vulnerable Santals to a forcible dispossession of property, personal violence and a variety of petty tyrannies.

However, though the Santals' demands which preceded the rebellion were concerned with the improvement of their general economic situation, the question of land had a special significance for them. As Culshaw points out:

> Economic factors alone will not give a solution to the question of why the Santals rebelled.... Hunger drove them to despair but their attachment to the land provided also an emotional basis without which the rebellion might not have taken place.[24]

For the Santal, land not only provides him with economic security but is also a powerful link with his ancestors. No land is taken possession of unless the spirits approve of it. This can be seen from the number of ominous beliefs associated with the

[24]Culshaw, W.J., 'The Santal Rebellion', *Man In India*, Ranchi, 25(4), Dec. 1945, p. 219.

selection of a site for a new village.[25] For the Santals, land is thus part of their spiritual as well as economic heritage. As a result of the extortion by landlords and money-lenders, the Santals had no security in the possession of the very lands they themselves had made fit for cultivation. The *Deku* settlers, in the course of time, acquired more and more land mortgaged by the Santals.

Another important element in the complex of factors which forced the Santals to rebel, was the yearning for independence, the dream of the ancient days when they had no overlords. Thus, Sidhu and Kanhu the main leaders of the rebellion, announced that 'we will kill and make an end of all the *Deku*, rule ourselves, and whoever does not listen, show him a sword'.[26] This urge for independence reached its climax when Sidhu and Kanhu proclaimed that they had received a divine message from Suba Thakur urging them to lead the Santals in a rebellion. It is well known that religion has often acted as an important motivating force and the claim of Sidhu and Kanhu that it was God's wish that the Santals revolt against their oppressors appeared to be the spark needed to kindle the conflagration. This religious sanction gave the leaders the authority they required to be accepted by the Santals.

In spite of all this, however, the rebellion did not get under way immediately. The leaders first petitioned the local authorities to redress their grievances by regulating usury and reducing land tax (Datta, 1940:10). The British Superintendent however did not pay any heed to these complaints. The Santal leaders then approached the Commissioner and told him plainly that if he did not redress their grievances, they would do so themselves. But again nothing was done. This resulted, in 1854, in a number of dacoities, directed against the money-lenders. As was reported by a contemporary, these robberies were 'well merited reprisals for their (money-lenders') unprovoked cruelties'.[27] The authorities, however, thought otherwise, and on the complaint of the money-lenders, these outrages were treated as ordinary dacoities and the Santal ringleaders were caught, tried and convicted.

[25]Refer to Campbell (1915:213-38).
[26]Culshaw, 'The Santal Rebellion', op. cit., p. 219.
[27]*The Calcutta Review* (1956:223-64).

Finally, Sidhu and Kanhu sent emissaries to announce a meeting at Bhognadi, and on 30 June 1855, more than 30,000 Santals armed with bows and arrows began their march towards Calcutta. A police inspector, instigated by some Hindu money-lenders, tried to arrest the leaders, but this so enraged the mob that they hacked him and nine members of his platoon to pieces. The cry *Hul*! *Hul*! (Rebel! Rebel!) was now heard everywhere and the rebellion got under way. After intermittent battles lasting over a year, the rebellion was eventually crushed by the British. The Santal insurgents suffered heavy losses. The ringleaders were rounded up, summarily tried and hanged.[28]

Though the rebellion was unsuccessful, it did draw the attention of the British Government to the extent of the oppressive conditions under which the Santals were living. It convinced the Government of the necessity of adopting ameliorative judicial and administrative reforms. Thus, by the Act XXXVII of 22 December 1855, the territory in and around the *Damin-i-koh* was formed into a separate non-regulation district called Santal Parganas which was placed under the control of the Commissioner of Bhagalpur.[29]

This new district created from the districts of Bhagalpur and Birbhum, lies between 23°48¹—25°18¹ North latitude and 86°28¹—87°57¹ East longitude. It has an area of 14,129 square kilometres.[30] As can be seen from Map 2.1 the district is bounded on the north by the districts of Bhagalpur and Purnea; on the south by Burdwan and Dhanbad; on the east by Birbhum, Malda and Murshidabad; and on the west by Bhagalpur, Hazaribagh and Monghyr. The river Ganges separates the district from Purnea and Malda, while the Ajai and Barakar rivers separate it from Burdwan and Dhanbad.

[28]For a further study of the Santal Rebellion see Diwakar, R.R. (ed.), *Bihar Through The Ages*, Bombay: Orient Longmans, 1959; Hunter (1975); Bradley Birt, op. cit., Archer, W.G., 'The Santal Rebellion', *Man In India*, Ranchi, 25(4), Dec. 1945, pp. 218-39; Datta, Kalikinkar, 'Original Records about the Santal Insurrection', *Bengal Past and Present*, Calcutta, 48(1), July-Sept. 1934, pp. 32-7; Thompson, E., and G.T. Garratt, *Rise and Fulfilment of British Rule in India*, Allahabad: Central Book Depot, 1958.

[29]This Act was, however, largely amended by Act X of 1857 which slashed down the district to a smaller area.

[30]*Census 1971*, Series 4, Bihar, Part X-B, Primary Census Abstract, Santal Parganas District.

Map 2:1

BIHAR

DISTRICT SANTAL PARGANAS AND SURROUNDINGS

The district was divided into four sub-districts—Dumka, Deoghar (including Jamtara), Godda and Rajmahal (including Pakaur)—and placed under a Duputy Commissioner and four Assistant Commissioners. By the Police Rules of 1856, the headman of every village (*manjhi*) and the *pargana* (head of a number of villages) were given police powers. The Deputy Commissioner was given the right to appoint and dismiss a *manjhi* or a *pargana*. A non-regulation system was thus introduced, the main feature of which was a direct communication between the people and their British rulers. The system did away with any intermediary between the Santal and the Assistant Commissioner since complaints were to be made verbally. This innovation was of great importance for, as Culshaw (1945:219) remarks, previously the Government was not only geographically remote from the situation but was also completely ignorant of the people's problems. Besides, the administration had previously almost been in the hands of the *Darogas* who were known to be corrupt. In 1872, Deoghar, Godda and Rajmahal became sub-divisions. The Duputy Commissioner went to stay in Dumka, the capital of the district. On 31 January 1881, Jamtara and Pakaur became sub-divisions (see Map 2.2). The Land Tenancy Act of 1885 further benefited the Santals since, by reason of this Act, no land could be bought by non-Santals from the Santals.[31]

Various changes have taken place in the administration of the district since Independence in 1947. Though the offices of *pargana* and *manjhi* still remain, their powers have been limited by the Police administration. There is no non-police tract in the district which is now covered by forty-two police stations. On 1 January 1963, for efficient police supervision, the district was sub-divided into two units—Dumka becoming the headquarters of the southern region and Sahibganj the headquarters of the northern region. For the purpose of revenue and development, the district is divided into forty-one Community Development Blocks, each of which is under a Block Development Officer. In the district, there are no Revenue Thanas. Instead there are Police Stations, Sardari Circles and Bungalows. The latter are to be found only in the *Damin-i-koh* areas. As

[31]Vice versa no Santal could sell land to a non-Santal.

Map 2:2

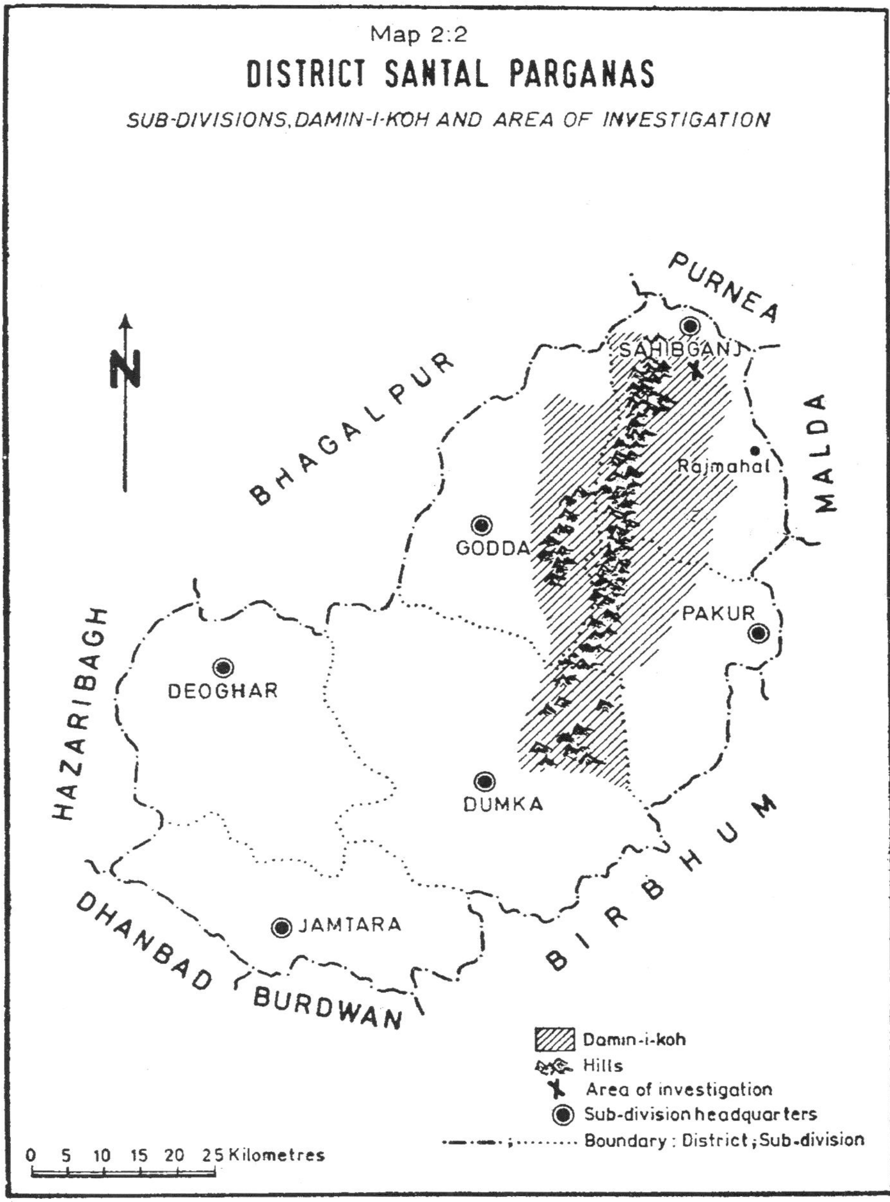
DISTRICT SANTAL PARGANAS
SUB-DIVISIONS, DAMIN-I-KOH AND AREA OF INVESTIGATION
N
PURNEA
SAHIBGANJ
BHAGALPUR
MALDA
Rajmahal
GODDA
HAZARIBAGH
PAKUR
DEOGHAR
DUMKA
BIRBHUM
DHANBAD
JAMTARA
BURDWAN
Damin-i-koh
Hills
Area of investigation
Sub-division headquarters
Boundary : District ; Sub-division
0 5 10 15 20 25 Kilometres

can be seen from Table 2.2, Dumka sub-division has all the three units.

TABLE 2.2 SUB-DIVISION WISE DISTRIBUTION OF DEVELOPMENT BLOCKS, POLICE STATIONS, SARDARI CIRCLES AND BUNGALOWS IN SANTAL PARGANAS DISTRICT.

Sub-division	*Community Development Blocks*	*Police Stations*	*Sardari Circles*	*Bungalows*[32]
Dumka	10	1	59	9
Jamtara	4	—	27	—
Deoghar	7	7	—	—
Godda	7	5	—	20
Rājmahal	7	3	—	27
Pakaur	6	4	—	13

Source: *Census 1971*, Series 4, Bihar, Part X-B, Primary Census Abstract, Santal Parganas District.

According to the 1971 Census, 1,003,819 Santals, or 57.5 per cent of the Santals in Bihar, live in the district of Santal Parganas which has been named after them and which the Santals regard as their own country. Contrary to the general impression, it is interesting to note that the Santals are outnumbered by the non-Santals in the district. They form 31.49 per cent of the total population of the district which has 3,186,908 inhabitants making it the tenth most populous district of Bihar.[33]

The Santals form 86.96 per cent of the total Scheduled Tribes' population in the district. Among the other seventeen Scheduled Tribes represented in the district, the Mal Paharias and the Sauria Paharias are the most numerous, as Table 2.3

[32]The number of Bungalows includes also the Sauria Paharia Hills Bungalows.

[33]The district of Santal Parganas has the largest number of villages —12,175—among all the districts of Bihar. There are 2943 villages in Dumka sub-division, 2705 in Deoghar sub-division, 2304 in Godda sub-division, 1807 in Rajmahal sub-division, 1250 in Pakaur sub-division and 1166 in Jamtara sub-division.

shows.[34] Another Scheduled Tribe largely confined to this district are the Mahlis.

TABLE 2.3: COMPOSITION OF THE SCHEDULED TRIBAL POPULATION OF SANTAL PARGANAS DISTRICT, 1971

Scheduled Tribes	*Population*	*Percentage to total Scheduled Tribal Population*
Banjara	56	Negligible
Gond	307	,,
Gorait	24	,,
Ho	44	,,
Karmali	525	,,
Kharia	523	,,
Kharwar	1,909	,,
Kisan	153	,,
Kora	3,537	,,
Korwa	1	,,
Lohara or Lohra	6,789	,,
Mahli	20,644	1.78
Mal Paharia	46,395	4.01
Munda	1,132	Negligible
Oraon	6,898	,,
Parhaiya	118	,,
Santal	1,003,819	86.96
Sauria Paharia	58,357	5.05
Unspecified	3,014	Negligible

Source: *Census 1971*, Series 4, Bihar, Part V, ST-II, (unpublished).

LOCATION AND POPULATION OF PANGRO[35]

Pangro is a Santal village within the *Damin-i-koh* situated at the foot of the Banjhi Hills about five miles southeast of

[34]Among the Mal Paharias small portions have migrated to other districts especially to Bhagalpur and Saharsa.

[35]According to the Census reports and maps, the village is recorded as Bara Pagaro to distinguish *it* from another village called Chota Pagaro. The inhabitants of the village, and the people of the surrounding area, however, call the village Pangro, a name which actually refers to the hill forest situated at the southern end of the village. This is the name adopted throughout this study.

Sahibganj Town, an important trade centre especially for jute which is received by river from the trans-Gangetic districts of Malda, Purnea and north Bhagalpur.[36] It forms part of the Rajmahal sub-division and for civil administration falls under the Borio Community Development Block, which, as Table 2.4 shows, is the second most populous Block in the sub-division.

TABLE 2.4: BLOCKWISE RURAL POPULATION DISTRIBUTION OF RAJMAHAL SUB-DIVISION ALSO SHOWING THE AREA IN HECTARES AND THE NUMBER OF VILLAGES

Community Development Block	*Population*	*Number of villages*	*Area in hectares*
Rajmahal	122,101	258	21,750.86
Barharwa	62,518	239	18,250.68
Pathna	41,546	150	16,315.93
Barhait	66,167	275	30,882.33
Borio	93,282	580	39,918.02
Sahibganj	29,160	32	16,856.00
Taljhari	41,192	273	15,828.15

Source: *Census 1971*, Series 4, Bihar, Part X-B, Primary Census Abstract, Santal Parganas District, pp. 350-623.

On the west side of Pangro, there is a metalled road leading from Sahibganj to Dumka. Another metalled road connecting Sahibganj to Rajmahal Town lies to its north. The river Ganges flows parallel to this metalled road as does the East Indian Railway Loop Line leading to Calcutta and Farakka, (see Map 2.3). Narrow paths along the field embankments connect Pangro with the two mentioned metalledr oads, both of which are about two kilometres from the village. It is impossible for any motorised vehicle to enter the village. The only means of transport are bullock-driven carts and horses. During the rainy season, owing to the big flow of water from the Banjhi Hills, Pangro is virtually cut off from the two metalled

[36]Since the opening of Farakka which made the jute transport by rail possible, Sahibganj has lost some of its importance.

Map 2:3

VILLAGE PANGRO AND SURROUNDINGS

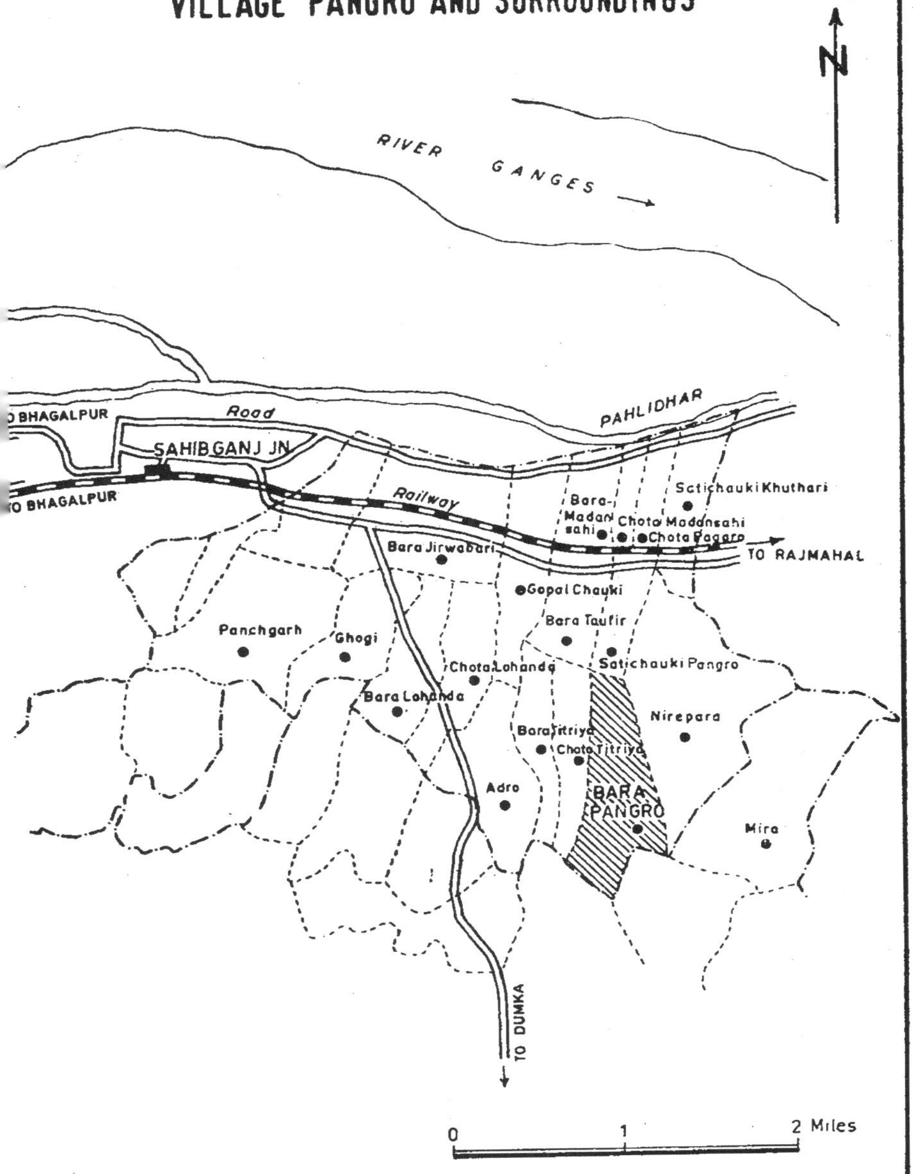

roads. Within a radius of two kilometres from Pangro, there are thirteen other villages, in which besides Santals, we find Bhuiya Ghatwals, Chamars, Doms, Karmakars, Mahlis, Mundas, Muriaris, Musahars, Oraons, Rajbanshis and Telis.

Pangro is made up of three hamlets (*tolas*): Rasi Tola, Manjhi Tola, and Ghatwal Tola. Like every Santal village, Pangro has one long street (*kulhi*),[37] which passes across Rasi Tola and Manjhi Tola, the other *tola* being situated to the west side of the street (see Map 2.4). There are fifty-six houses built along the village street, twenty-one on the west side and thirty-five on the east side. Pangro, which has an area of 120.26 hectares (*Land Settlement Report*, 1924-25), was founded around the year 1850. Lakhin Murmu was the first headman and settled down in Manjhi Tola. At the time of the fieldwork, the total population of the village was three hundred and twenty-six, of whom a hundred and fifty-nine were males, and hundred and sixty-seven females. Of the seventy-six households in the village, sixty-eight belonged to Santals, while of the remaining eight, five belonged to the Bhuiya Ghatwals and three to the Karmakars.[38]

TABLE 2.5: HAMLETWISE POPULATION DISTRIBUTION OF PANGRO VILLAGE

Hamlet	*Total Population*	*Total No. of households*	*Santal households*	*Karmakar households*	*Bhuiya Ghatwal households*
Rasi	273	64	61	3	—
Manjhi	26	7	7	—	—
Ghatwal	27	5	—	—	5
Total	326	76	68	3	5

[37]A *kulhi* is not merely a link between houses. It serves as a dance floor and a court of justice (*Kulhi Durup*). Each household is responsible for the cleanliness of the part of the village road in front of their house.

[38]In this study, the word household refers to the residential form of a family. It is a domestic group whose members live under the same roof and share the same hearth.

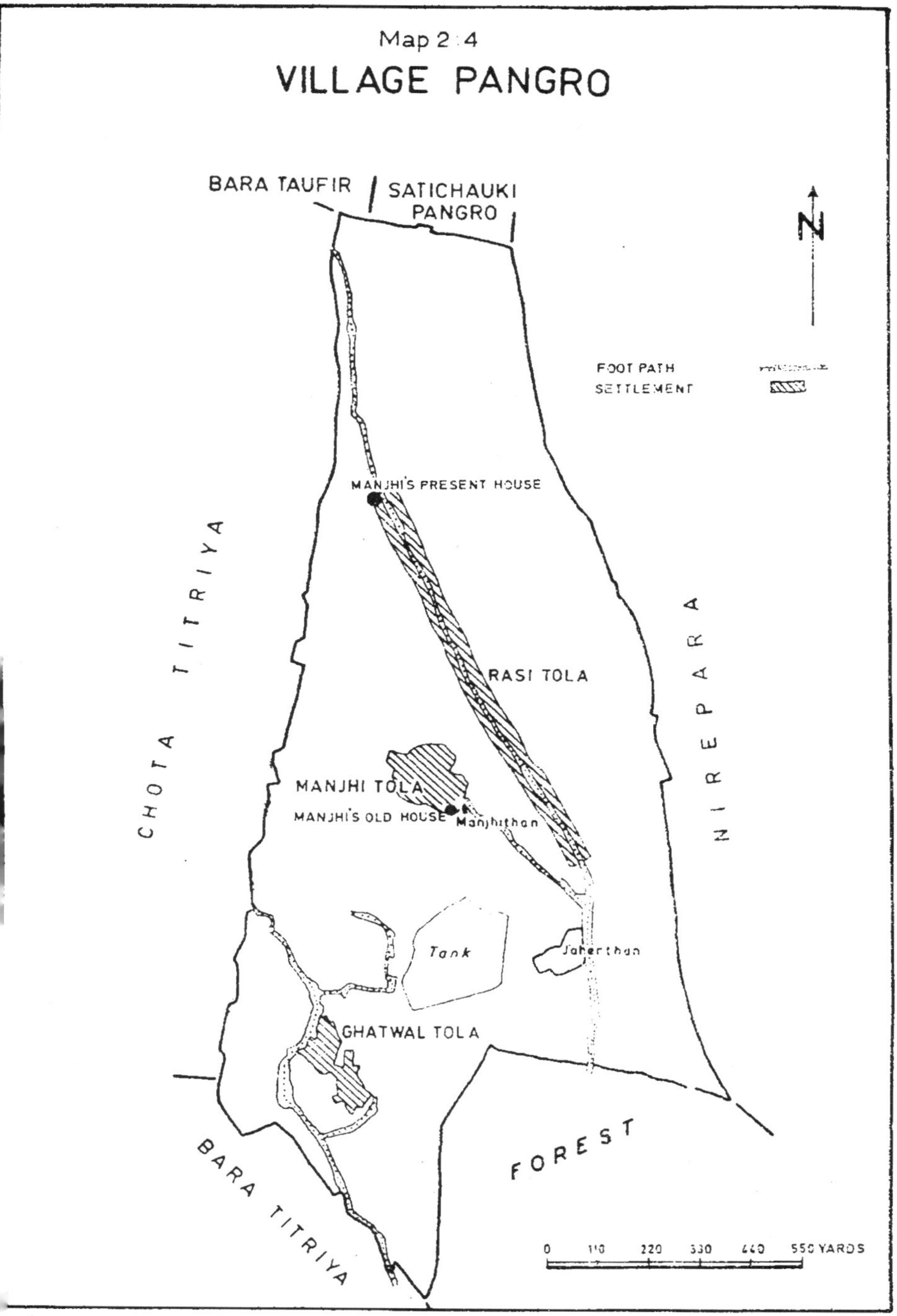
Map 2:4
VILLAGE PANGRO
BARA TAUFIR
SATICHAUKI PANGRO
N
FOOT PATH
SETTLEMENT
MANJHI'S PRESENT HOUSE
CHOTA TITRIYA
NIREPARA
RASI TOLA
MANJHI TOLA
MANJHI'S OLD HOUSE
Manjhithan
Tank
Jaherthan
GHATWAL TOLA
FOREST
BARA TITRIYA
0 110 220 330 440 550 YARDS

TABLE 2.6: POPULATION COMPOSITION OF PANGRO VILLAGE

	Population
Santals	283
Karmakars	16
Bhuiya Ghatwals	27

Though Karmakars are not tribals as the Santals are, they are said to live mostly where the Santals are to be found. As Culshaw points out: 'Every moderate-sized village contains a family of Kamars who have been granted a piece of land from the village' (1949:18-19). The three Karmakar households in Pangro were related to one another. Babulal and Suklal were brothers while Sikdar was their first cousin. The first two had their ancestral home and fields in Pangro while Sikdar's ancestral home was in Chasgawa, a village situated in Borio Bungalow and he had no land in Pangro. These three households formed an integral part of the social structure of the village. Though their mother tongue was different, they spoke Santali fluently, dressed in the same manner as the Santals and their houses were patterned on the Santal model. During the village festivals, they not only handed in their contribution along with the others but also participated fully in the festivities. They brought their disputes to be settled in the *Kulhi Durup* (village assembly). The menfolk also played an active part in the annual hunt (*Disom Sendra*) and in the lesser hunts held by the village (*Por Sendra*). Following the Santal custom, they shared game with the other villagers of Pangro. Karmakar men were often to be seen partaking of cooked food with Santal men and drinking *handi* (rice-beer) with them.

Though their traditional occupation is blacksmithing, only Sikdar was actually engaged in this occupation. Babulal and Suklal were engaged in farming. Besides doing various jobs for the people of Pangro, Sikdar also took up jobs for the people of Nirepara. He was paid twice a year for all the repairs done and the sharpening of the various agricultural implements. Every household which used his services paid according to the number of ploughs it had. Thus, for every plough, each household paid half a maund of rice in the month of *Aghar* (November-December) and one *hatak* (winnowing fan) of *jondra* (maize) in the month of *Bhador* (August-September).

If we can speak of an integration between the Karmakar and Santal households in Pangro, the same cannot be said of the Bhuiya Ghatwal households found in Ghatwal Tola which is named after them. In former times, the Bhuiyas along with the Mal and Sauria Paharias were in possession of the forests and land in the Santal Parganas when the Santals moved in.[39] As we have seen, Ghatwal Tola is cut off from the other two *tolas*. Though the Ghatwal menfolk did occasionally attend some of the village festivals, they rarely mixed with the other villagers. Apart from agriculture they still followed their traditional occupation of making *taben* (a kind of flattened rice) which they sold to all the villagers in the area.

ECONOMIC ORGANISATION OF PANGRO

The economy of the Santals of Pangro, like that of many Santals elsewhere, is primarily based on plough cultivation. Food gathering, hunting and fishing, though formerly very important scurces of living, are now subsidiary occupations. During the rainy reason, the Santals of Pangro, like other villagers situated at the foot of the Banjhi Hills, still practice slush—and-burn cultivation (*kurau*) as a subsidiary occupation.[40] They, however, depend mainly on paddy cultivation as their chief source of livelihood. According to the Settlement Report of 1924-25, the total cultivable area of Pangro is 759 *bighas*, 10 *kathas* and 17 *dhurs*, amounting to roughly 253 acres.[41] Of these, 653 *bighas*, 7 *kathas* and 4 *dhurs* belong

[39]See Bradley-Birt, op. cit.

[40]Those who practice slush-and-burn cultivation on the hill slopes, rent the land from the Mal and Sauria Paharias. Usually *jondra* (maize), *raher* (a kind of pulse), *bajra* (giant millet) and some smaller millets and pulses are sown. To cultivate these crops, the Santals hire Paharias who receive one rupee for half a day's work and two rupees for a day's work.

[41]One *bigha* is approximately one-third of an acre. There are twenty *dhurs* in one *katha* and twenty *kathas* in one *bigha*.

to the Santal and Karmakar households in the village. Six Santal and one Karmakar households do not own land in the village. Four of these households have land in other villages. The other three households earn their living by ploughing the fields of others and by selling milk at Sahibganj. As can be seen from Table 2.7, the five Bhuiya Ghatwal households own 6 *bighas*, 6 *kathas* and 6 *dhurs*. The rest of the cultivable land is owned by villagers from the adjoining villages of Bara Titriya, Bara Taufir, Nirepara, Satichauki Pangro and by four Paharia households living in Tetria, a Paharia village.

TABLE 2.7: OWNERSHIP OF CULTIVABLE LAND IN PANGRO

	Bighas	*Kathas*	*Dhurs*
Santals	634	18	6
Karmakars	18	8	18
Bhuiya Ghatwals	6	6	6
Bara Titriya*	53	2	18
Bara Taufir	18	3	11
Nirepara	19	10	13
Satichauki Pangro	3	13	15
Tetria (Paharia)	5	6	10

*Sections from one marked with asterisk refer to households from these villages that own land in Pangro.

Paddy cultivation keeps the Santals of Pangro engaged for nine months of the year. From the month of *Baisak* (April-May) to the month of *Pus* (December-January)) the Santals are engaged in manuring, ploughing, sowing, transplanting, weeding, harvesting and threshing as Table 2.8 shows.

Bullocks and buffaloes are commonly used for ploughing and levelling. Some poor families also use cows. Ploughing and the making of *bandhs* (embankments) are restricted to the menfolk, while transplanting and husking are exclusively women's work. In the other agricultural operations, men and women share the work.

The domestication of animals and birds such as fowls, pigs, cows, buffaloes, bullocks and goats, is another secondary occupation of the Santals of Pangro. Three households also

TABLE 2.8: CALENDAR OF RICE CULTIVATION FOLLOWED BY THE SANTALS OF PANGRO

Month	*Agricultural operation*
Baisak (April-May)	Manuring
Jhet (May-June)	Ploughing Sowing the *bhadai* (summer paddy)
Asar (June-July)	Sowing the winter paddy Weeding the *bhadai*
San (July-August)	Transplanting the winter paddy
Bhador (August-September)	Harvesting the *bhadai* Weeding the winter paddy
Aghar (November-December)	Harvesting
Pus (December-January)	Threshing

domesticate pigeons.[42] Cattle are of great use to them in agricultural operations. Chickens, pigs and goats provide them with meat as well as sacrificial offerings to the spirits. Buffaloes, goats and cows also provide them with milk, most of which is sold at Sahibganj.

While the *kulhi* (village street) expresses Santal unity, the houses give the village its uniquely Santal air. Commenting on Santal houses, Archer remarks:

> Of all the other tribes of eastern India, none has quite the same relish for neatly ordered buildings, the same capacity for tidy spacious living or the same genius for domestic architecture (1974:20).

Generally, the entrance to the houses never faces the *kulhi* but the courtyard (*raca*), which serves as the social centre of the family. The outer walls are beautifully decorated with different colour designs.[43] The floors are made of beaten

[42]Quite a number of people from Pangro and the surrounding villages buy pigeons from these three households mostly for sacrificial purposes.

[43]Though built of mud, Santal houses are kept very clean and they are beautiful to look at. Village women compete with one another to beautify their houses. In various places one can see the walls painted

earth with a cowdung coating on top. The roof framework is made of *sal* logs, bamboo splinters and rafters.

Two characteristic features of every Santal village are the *jaherthan* and the *manjhithan*. Both these localities are held in great respect. The *jaherthan* or sacred grove is regarded as the abode of the principal Santal spirits and is situated at the end of the village. It is here that, on important occasions, the village community through its *naeke* (village priest) offers sacrifices to its principal spirits for its general well-being. In Pangro, the *jaherthan* is situated at the southern end of the village. It contains a cluster of trees among which, there are four *sal* trees and one *mahua* tree. These are believed to be relics of the primeval forest. The association of a village with the *jaherthan* expresses the ritual unity of the group. The location for the *jaherthan* is established by the original settlers after careful divination.[44] No two villages share the same sacred grove though the *jaher* spirits are everywhere the same. It thus serves as an important criterion to ascertain village membership and geographical boundary.

The *manjhithan* is the place erected in honour of *Manjhi Haram* (see Chapter III). As a rule, it is situated outside the headman's house on the opposite side of the street, 'and if the headman moves away from his old place, the *than* is also moved to his new abode' (Bodding, 1935b: 258). In Pangro, however, for reasons which we shall shortly explain, this is not the case. While the *manjhithan* is located in Manjhi Tola, the present headman's house is the first house in Rasi Tola. Normally, it is the village headman and not the village priest who officiates at the *manjhithan*, but in Pangro the headman pays the *naeke* to officiate in his place. The duty of taking care of the *manjhithan* falls on an unmarried girl belonging to the headman's household. Traditionally, village community meetings take place here but in Pangro these are held in the

with a variety of colours, white, black and red being the most common. Certain houses also display on their walls pictures of animals, flowers etc. which stand out against the white background. For further details refer to Bose, P.N., 'Three specimens of Santal Drawing', *Man in India*, Ranchi, 5(3-4), Sept-Dec. 1925, pp. 227-8.

[44]Bodding, P.O., 'How the Santals Live', *Memoirs of the Asiatic Society of Bengal*, Calcutta, 10(3), 1940, pp. 429-30.

courtyard of the *manjhi's* house. In Pangro, the *manjhithan* consists of a raised mud platform at the centre of which there is a post with a stone at its base. When asked about the significance of this stone, the people were not sure as to whether it represented the original headman or the office of headmanship in general.

SOCIAL ORGANISATION OF PANGRO

As we have already seen, the Santal tribe is divided into eleven clans or *paris*. Though it is very rare for all these clans to be represented in a single village every Santal village includes members of different clans. In Pangro, eight of these clans are represented, making it a highly representative village. The clan which is numerically the largest in Pangro is the Murmu clan as Table 2.9 shows.

TABLE 2.9: CLAN AND SUBCLAN DISTRIBUTION OF THE SANTALS OF PANGRO

Clan	*Number of Persons*	*Subclan*	*Number of Persons*
(1)	*(2)*	*(3)*	*(4)*
Hasdak	21	Cil-Bindha	2
		Obor	1
		Sada	3
Murmu	66	Nij	7
		Bitol	12
		Gar	1
		Handi	15
		Jugi	20
		Sada	2
		San	2
		Gar	2
Kisku	17	Gar	8
Hembrom	58	Nij	6
		Gua	39
		Sada	1
Marndi	44	Nij	1
		Hesel	2
		Manjhi khil	7

(1)	(2)	(3)	(4)
		Naeke khil	27
		Sada	1
Soren	41	Obor	12
		Sidup	20
		Turkulumam	1
Tudu	32	Sada	14
Besra	4	Son	3

Of the sixty-eight Santal households in Pangro six, four of which belong to the headman's family, are Protestants, belonging to the Church Missionary Society of England. The missionaries belonging to this Protestant society have worked a lot in Santal Parganas, as we shall see later. In Pangro, they have a small chapel in which Sunday services and other functions like baptisms and marriages are held. Once a month, and on special occasions like Christmas, baptisms and marriages, a Santal Protestant pastor from Mahadevganj, a village on the other side of Sahibganj town, came to conduct the services. These were also attended by Protestants from the neighbouring villages of Nirepara and Adro. On the other three Sundays, Bhattu Murmu, whose great-great-grandfather was the first headman of the village, conducted the services which normally started after lunch and lasted for about an hour and a half. Besides the members of these six households who numbered forty-one persons, there were three other persons who belonged to this Protestant society. There was also one woman who was a Seventh Day Adventist and one Catholic household.

Till 1947, there was a big school in the village run by the Church Missionary Society of England. This was a private school and there were five classes. Adjacent to the school there was also a church run by the same society. Both buildings were, however, destroyed during the monsoon due to heavy rains and the enormous flow of water from the surrounding hills. Though in 1964, the Government started a primary school in the village, there was still no separate building. Classes were held, if at all, in the veranda of one of the houses, and they were attended by thirteen children. There was only one teacher, a Santal who hailed from

Laotana village in Godda sub-division. It is interesting to note that a Santal woman from Pangro was employed as a Government teacher in Rangamatya, a village situated about thirty miles away.

There is a Government middle school in Adro and another one in Bara Madansahi. In Pangro, there were thirty-six literate persons, twenty males and sixteen females, twenty-five of whom were Protestants and two Catholics. Of these, seven have passed their matriculation examination. One of these, after finishing his intermediate from Sahibganj college, went to Bhagalpur for a course in homoeopathy. He is now a registered homoeopathic doctor with a private clinic-cum-dispensary at Satichauki Pangro. Two boys were studying at Sahibganj College, one doing the final year in economics while the other was doing his second year science. One girl was undergoing a nurses' training course at Bhagalpur. At the time there were also five boys and eight girls studying in Protestant or Catholic schools outside the village.

Of the sixty-eight households in Pangro, sixteen employed servants on an annual basis. There were twenty-two servants, most of whom were Muriaris and Oraons belonging to Kulhu Tola and Jharna Tola. These two *tolas* form part of the neighbouring villages—Bara Taufir and Chota Titriya. Usually, if there is no one in the household able to take care of the cattle, a servant is employed as a *gupi*. Normally, such servants are employed in the month of *Magh* (January-February) the last month of the Santal agricultural year. During this time, a *darmaha garmarao* (wage consultation) is held at the employer's house to which the servant's parents or other relatives are invited. Rice-beer, brewed for the occasion, is drunk, after which contracts are renewed or terminated. Often, an increase in wages is discussed. If employed, the servant becomes a member of the employer's household, where he lives and is well treated. For his work he is paid annually in kind or in cash. Different households decide on different wages (*darmaha*) with their servants. The wages vary according to the type of work done and the number of years one has been working in a household. Clothes are also provided to them throughout the year.

Besides these 'permanent' servants, there were others who

were employed on a short-term basis, say for the repairing of a house, the building of a cowshed or for plastering house walls with cowdung. These received two seers of rice plus one meal, or two rupees daily during the time they were working. During the transplanting and the harvesting season, various agricultural labourers were employed to help in the work.[45]

POLITICAL ORGANISATION OF PANGRO

Pangro, like other Santal villages and those of other neighbouring tribes, is a well-defined political and administrative unit governed by a council of village elders which not only regulates life within the village but also orders the villagers' relations with the outside world. The Santali term *more hor*, which literally means 'five persons', is used to refer to this village council as a representative body of the community. Until recently, Santal villages enjoyed a large measure of internal autonomy. They were largely governed by their own laws and had their own methods of dealing with different kinds of offences. The authority of their traditional headman was further strengthened, as we have seen, by Government recognition in 1856. Since independence, however, a lot of changes have taken place in the district's administration and though the headman is still recognised as a Government officer, his powers have been curtailed by the Police Administration.

The village council of Pangro is a full-fledged one consisting of seven officials: a headman (*manjhi*); a deputy headman (*paranik*); an overseer of village morals (*jog manjhi*); his assistant (*jog paranik*); a messenger (*godet*); and two religious functionaries namely the *naeke* (village priest) and his assistant the *kudam naeke*. These officials were traditionally chosen by the villagers themselves at the time of the foundation of a village. Though their offices were considered hereditary, the villagers had the right to dismiss the incumbents for serious

[45]In Pangro, those who help in the transplanting get three rupees for a full day's work. Those who help in the final ploughing get four rupees daily. They bring along their ploughs. For helping out in the harvesting and threshing, a worker gets five seers out of every maund of paddy irrespective of the number of days spent.

misconduct. Formerly, during the annual *Magh* Festival, these officials used to 'surrender' their offices, and, though this was largely a formality, the ceremony used to serve as a pointer to the fact that their office-tenure depended upon the wish of the villagers. All these officials used to receive rent-free land (*man*) given to them by the villagers themselves as remuneration for their services. Nowadays, however, it is only the *manjhi* and *godet* who enjoy this privilege.

The headman of every Santal village is called *manjhi.* Traditionally he used to be elected by the entire village community. The final appointment, nowadays, is made by the Deputy Commissioner who, however, takes into consideration the villagers' choice and the traditional custom of appointing the nearest male heir to the office.[46] Otherwise, the office is by custom hereditary, descending from father to son. When the direct line of succession fails, either through the absence of male offspring, or through an incapacity of the natural heir, the office passes on to a brother or near relative on the paternal side. In this manner, the history of the village is preserved in the tradition handed down concerning the headman's ancestry. A headman can also be dismissed by the Government, in which case his heir has no claim to the office.[47] This is exactly what happened in Pangro in 1926 when Bhattu Murmu was removed from the office of *manjhi* for keeping the village rent to himself instead of handing it to the Government. Lakhin, Bhattu's first cousin was appointed as headman instead. He was succeeded by his son Thomas who died, leaving no male offspring. On his death, in 1957, Sona, Thomas' wife, asked the Government after obtaining the village's approval, to continue as *manjhi* till her death. The permission was granted. It is interesting to note that though Sona has a son-in-law, Gangaram, the headman's family who were not eager to let the *manjhi's* service lands go to another family, did not accept him as a *ghar jawae* or house

[46]It is only in exceptional cases that the Sub-Divisional Officer, though he has the right to appoint and dismiss a village headman, does so contrary to the wishes of the villagers. Schedule V of the Santal Parganas Tenancy (Supplementary) Rules 1950 has mentioned the rules for the appointment of headmen.

[47]See Sachchidananda (1968:75-6).

Diagram 2:1

GENEALOGY OF HEADMAN'S FAMILY

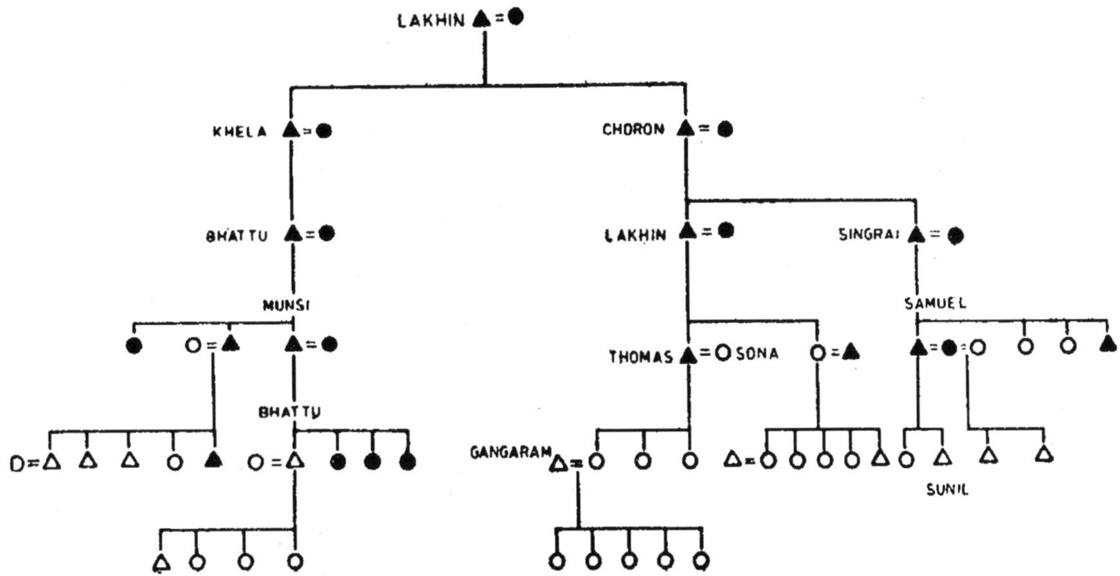

son-in-law.[48] He cannot thus inherit the village headmanship which, on Sona's death, will be filled by Sunil Murmu, Thomas' first cousin's son (see Diagram 2.1 of the headman's family). This change of headmanship from Bhattu to Lakhin also explains the fact that, in Pangro, the present headman's house is not to be found opposite the *manjhithan* as is the case in other Santal villages.

According to Sachchidananda, 'Among none of the tribes under review is the office of the headman so important as among the Santal and in no other case have his rights and duties been so elaborately laid down' (1969:73). He is the representative of the village both in its external and internal affairs. Nothing of a public character can be properly performed without his actual presence or at least without his consent and the presence of his substitute. With the assistance of the village elders, he decides the dates for village festivals and also the nature of the *Sohrae* (Harvest festival)—whether it is going to be a *sari Sohrae* or a *nase Sohrae*, meaning a full *Sohrae* or not. He is informed and also is present at name-giving, initiation, marriage and death rituals and ceremonies. His permission in fact is essential in negotiating a marriage. A marriage party always pays its respects first to his house. When a new bride is brought into the village, the headman gets one rupee from the bride's father. At festivals, the dancing starts from his house. He gets portions of the animals killed in sacrifice. During the hunt, he receives a special portion of the flesh of every animal slain by his village members. Because of his importance, if a village has a headman of another tribe, the Santals of that village, whatever be their number, will have for themselves an official called a *handi manjhi* (literally a liquor headman) who ratifies everything of a ceremonial character. This was the case in Adro village where the headman was an Oraon.

In relation to the Government, a *manjhi's* main duty is the collection and punctual payment of the village revenue to the Government. There are sixty-nine *raiyats* (tenants) in Pangro

[48]Contrary to patrilocal residence, a *ghar jawae*, at his marriage takes up residence in his father-in-law's house where he stays for good.

who together pay 381 rupees 25 paise as rent (*khajna*).[49] The *manjhi* tries to collect the *khajna* before the first week of March so that he could present this to the Circle Inspector at the Community Development Block of Borio before the fifteenth of the month. He is helped by a *karamchari* who sees to it that the rent is delivered on time.[50] For this work, the *manjhi* gets an 8 per cent commission on the annual rent collected from his village.[51]

Besides this work, the *manjhi* has other administrative and political duties to perform. He is held responsible for the maintenance of law and order in the village. He is bound to report any crimes which take place in his village. The police cannot enter a Santal village nor search the houses without first getting the *manjhi's* permission. He also keeps with him a map of the village territory showing the amount of land each *raiyat* has. He is also responsible for constructing and repairing water reservoirs, embankments, village roads, etc. As a remuneration for his work, he holds certain lands on service tenure called *manjhi man*. The *manjhi* of Pangro has 19 *bighas*, 4 *kathas* and 16 *dhurs* as *man*. This rent-free land is attached to the office. The *manjhi* must keep his private holdings separate from his official holding. When a headman is dismissed by the Government, he loses his official holding which passes to his successor and not to his heirs. If he is found guilty of not having paid rent on his private holdings, then even these are liable to be

[49]The village rent and the rent payable by a *raiyat* remain unchanged till a fresh rent roll is prepared under the Santal Parganas Settlement Regulation of 1872 or The Santal Parganas Rent Regulation of 1886.

[50]We have seen that to facilitate revenue administration, the district of Santal Parganas is divided into forty-one Community Development Blocks. These in turn are divided into 410 *halkas* each of which is under the charge of a *karamchari* whose job is to collect rent and agricultural statistics. There are ten Community Development Blocks in the *Damin-i-koh* area which are divided into 97 *halkas*.

[51]In the *Damin-i-koh* area, the commission which a *manjhi* gets for the collection and deposit of rent is fixed according to the following rates if full payment is made:

On or before the 15th March	8 per cent
Between the 16th and the 20th March	$7\frac{1}{2}$,, ,,
Between the 21st and the 25th March	7 ,, ,,
Between the 26th and the 31st March	6 ,, ,,

taken away from him as happened in 1973 to the *pradhan* of Jharna Tola in Bara Taufir village. He was found guilty of not having handed in the village rent and also of not having paid rent on his private holdings for a number of years. All his land holdings, both private and official, were taken away from him and auctioned to the highest bidder at the Sahibganj Municipality office.

In his civic functions, the *manjhi* is assisted by the *paranik* who has the right of succession if the *manjhi* dies without leaving any male offspring or brother to succeed him. In the *manjhi's* absence, he presides over the village council and does the work of the headman. In the discharge of his moral functions, the *manjhi* is assisted by the *jog manjhi* who is considered to be the village guardian of tribal morals and is held responsible for the observance of the tribal endogamy and clan exogamy rules. He is also called upon to investigate allegations of immoral behaviour. At the beginning of the *Sohrae*, the young lads of the village go to him and entreat him to turn a blind eye tò any of the faults they commit during that time. If an unmarried girl becomes pregnant, it is the duty of the *jog manjhi* to locate the genitor. He also acts as the master of ceremonies at birth, marriage and funerary ceremonies. The *jog manjhi* has an assistant called the *jog paranik*. Being the main officials in Santal marriages, both of them receive a yellow turban, four feet long, for every marriage at which they officiate besides the food and drink which every village official gets on such occasions. The *godet* is the village messenger of the Santals. At the instance of the *manjhi*, he summons the villagers when some business has to be discussed. In the meeting of the village council he acts as a public prosecutor. He also carries news such as of birth, deaths and marriages to the villagers. He collects sacrificial offerings from the villagers during village festivals. Like the *manjhi*, he has some rent-free land. In Pangro the *godet* has 2 *bighas*, *8 kathas* and 18 *dhurs* as *man*.

Among the Santals, there are two priestly functionaries—the *naeke* (village priest) and his assistant and co-priest the *kudam naeke*. The *naeke* is responsible for the ceremonial rituals that take place in the village.[52] According to Santal belief, the selection of the *naeke* is made by the spirits themselves who are said to possess an individual and express their choice through him. The continuity of the office in the *naeke's* family is, however, generally assured. If a *naeke's* son takes up the work after his father, no fresh appointment by possessed mediums is considered to be necessary. His special duty is to worship the principal Santal spirits on behalf of the village community during the annual festivals. Prior to all kinds of worship he observes a certain ritual segregation from the other villagers. Formerly, he used to receive rent-free land given by the villagers themselves. Nowadays, however, he annually receives paddy and other grains from each family in the village for his services. He also gets the heads of the animals sacrificed. His share at the annual hunt consists of a strip of flesh cut from the backbone of the animals killed.

The *naeke's* assistant and co-priest is called the *kudam naeke*. He is responsible for propitiating the *Pargana Bonga* and the spirits of the outskirts and village boundaries. On such occasions, he offers drops of his own blood (*Bul Mayam*) which he produces by pricking his body with a thorn. According to Culshaw, 'while the function of the priest is to deal with the tribal spirits, it would seem that his co-priest has to propitiate relatively unknown and fearful spirits' (1949:80). The members of the community usually reward the *kudam naeke* with various gifts.

As we have seen, the village is administered by a number of officials, each with clearly prescribed duties. Tribal custom has endowed them with authority and influence. Under this traditional authority, the village life proceeds smoothly and the villagers feel a certain sense of security, believing themselves to be under the proper leadership advocated by their forefathers. Among the Santals, however, so intense is their belief in democracy that the village *panchayat* is never complete without the assembly of all the adult males of the village. As

[52]According to A.C. Sinha 'Leadership in a Tribal Society', *Man in India* 47(2), Sept. 1967, pp. 222-7, traditionally, the secular and religious leadership among the Santals were combined in one person incorporating the functions of legislature, judiciary and executive.

already mentioned, the term *more hor* which originally signified the headman and the other village officials, also denotes the village community. Disputes, breaches of peace, divorce cases and social offences in a village, are settled by the villagers themselves gathered under the chairmanship of the *manjhi*. The Santal village court called *Kulhi Durup* is a general village assembly in which all male household heads act as judges [53]

Most of the cases that come under the village jurisdiction are concerned with social and sexual offences. During my stay in Pangro, three breaches of clan exogamy were judged. Twice the *Kulhi Durup* met to dispose of partition cases between the sons of the deceased. The *Kulhi Durup* also has jurisdiction over divorce proceedings. In the case of disputes between villages, one of the persons involved goes to the *manjhi* and, after explaining the case to him, asks for redress in a *Kulhi Durup*. The *manjhi*, if he agrees, sends the *godet* to each house in the village, informing everyone about the day and time when the *Kulhi Durup* is to meet. In Pangro, a *Kulhi Durup* is held in the courtyard of the *manjhi's* house usually at night. The prosecutor comes forward and explains the case to all present. The defendant is then given a chance to present his position. Once this is done, the case is opened to all present. It is the villagers themselves who decide who is guilty and what type of punishment should be given. The *manjhi*, however, always has the final word. Traditionally, punishments for most breaches of customary law consist of fines (*dandom*) in either kind or cash which the person found guilty has to pay within a certain specified time. Formerly, very serious breaches of the customary law, carried with them heavy fines. Nowadays, however, the *Kulhi Durup* of Pangro has decided that in dispute cases there cannot be any *dandom* of more than fifty rupees. These are divided equally between the aggrieved person and the *Kulhi Durup*. The latter's portion is kept with the *manjhi* who, after deducting a portion of money for himself, uses the rest of the money to buy rice-beer and foodstuff for all.

Though the Santals take a rather long time to settle a case,

[53]Though usually only the menfolk take part in a *Kulhi Durup*, women are called for when they are involved. The same is the case with widows when their children are involved.

as a rule the ultimate decision reached is accepted. If, however, the complainants get no satisfaction from the village *Kulhi Durup*, they are free to take their case to the police station or to the Government's courts. As far as possible, however, villagers try to settle all their internal disputes within the village itself. It is considered rather improper for anyone to take a case outside the village boundary.

EXPANDING SOCIO-ECONOMIC AND POLITICAL FRONTIERS

Till now we have considered Pangro as an isolated, independent unit. It would be erroneous, however, not to take into consideration the wider sphere of which Pangro is only a part. Beteille in his discussion of the distribution of power in Sripuram has shown how the village must be treated as a point at which many external political processes intersect.[54] A complete understanding of a village can, therefore, only be brought about when one relates its local power dynamics to the larger political movements and structures.

Pangro is a part of a larger political group called *Bungalow* or *Bangla*, a confederacy of village communities, under the leadership of a *pargana* who is usually elected from among the headmen of the constituent villages. By the Police Rules of 1856, the *Pargana's Panchayat* was recognised by the Government. The *pargana* was given the power and functions of a sub-inspector of police. He had the power to punish people and to send the accused to the Sub-Divisional Officer's court. With the introduction of the Thana System in the *Damin-i-koh* in May 1950, however, the powers of the *pargana* as sub-inspector of police were taken away.

Though a *pargana* is appointed by the Government, the post, like that of the *manjhi's*, is customarily hereditary, as the Santal Parganas Tenancy (Supplementary) Rules, 1950 lays down (359): "If possible the son would be appointed to succeed the father', and (360) 'in case of minority, the office will be filled up temporarily till the son becomes capable to take charge of the office'.

[54]Beteille, A., *Caste, Class and Power. Changing Patterns of Stratification in a Tanjore Village*, Bombay: Oxford University Press, 1966.

As we have seen (Table 2.2), *Bungalows* are only to be found in the *Damin-i-koh* area. There are sixty-nine *Bungalows* in the area, twenty of which belong to the Sauria Paharias. In the Borio Community Development Block, there are five *parganas* in charge of the five *Bungalows* namely Sakrigarh Bangla, Banjhi Bangla, Borio Bangla, Mandro I and Mandro II. Borio Bangla is the biggest (Table 2.10).

TABLE 2.10: BUNGALOW COMPOSITION OF BORIO COMMUNITY DEVELOPMENT BLOCK

Bungalow	*Population*	*Number of villages*	
		Plains	*Sauria Paharias*
Borio	26,079	92	68
Banjhi	20,365	112	17
Sakrigarh	18,245	53	61
Mandro I	14,201	51	45
Mandro II	13,894	51	30

Source: *Census 1971*, Series 4, Bihar, Part X-B, Primary Census Abstract, Santal Parganas District, pp. 578-604.

Pangro forms part of the Sakrigarh Bangla. As Thomas Murmu, the former *pargana* (see diagram of headman's family) died without leaving any male issue, he was succeeded by Sunil Murmu, Thomas' cousin's son. Since he was still a child, the office was discharged by Sunil's mother's brother who acted as *sarbarakhar*. Sunil was to take over as soon as he finished his college studies.

The *pargana* is responsible for the good behaviour of the *manjhis* within his *Bungalow* area. He also sees to their punctual payment of the village rent (*khajna*) to the Government. When any headman fails to deposit the money, the *pargana* has to see to its collection and deposit. The *pargana* of Sakrigarh Bangla gets 1000 rupees as commission. Besides this revenue work, the *pargana* is also bound to see that crimes which take place in his area of jurisdiction are immediately reported to the police. Like the *manjhi*, the *pargana* also has an assistant called *des-manjhi* and his messengers are called *chakladars*.[55]

Besides these officials, the *Pargana Panchayat* is made up of all the village headmen of the *Bungalow* and the village elders of the locality. In the case of unresolved disputes between villagers of two separate villages, an appeal can be made to this *Panchayat* through their respective headmen. This was the case when Singrai Hembrom, a resident of Pangro, accused Mohan Hasdak, a resident of Nirepara, of encroaching in his fields while ploughing. No agreement could be reached and the case was brought in front of the *Pargana Panchayat*. Readmission of an excommunicated Santal into the tribe (*Jom Jati*), is also the work of this *Panchayat*.

The Santals have a still higher court of appeal called *Lo Bir* or Hunt Council which meets once a year during the annual hunt or *Disom Sendra*. The *Lo Bir* Council presided over by the *dihri* or hunt superintendent, usually arbitrates in quarrels arising primarily out of the hunt itself, as for example, the rights over a slain animal. Any other matter, however, may be raised here and is fully discussed by all those interested. Previous decisions taken by the village and *Pargana Panchayats*, may be brought for a fresh trial before this council, whose decisions are binding on all. The decision of excommunicating a Santal from the tribe (*Bitlaha*) can only be taken and executed by this council.

Since independence, the traditional political organisation of the Santals has been threatened by the increasing encroachment of the Government's administrative control. In addition to the traditional *Pargana* and *Lo Bir Panchayats*, the village forms part of three other administrative agencies—the Community Development Block; the Police Thana; and the Statutory Gram Panchayat. As we have seen, Pangro forms part of the Borio Community Development Block. Though the Block is mainly concerned with the socio-economic development of the people, the Block Development Officer is also in charge of the maintenance of law and order, and of revenue collection in his area of jurisdiction. Police stations or *thanas* have been opened in all

[55]The *des-manjhis* and *chakladars* are appointed by the Government though, like the *pargana*, custom has made their office hereditary.

tribal areas. Each *thana* consists of a *daroga* (sub-inspector) and a number of *sipahis* (constables). There are also *chowkidars* (watchmen) who look after police work in the villages. The latter are local men whose job is to report births and deaths, and any thefts or murders which occur in their villages. Pangro forms part of Borio Thana and its *chowkidar* is a Dom.

Following the Bihar Panchayat Raj Act of 1948, *Gram Panchayats* have been established on a statutory basis in Chotanagpur and Santal Parganas.[56] A *panchayat* is set up for a population of about 1,000 people living within a radius of two miles. The main functionaries of the *Gram Panchayat* are the *mukhiya*, *sarpanch* and the *gram sevak*, who is also known as *panchayat sevak*. While the first two are elected, the *gram sevak* is a paid Government servant. The *mukhiya*, the executive head and chairman of the *Gram Panchayat*, is assisted by an executive committee or *Karya Karini Sabha* normally consisting of eight members, two of whom are co-opted members while the rest are elected by the respective villages. They look after the developmental and other socio-economic functions of the *Gram Panchayat*.

Besides discharging these functions, the *Gram Panchayat* is also a judicial body. The *sarpanch* or the judicial head, is elected and assisted by fifteen *panches* each of whom is in turn elected for a period of three years. The *sarpanch* has been vested with the powers of a third class magistrate. The *Gram Panchayat* acts as an appellate court over the traditional village *panchayat* and the traditional *Pargana* and *Lo Bir Panchayats*. It also settles intra-tribal disputes as well as those between tribals and non-tribals.

Pangro falls under Bara Madansahi *Gram Panchayat* which consists of ten villages.[57] The *mukhiya* lives in Satichauki Kuthauri. A woman from Pangro is an elected member of the executive committee. On the whole, however, the impact of this *Gram Panchayat* is not felt very much in Pangro. This is also the case in those areas where the village *panchayat* and the

[56]As of the 31 January 1964, the number of such *Gram Panchayats* in Santal Parganas district was 375.

[57]Bara Madansahi, Bara Pangro, Bara Taufir, Bara Titriya, Chota Madansahi, Chota Pangro, Chota Titriya, Nirepara, Satichauki Pangro, Satichauki Kuthauri.

Pargana Panchayats are still in force. As we have seen, village disputes are usually settled within Pangro itself. Besides, the local development work done in the village is taken care of by the *manjhi* or the Block Development Officer.

In what follows, we shall see how Pangro forms part of a larger economic and social sphere. As in the case of Bisipara,[58] Pangro's economic frontier is an ever expanding one. We have already seen that there were twenty-two servants working in Pangro, all of them recruited from other villages. There were six villagers from Pangro whose place of work was outside the village.

Twice a week, on Thursday and Sunday, Santals from Pangro and the neighbouring villages go to the *hatia* (market) held at Sahibganj. Hindus, Muslims, Santals and others, flock to this place in the hope of selling their wares and buying what they need. Among the local products which the Santals of Pangro sell in the *hatia*, are firewood, leaves for making *bidis* (small country-made cigarettes), mangoes and jackfruit, maize, mustard, rice and milk. The *hatia*, especially the one on Sunday, serves also as a clearing house for all news. Friends and relatives meet one another. Marriages are also often arranged here.

Since there are no shops in Pangro, various things have to be bought from the *hatia*. Such edible goods as salt, potatoes, onions, fish, meat, pepper, spices, cooking oil and vegetables used for making curry, are purchased there. Other items purchased are kerosene, clothes, earthenware pots, tiles for roofing the houses, brass plates and cups, cooking utensils, etc. Although the people of Pangro get most of the things they need from the *hatia*, they also buy from vendors who regularly frequent the village. After harvest time, quite a number of outsiders come to Pangro to buy straw and paddy.

The Santals' epicurean outlook of 'eat, drink and make merry while you are prosperous and never care for the future' has been the ruin of many Santal families who fell in the clutches of the money-lenders (*mahajans*). During the months of *Aghar* (November-December) and *Jhet* (May-June) various Muslim

[58]Bailey, F.G., *Caste and the Economic Frontier*, Bombay: Oxford University Press, 1958.

and Hindu money-lenders visit Pangro either to collect their share of the crops or to see that 'their' fields are ploughed. Others come to settle new deals.

Once a week, a barber comes from Bara Madansahi. Various people in the village make use of his services. Some pay him in kind after each shave or haircut, others pay him annually. From the latter he gets half a maund of paddy in the month of *Magh* (January-February). His services are also called on for such occasions as the *Bhandan* (a feast where sacrifices are offered to ancestral spirits, for which the relatives of the deceased and the villagers are invited) and the *Janam Chatiar* (name-giving ceremony). Another person who comes from Bara Madansahi once a week is the postman.

A midwife who belongs to the Dom caste (a semi-Hinduised caste of aborigines) is often called by the villagers to attend at births. She comes from a nearby village. For her work, which, besides attending at births, includes taking care of the mother and child till the day of the *Janam Chatiar*, she gets the following: in the case of a boy she gets half a maund of rice, a piece of cloth about three feet long and two rupees. In the case of a girl, she gets ten seers of rice.

The intimate relationship between Pangro and the wider society is much more evident when one examines the social inter-relations between Pangro and other villages. Marriage is one of the major ways of uniting people from different places. This is due to the fact that, in most cases, among the Santals, not only two individuals and their families but also two villages are united by a new relationship whenever a marriage takes place. This is evident from the parting speeches made by the headmen of the two villages concerned, when the bride leaves her home to take up residence in her husband's village,[59] as well as from the attendance of people from both villages at the ceremonies associated with a Santal marriage. Through marriage alone, the people of Pangro are socially related to people from forty-four other villages scattered in twelve *Bungalows*, three Sub-divisions—Godda, Jamtara and Rajmahal; two districts—Birbhum and Santal Parganas; two States—Bihar and West Bengal; and one Union Territory—Delhi.

[59]Archer, W.G., (1974:184).

On other occasions like birth, death and *Bhandan*, relatives from all over the district meet to join in the ceremonies. If marriages and other rites of passage ceremonies bring people from various villages together, the same can be said, and perhaps to an even greater extent, of the annual festivals and of the *Disom Sendra* (annual hunt). But about these we shall speak in greater detail in Chapters IV and V.

So far we have focused on who the Santals are and their migration and settlement in the district of Santal Parganas which is named after them. We have also described in the context of Pangro, various social institutions which constitute the social structure of Santal society. In the following chapters, an attempt will be made to study the role of Santal religion as manifested and expressed in its beliefs and ritual practices and the way it interacts with some of the social institutions of Pangro. Special emphasis will be placed on the relationship between religion and agriculture since, as we have seen, agriculture, especially paddy cultivation, is not only the main economic organisation of the Santals but also affects, directly or indirectly, almost every other activity. We shall start by describing and analysing the nature of the Santal religious universe in the following chapter.

Chapter III

The Religious Universe: Supernatural Spirits and Powers

The aboriginal tribes of Chotanagpur and Central India, see the world as being inhabited by invisible supernatural beings and powers. According to Santal belief, the world is inhabited by a large number of spiritual beings of various kinds. The Santals regard themselves as living, moving, and having their being in this world of supernatural entities. As Datta-Majumder noted, 'The Santals live not only in their human tribal society but in a greater society consisting of supernatural beings as well' (1956:101).

So intimate is the relationship between a Santal and these supernatural beings and powers that one cannot fully analyse the Santal social structure unless one understands their religious universe. With the passage of time, the Santals have gradually evolved a system of beliefs and rituals so as to cope with the unknown supernatural world. Though the system does have a coherence, one must be careful not to fall into the common anthropological trap of attributing to it the same kind of sophisticated coherence which is to be found in highly civilised societies. This coherence has been recognised by Levi-Strauss who points out that the primitive peoples were able to invest their activities over time with a certain religious meaning that remained 'within the stream of intelligibility'. It is because of this coherence which characterises primitive religions that he proposes an alternative to the extreme positions taken by Frazer and Malinowski, pointing out that:

> Between the basic absurdity Frazer attributed to primitive practices and beliefs and the spacious validation of them in terms of a supposed common sense invoked by Malinowski, there is scope for a whole science and a whole philosophy.[1]

Though it is true that, by and large, the Santals are unable to have precise terms and concepts regarding the exact nature and function of all their spirits, this does not mean that they do not differentiate between the various spirits. As we shall see in the course of this chapter, the Santals do have individual attributes associated with many of their spirits. In other words, one can rightly say that Santal spirits are more than mere abstractions. With the exception of the sacred grove spirits to whom both personality as well as a more or less definite form and individuality are ascribed, the other spirits, though endowed with personality, are in fact group spirits. Each class contains more than one spirit bearing similar attributes.

As in all primitive societies, so also among the Santals, religion performs an important social role. This, however, does not mean that the Santals do not relate to their agrarian activities from a pragmatic perspective. Through elementary reasoning based on one's own observation of the processes of nature, the Santals have acquired a certain amount of rudimentary scientific knowledge. They are thus conscious of the natural course of growth, the variations of the weather, the properties of plants, fruits and flowers, the qualities of different kinds of soil, as well as the ordinary pests and dangers to be warded off. They are also cognisant of the fact that the uniform action of natural laws coupled with human work and industry produces definite results.

But experience has also shown them that even when one has

[1]Levi-Strauss, Claude, *The Savage Mind*, Chicago: Chicago University Press, 1968, p. 74. Speaking of religious beliefs and practices in primitive societies, W. Dubre points out that, 'The religious phenomena in primitive cultures, however, do not present themselves, as do the so-called world religions, within a doctrinal system and a set of ideas that claim universal or cross-cultural recognition' (1975:245).

a rational approach to agriculture and life, there are still many aspects over which one has little or no control and whose outcomes cannot be predicted. Among the Santals, the *bongas* or spirits are believed to exercise power over these contingencies of nature and, therefore, Santals have recourse to them through magical or religious practices. Broadly speaking, the Santals' beliefs in these personal supernatural spirits and the ways of entering into relations with them constitute their religion. This fits in with Radcliffe-Brown's view that 'religion is everywhere an expression, in one form or another, of a sense of dependence on a power outside ourselves' (1959:157). It is precisely this urge to communicate and to enter into alliance with the higher supernatural world which has led the Santals to personify and, in certain cases, even individualise their spirits.

In religion proper, the Santals' relation towards these supernatural spirits is one of reverential fear, dependence, submission and propitiation. Communion with these spirits is concretely manifested mainly through supplications, rice-beer offerings and animal sacrifices made on behalf of a particular group, be it the whole village, subclan or household. To these must be added the ceremonial sharing of sacrificial food and rice-beer libations, besides certain special observances and taboos.

In the worship of the *bongas*, we can distinguish analytically two inter-related aspects, namely the instrumental and the expressive. On the one hand, the performance of the religious rites expresses the recognition of the existence of the supernatural powers that can be exercised by the *bongas*. On the other hand, the powers of the *bongas* are generally invoked to secure the goodwill of the beneficent ones and to avert the ill-will of the maleficent ones. In other words the instrumental aspect behind these religious rites expresses an alliance with the benevolent *bongas* and through them control of the harmful spirits. The expressive aspect is symbolised and manifested in a special manner in the various seasonal rites and festivals correlated to the annual agricultural cycle and the recurring rites of passage. Through these feasts, the Santals acknowledge in an emphatic way the spirits as their lords and protectors. They also offer the Santals an occasion to thank their spirits and to rejoice with them. How the instrumental and the expressive character of the religious beliefs and values of the Santals are manifested in the rites and ceremonies associated with their life-cycle events will be discussed in Chapters IV and V. In Chapter VI, we shall discuss the nature and function of Santal magic. In the present chapter, an attempt will be made to describe and analyse the beliefs of the Santals associated with supernatural spirits and impersonal powers.

THE SUPREME DEITY

Like other tribes, the Santals recognise a supreme deity to whom they attribute a pre-eminent position among all the religious beings.[2] According to their tradition, the Santals' belief originally centred on a supreme deity whom they called *Thakur* (Bodding, 1942:132). Though undoubtedly this word is the same word as *thakkura*, found in very late Sanskrit, Risley's association of the word *Thakur* with a later stage of Santal theological development seems to be rather unfounded.[3] O'Malley (1910:118), taking into consideration the Santals' custom of avoiding the mention of anyone's proper name, explains the assimilation by saying that the Santals took the word *Thakur* to replace an older name which they had forgotten. Similarly, Datta-Majumder (1956:11) speaks of the application by the Santals of the Hindi word *Thakur* to their supreme deity as an instance of syncretism.[4] This theory appears more plausible, especially when one considers the fact that, since the Santals had wandered from one place to another prior to their reaching Chotanagpur, their language, naturally enough, was influenced by the people with whom they came in contact.

[2]Andrew Lang, *The Making of Religion*, London: Longmans, Green & Co., 1898, indicated the existence among sóme Australian tribes of the belief in what he called a 'high god'; Pater Schmidt, *The Origin and Growth of Religion· Facts and Theories*, London: Methuen, 1931, adduced a lot of evidence to prove that this belief in a supreme deity was universal among all the peoples of the simplest cultures.

[3]Risley, H.H., *The People of India*, Delhi: Oriental Books Reprint Corporation, 1969, App. VII.

[4]Herskovits, M.J., 'Problem, Method and Theory in Afro-American Studies', *Afroamerica*, 1, 1945, p. 19.

The most common Santal term now used for the supreme deity is *Cando* which also means the sun. The use of the same term has led many writers to believe that the Santals identify their supreme deity with the sun.[5] This, however, is inaccurate. What the Santals have in mind when using the word *Cando* to denote the supreme deity and the sun, is not that the sun itself is the supreme deity but that it is a manifestation of divine activity, a sign of the divine in relation to man and of significance to him. Because of this, the East, the place of the rising sun, has great significance in Santal rituals and practices. Thus, when worshipping their spirits, they always face the East. The East is associated with life. The association, not identification, is also shown when most solemn oaths are taken. In such cases *Cando* is called upon to act as a witness, while the man taking the oath stands facing the East. To show further the distinction which the Santals themselves make between their supreme deity and the sun, it is worth noting that while the Santals consider the sun to be a *bonga*, they do not consider their supreme deity to be so. 'The old gurus', remarks Bodding 'are positive that the supreme being is not a *bonga* but stands above all' (1932:324).

When referring to their supreme deity, the Santals of Pangro, besides the term *Cando*, use also the term *Thakur Jiu*. *Jiu* is the Santal word connoting 'spirit' in the sense of the life principle. They call the sun *Sin Cando* and the moon *Ninda Cando*. The Santals do not claim to see their supreme deity. When I asked some Santals of Pangro to tell me what *Thakur Jiu* looked like, I was told that 'He is not seen by any human eyes. Yet He himself sees all'. Nor do they think that anyone in this world is able to know what he is like in himself. In fact when they speak about his nature, they do so using adjectives which refer to attributes such as 'great' and 'good', or in metaphors taken from the

[5]E.G. Man (1867: Ch. VII) referred to the Santal supreme deity as *Cando* and as *Cando Bonga*. W.W. Hunter (1975:184) remarked that, '*Cando*, the sun god, although he seldom receives sacrifice, is theoretically acknowledged as supreme'. According to S.C. Mitra, *Thakur* is *Sin Cando*, or the sun and the moon is his wife, 'On A Far-Travelled Star-Myth', *Man in India*, Ranchi, 8(4), Oct.-Dec. 1928, p. 250. Similarly S.C. Roy (1972:15) has analysed the Oraon high god, *Dharmes*, as the sun god.

world around them, likening his greatness to the universe he has created.

The Santals believe that *Thakur Jiu* is the creator and sustainer of the universe. He is considered to be a benevolent deity. As Kolean remarks, 'God is thought to be fairly well satisfied with the Santals and will not distress them except when it may be absolutely necessary' (Bodding, 1925:1). Since he is good, the Santals are of the opinion that they do not have to worry about him very much. In fact, *Thakur Jiu* has no specific worship but is reverentially remembered in every important religious festival and in other important occasions such as marriage and death. In the latter, he is mentioned as the master of life and death. He is also called upon to act as a judge in solemn oath takings and at the re-entry of an ostracised person into Santal society. In such calamities as droughts and famines, he is specially invoked and a white fowl is sacrificed to him. But apart from this, no sacrifice is offered specifically to *Thakur Jiu*.[6]

In his study of primitive religion in Chotanagpur, S.C. Roy remarks that:

> Though there is a general similarity in the religious systems of the tribes of Chota Nagpur, what they really differ in, is the relative weighting of the different classes of supernatural powers recognised in their respective pantheons (1928:67).

Thus, while the Oraons focus most of their religious thought and attention on their supreme god *Dharmes* and on the powers of the evil eye, the Santals and other Munda speaking tribes are particularly solicitous about spirits or *bongas*.

[6]Datta-Majumder appears to have been misinformed when he speaks of a sacrifice called *Jom Sim* which every Santal must perform once in his lifetime in honour of *Thakur Jiu* (1956:49). Bodding (1935a:337) and G. Campbell, *Santali-English Dictionary*, Benagaria: Benagaria Mission Press, 1953, p. 363, show that the *Jom Sim* is a festival in honour of *Sin Cando Bonga*. See also Culshaw (1949:64) and Dalton, Edward Tuite, *Tribal History of Eastern India*, Delhi: Cosmo Pulications, 1973, p. 213.

SPIRITS: GENERAL CHARACTERISTICS

The belief of the Santals in the power of the *bongas*, who are said to constantly manifest themselves to men and to intervene in men's enterprises and affairs, is so strong that it colours their whole life. They believe that they are completely surrounded by these *bongas*. Gausdal (1960) records the names of one hundred and seventy-eight different *bongas* who are said to be prevalent among the Santals.

Santal tradition asserts that in primeval times the Santals had no *bongas* and that belief in these spirits and the propitiatory or religious ceremonies connected with them were instituted sometimes during their ancestors' wanderings.[7] Several ethnographers, basing themselves on Santal mythology, have paid exaggerated attention to speculations regarding the origin of *bonga* worship among the Santạls.[8] They, however, failed to portray the symbolic significance expressed through these myths which presented *bonga* worship as a necessary condition by which the Santal ancestors overcame the critical situations they encountered in their wanderings. On their flight from Campa and from the tyrant Mando Sin, whether when ecountered the Sungh door or the Bahi door which they could not force open, or the river which they could not cross, it was the *bongas* who came to their help and rescue.

It has often been said that fear is the father of religion. Mary Douglas (1966:13) points out that one of the peculiarities which made the nineteenth century sociologists and anthropologists separate primitive religions as a group from the great world religions was precisely the fact that the former were inspired by fear. A Study of Santal *bongas* and their attributes has led various authors to think of Santal religion as an almost

[7]S.C. Roy remarks that according to Oraon and Munda traditions in the beginning there was only a supreme being and that the cult of the deities and spirits and the ceremonies associated with them were instituted later on, namely in the second part of their legend of creation (1928:65-74).

[8]For some of the versions regarding the origin of *bonga* wo ship among the Santals, see Campbell, A, 'The Traditions of the Santals', op. cit., p. 28; Archer (1974:60); Mukherjea (1962:19): and Bodding (1942:9).

typical example of faith based on neurotic dread and apprehension which is most clearly expressed in the German word *angst*. Thus, for example, Hunter (1975:181) classifies the Santals' religious system as one of terror and depreciation. He represents the Santals as worshippers of malevolent spirits whose sole aim is to cause drought, disease and death. Similarly, according to Bodding (1925:1) the *bongas* are, without exception, all malevolent and the enemies of man. They can work only evil. They are supposed to harass humanity, to be the cause of all sickness and of all deaths resulting from evil.

A careful inquiry into the Santals' religious beliefs and ceremonies, however, shows such views to be inaccurate. It is true that all *bongas* have to be regularly appeased and kept satisfied, otherwise, if offended, they may cause any type of mischief. It is also true that all the *bongas* are very sensitive to all kinds of neglect and disobedience and that they are fussy about their rights. That there are some *bongas* who are by nature vicious and from whom inaction is all that can be hoped, cannot be denied. This, however, does not lead to the conclusion that all *bongas* are by nature spiteful. As we shall see, there are *bongas* who are intimately concerned with the Santals' welfare and integrity.

The idea that the Santals are mere worshippers of malevolent spirits and that the sole object of their worship is to avert disasters with which their spirits delight in afflicting mankind, appears to have arisen from confounding these two classes of spirits, namely, those who are naturally malevolent and those who are beneficent. It was, therefore, a mistake of the early Christian missionaries to regard all the *bongas* as demons. Just as in other religions there are good and bad angels, so also in the Santal religious system one can speak of good and bad *bongas*. Thus, for example, the Mundas distinguish between the *manita bongas* or the beneficent spirits and the *banita bongas* or the malevolent ones (S.C. Roy, 1970:268).

The various spirits recognised by the Santals may be broadly classified into ten categories or classes. This classification does not imply any notion of hierarchy in which one class is superior to the other.[9]

[9]The Santal spirits or *bongas* could also be differentiated on other

1. Village tutelary spirits consisting of *Maran Buru*, *Moreko-Turuiko*, *Jaher Era*, *Gosae Era*, *Pargana Bonga*, and *Manjhi Haram Bonga*.

2. The *abge bongas*, or subclan spirits.

3. Household spirits known as *orak bongas*.

4. The spirits of ancestors, known as *hapramko bongas*.

5. *Saket bongas* or the tutelary spirits of the Santal *ojhas*.

6. The *jom sim bongas*.

7. The *deku bongas*, or the Hindu deities found in the Santal pantheon.

8. The spirits who are by nature malevolent and spiteful and from whom inaction is all that can be hoped for. To this class belong the village boundary spirits (*sima bongas*), the spirits of the village outskirts (*bahre bongas*), mountain and hill spirits, water spirits, *Rongo Ruji* and *Baghut Bonga*.

9. The spirits who, through *ojha* divination, are found to be the cause of disease or other mischief and who have to be exorcised by the *ojha* himself otherwise the mischief caused by them will continue. These include the *naihar bongas*, *kisar bongas*, *thapna bongas*, and the *bonga* husbands of witches.

10. The tramp or stray mischievous spirits and impersonal powers which are not objects of worship but have to be scared away through exorcisms or magic. Among these we find *curins*, *bhuts*, *ekagudias* and *rakas*. Also included in this group are the impersonal powers believed to reside in or to be connected with certain objects. They are not directly connected with the Santals' religion, though the help of the benevolent *bongas* is sought to neutralise their evil effects. These, however, will be studied in a general manner when dealing with the nature and function of magic (Chapter VI).

To help us understand better the role and function which these spirits and impersonal powers have in Santal society, I shall now describe and analyse the beliefs connected with them.

criteria such as locality, nature and function of the spirits, the characteristics of the rites performed and the specific people who perform these rites.

VILLAGE SPIRITS (JAHER BONGAS)

MARAN BURU

He is the chief of the Santal *bonga* pantheon.[10] According to Santal mythology, he is supposed to have instructed the first Santal couple—*Pilcu Haram* and *Pilcu Budhi*—in sex and taught them how to brew rice-beer exhorting them to offer him rice-beer whenever they invoked his name. Following this, whenever offerings or libations are made, the Santals always invoke his name together with that of their ancestors.

He is believed to be the most powerful *bonga*. The Santals have always venerated him as a genial and kind grandfather and he is propitiated on all festivals and in rites of passage. The Santals also believe that there is a close affinity between *Maran Buru* and their ancestors. This is clearly shown in what is called the *Umul Ader* ceremony which occurs on the death of an individual (Chapter V).

In Santal mythology, as we have seen, the anthropomorphic image of *Maran Buru* is identified as one from whom the first human Santal couple received instructions on the making of rice-beer and the enjoyment of sex. Because of this the Christian missionaries forbade their converts to worship *Maran Buru* whom they identified with Satan, the principle of all evil, and exhorted their converts to abstain from drinking rice-beer. This was a tactic by which it was hoped that the new converts would be weaned from their former allegiance to *Maran Buru* and make them conform to Christian norms of sexual behaviour.[11]

MOREKO-TURUIKO

Though addressed in the plural (literally the name means

[10]He is also worshipped by the Bhumij, Birhors, Hos and Mundas. The Hos consider *Maran Buru* as a minor deity, Majumdar D.N., *The Affairs of a Tribe: A Study in Tribal Dynamics*, Lucknow: Universal Publishers Ltd., 1950, p. 258. Among the Birhors he is reckoned as a household spirit, S.C. Roy, ' 'The Religion of the Birhors' ', *Journal of the Bihar and Orissa Research Society*, Patna, 14(4), Dec. 1918 pp. 455-82.

[11]The tendency to equate *Maran Buru* with Satan came largely from the conservative and puritanical strands regarding drink and sex to be found in some of the Christian traditions of the missionaries.

'the five-six'), this spirit is worshipped only as one. Very little is known about this spirit whose identity is shrouded in mystery.[12] Various myths try to explain the curious number. According to one tradition, it is believed that they are five brothers and one sister (Bodding 1935b:324). Another myth cited by Mukherjea (1962:279) presents them as five brothers (*more* meaning 'five') who were wedded to six sisters (*turui* meaning 'six'). In other myths, they are referred to as being five brothers with *Jaher Era* as their mother.

Whatever be the actual identity of this composite spirit, he is believed to preside over the welfare of the village and to have control over rain, crops and epidemics. This is shown in some of the songs sung during the *Baha* or Flower festival.[13] Whenever a severe epidemic ravishes a village, the villagers placate this spirit by promising him special sacrifices to be offered on a special occasion known as *Mak More*.[14]

JAHER ERA

This spirit, as the name implies, is said to be the Lady of the Sacred Grove (*jaherthan*) over which she presides. The cult of the Old Lady as a tribal spirit is also prevalent among other tribals.[15] The Santals consider her a good-natured spirit who never does them any harm but who, on the contrary, is concerned about their bodily needs. A fowl is offered to her at all the festivals for the general welfare of the village, especially for obtaining good crops and for the good health of the villagers and their cattle. She is also invoked, whenever any cattle disease ravages a village. The Santals regard her not only as a personal spirit but also as a distinctively individualised one. This is clearly seen during the *Baha* or Flower festival (Chapter IV).

These three spirits, namely *Maran Buru*, *Moreko-Turuiko* and

[12]Hunter (1975:188) describes him as the husband of *Jaher Era*.

[13]See Bodding (1942:155)

[14]See Bodding (1942:212-213).

[15]Among the Oraons 'The Old Lady of the Grove' or *Chala Pachcho*, is the most popular deity. Known also as *Sarna Burhia* or *Jhakra Burhia*, she is considered as a sociable Oraon deity. S.C. Roy (1972:30). The Mundas call her *Jaher Buri*.

Jaher Era are, according to Santal belief, very closely associated with one another. Thus, in the *jaherthan*, where they are said to abide, there are three *sarjom* trees (*shorea robusta*) which should be in a row, the tallest two: the one for *Maran Buru* and that for *Jaher Era* being close together, while the third is for *Moreko-Turuiko*. At the foot of each tree, there is a stone representing each spirit which, according to Santal belief, is deposited by the respective spirit itself.[16]

The close connection of these three spirits is also manifested in various rituals. Thus, for example, on the occasion of restoring an outcasted Santal to the tribe (*Jom Jati*), these three spirits are propitiated by the village priest who offers three fowls, imploring the three spirits to purify the village from the guilt and defilement which the outcasted man has brought upon his whole village. Another instance which clearly manifests their close connection occurs during the *Baha* or Flower festival during which two huts or sheds are erected in the *jaherthan*, by the *kudam naeke* (assistant priest) and the other villagers. One of these huts is shared by *Maran Buru*, *Jaher Era* and *Moreko-Turuiko*.

Gosae Era

The second hut erected in the *jaherthan*, during the Flower festival, is in honour of this spirit who is worshipped along with the other spirits of the sacred grove. She is represented by a *matkom* tree (*bassia latifolia*) at the foot of which there is a stone. The Santals propitiate her against sores. A white fowl is sacrificed in her honour by the *naeke*. This spirit is worshipped by the Murmu and the Naeke khil (a subclan of the Murmu clan) as their *abge bonga* (subclan spirit). The Nij, Gar, Jugi and Sada subclans of the Murmu clan worship her as their *orak bonga* (household spirit).

When asked about the identity of this spirit, the people told me that she was a girl belonging to the blacksmith community. Because of this, when a Santal boy wanted to marry her, his mother objected. Being in love with the girl, the boy set up a separate hut and lived with her.[17]

[16]O'Malley (1910:116).

[17]A similar account is given by Archer (1974:240).

PARGANA BONGA

This spirit also is said to reside in the sacred grove where he is represented by a stone at the foot of one of the *sarjom* trees (*shorea robusta*). The Santals of Pangro were not clear as to whether this spirit was the symbolised spirit form of the office of the *pargana* or whether he represented the spirit of the first *pargana* of which the village was a part.[18] What is however sure is that this spirit has great significance for the Santals who believe that he has special powers over witches. Because of this, whenever there is any general illness in the village which is attributed to witches, this spirit is propitiated by the *ojha* who implores the spirit to rid the village of all malady and misfortune.

The spirits of the *jaherthan* are often considered by the Santals as their national spirits since they are worshipped by all. Sacrifices are performed during the principal festivals, namely the *Sohrae* (Harvest festival), the *Baha* (Flower festival), the *Erok Sim* (Sowing festival), *Hariar Sim* (Sprouting festival) and the *Janthar* (First Fruits festival). While *Maran Buru, Moreko-Turuiko, Jaher Era,* and *Gosae Era* are propitiated by the village priest (*naeke*), the *kudam naeke* (the priest's assistant) propitiates the *Pargana Bonga* through a blood-offering called *Bul Mayam*.[19]

MANJHI BONGA

Sometimes also called *Manjhi Haram*, this spirit is believed to preside over the village. As in the case of *Pargana Bonga*, the

[18]According to Datta-Majumder (1956:100) this spirit seems to be a spiritual counterpart of the Santal social institution of *pargana* or headman of a group of villages. V.K. Kochar remarks that 'the nomenclature similarity of the *bonga* with the particular office incumbent in social organisation is only an analogy', 'More village Bongas of the Santals', *Folklore*, Calcutta, 5(12), Dec. 1964, p. 451. To substantiate his argument, the same author also shows how the worship of this spirit has been found in areas where there was no *pargana*.

[19]Pricking various parts of his body with a thorn, the *kudam naeke* mixes the ensuing drops of blood with some grains of *adwa caole* (rice husked without previously having been boiled) and offers them to *Pargana Bonga*. This practice is believed to make the rite more

Santals of Pangro are not sure if this spirit represents the original headman or founder of their village or whether he is the spirit of headmanship in general.[20]

As in all Santal villages, this spirit does not reside in the *jaherthan* but has a special place built for him facing the headman's house. This is called *manjithan*. Here he is represented by a stone at the foot of the central wooden post.[21] He is believed to act as the spiritual adviser to the current headman. In fact, it is the headman himself who is supposed to propitiate this spirit by offering libations of rice-beer and sacrificing two pigeons, which are provided by the headman himself. The heads of the sacrificed pigeons are eaten only by the headman. It is believed that through this ritual communication, the present headman derives his authority from his predecessors.[22] The offering of sacrifices to the dead headman of a particular village is a matter of vital concern to the members of that particular village. In fact, during the course of my fieldwork in Pangro, the villagers at one time accused the acting *manjhi* Sona Marandi of not having given the two pigeons necessary to propitiate the *Manjhi Bonga*. A *Kulhi Durup* was called and Sona was made to pay a fine of fifty rupees. This spirit is considered to be a benevolent *bonga*. In fact, it is very rarely divinised by the medicine-man to be the cause of any general calamity. Both the *Pargana* and the *Manjhi Bonga* are believed to have supervisory powers over other *bongas*.

The Santals acknowledge the mentioned spirits not only as protectors of their villages, but also as intimately concerned with their well-being. They are believed to guide the Santals in every concern of life and also to order every human event.

efficacious since the blood flowing in a person's veins is said to have fecundating powers. It is also common among other Munda tribes. See also Durkheim (1967:371).

[20]Bodding (1932:324) speaks of him as the spirit of the original headman or founder of the village. O'Malley (1910:116) remarks that he is the spirit of the *manjhiship* in general.

[21]Culshaw (1949:82) remarks that in Bankura district of West Bengal clay effigies of elephants or horses are set up in the *manjhithan* in honour of the spirits of the departed headmen.

[22]In Pangro, however, it is the *naeke* who propitiates the *Manjhi Bonga*. This is because the present *manjhi* is a woman and all sacrifices are considered taboo for women.

Through their aid, good omens are said to be acquired when searching for a new village. When appealed to, they are also said to stop any kind of epidemic. They are also credited with the supervision of the Santal tribe as a tribe. Some scholars have chosen to describe them as the 'national deities' of the Santals. Because of the importance given to these *jaher* spirits, the Santals are very careful not to make these spirits feel neglected or insulted. They must also on no account be polluted since it is believed that once the village becomes polluted, these *bongas* immediately withdraw their protective power and concern, thus leaving the villagers vulnerable to harm brought about by mischievous spirits. As a consequence, no festival is performed unless a village is judged to be totally cleansed from defiling impurities.

This urge for village ritual cleansing so as to regain these spirits' protective power can be seen whenever a birth or death occurs in a village. Since both events are considered unavoidably polluting, the purifying rituals, *Janam Chatiar*, in the case of a birth, and *Tel Nahan* or *Nai Gada*, in the case of a death, are promptly performed so that the village may again enjoy the aid and care of their *jaher bongas*.[23] Until these ceremonies are performed, the whole village remains polluted and no festivals, weddings or sacrifices can take place. The household members cannot offer sacrifices to their *bongas*, nor can they eat or drink with others. Village worship is at a standstill. The inconvenience is so great that it is everybody's wish to end it quickly. Thus, though according to Santal custom, the *Janam Chatiar* ceremony is to be performed after five days in the case of a male child and after three days in the case of a female, this ceremony is anticipated if a festival is imminent. This is what happened in 1973 when Salgi Murmu, wife of Bajal Soren, gave birth to a boy two nights before the *Sohrae* festival. Since no one wanted to delay the celebrations, the *Janam Chatiar* was performed the next morning and the *Sohrae* began on the fixed day. Pollution may also be the result of the individual's faults. Thus, a village is also polluted when the tribal rules of endogamy are infringed, as when, for example, a Santal has sexual

[23]The spirits' protection is regained once the appropriate ritual has been performed.

relations with a non-Santal and persists in it. The *bongas* are defiled, and withdraw their protection.

Another point worth mentioning is the fact that although the *bongas* of the sacred grove are the same for all the Santals living in different villages, no two villages share the same *jaher bongas*. Their worship is valid for the members of a particular village only. Thus, if during a certain festival in a particular village there are visitors from another village, the latter are not permitted to worship the sacred grove spirits of that village. Besides, if one family were to move to another village, the members of that family acquire a relationship with the new sacred grove. This association of a village with the *jaher* expresses the ritual unity of the group.

SUBCLAN SPIRITS (ABGE BONGAS)

While the *jaher bongas* protect the Santals as a tribe, there is another class of *bongas* known as *abge bongas* which act as tutelary spirits to each different subclan or *khut*. We have already seen how the Santal tribe was originally divided into twelve exogamous clans of which one, the Bedea clan, has been lost. These clans are further sub-divided into a number of subclans known as *khuts*, the number of which varies from clan to clan. Enquiries made by Gausdal (1960) in the district of Santal Parganas led to the tabulation of 405 different subclans distributed among the eleven prevalent clans.

That the *khut* system is intimately connected with the worship of the *bongas* is evident. As the saying quoted by Bodding (1935a:750) points out, 'Mitkhutren kanale, mit khondrele bongaka', meaning, 'We belong to the same subclan, we perform sacrifices in the same magic circle (i.e., to the same *bongas*)'.[24] In actual practice, however, the sphere of participation in *abge bonga* worship is not the same for the whole *khut* group. In this connection, the term I often heard in the village

[24]S.C. Roy (1972:49) remarks how the Bhunkars, the descendants of the original founder or founders of an Oraon village, are divided into *khunts* (branches amongst whom the original clearances were divided). They are entrusted with the propitiating of their respective *khunt-bhuts* or spirits attached to their respective *khunt* lands.

of Pangro during *abge* worship is *gutia*, which can perhaps best be translated as the local patrilineal lineage. Women are excluded from partaking in *abge* worship for reasons which we shall soon explain.

To be admitted to a Santal subclan is to be associated with its *bongas*. Because of this, the formal giving of a name, clan and subclan, to the newborn child is an essential part of the *Nim Dak Mandi* ceremony. The announcement of the name formally admits the child to his father's clan and gives him the protection of his own *abge bongas*. A child cannot remain without *bongas* and hence it is extremely important for him to have a legal father who gives the child his clan and admits him to his *bongas*. If a child has no father, then it has no subclan and hence it cannot worship any *abge bongas*. So long as the child is known to be illegitimate, it cannot even marry within the tribe. In short, it is not considered a Santal. The *Nim Dak Mandi* ceremony or formal acceptance of a child by a father removes all traces of illegitimacy.

In the case of adoption, if the adopted son is of a clan or subclan different from his adoptive father's he must change his *bongas* and adopt those of his foster father.[25] To do this he must undergo a ceremony called *Bonga Tala*, which literally means 'to put between the *bongas*', that is, to adopt formally, to naturalise. The ceremony is a replica of the *Nim Dak Mandi*, or naming ceremony. Having passed through this ceremony the adopted son is considered to have shed his former *bongas* and so he is allowed to share in his adoptive family's sacrificial meal. It is in fact this change of *bongas* which makes him the man's own son. The adoption cannot be negated or cancelled once the son has been 'brought into his father's *bongas*'. If the adopted son belongs to the same subclan as that of his adoptive father then, since he already has full access to his 'father's' *bongas*, a formal approval by the village elders is enough and he has not to undergo the *Bonga Tala* ceremony. Similarly no *Bonga Tala* ceremony is performed when the adopted son's mother is one with whom sexual relations by the adoptive

[25]Since the boy is of a different clan or subclan, his *bongas* are different from those of his adopting father. To be formally recognised as a son by the villagers, he must change his *bongas*.

father are forbidden.[26] The adopted son would continue to retain his own name and clan.

The *abge bongas* are a class of *bongas*. They are considered to be the most sacred and the most guarded household spirits and are said to give earthly blessings and to save in time of danger.[27] In the case of disease and distress within a household, the Santals appeal to them, believing that once this is done the disease will suddenly disappear. They are also said to look after the crops and other belongings of their worshippers.

They are the most personal spirits of the Santals. Their names are not, under any circumstance, to be known to other people. They are only known by the head of a household who keeps them secret till just before his death when he whispers them to his eldest son. If a Santal were to die without disclosing the names to his eldest son, then the latter must take into confidence another member of his subclan who already knows them. This is very important, since he can solemnise the sacrifice to the *abge bongas* only after he has learnt their names. The Santals believe that even uttering the names of such *bongas* may cause them to appear and cause the greatest calamity. Special care is taken to keep this secret away from women for fear that if a witch gets hold of an *abge bonga*, then the members of the household will die.[28] In such cases, an *ojha* has to be consulted and special sacrifices must be performed.

Though Skrefsrud (1968:166) reports that from primeval times the *gurus* knew the names of the *abge bongas*, very little is known about how the Santals began to worship these spirits. A study of their folklore reveals that whenever the Santals had fallen into great misfortune, they were rescued by these spirits who appeared to the afflicted persons in human form and asked them to worship them as their protectors.

[26]Sister's son, son of a daughter of a paternal or maternal uncle or aunt, son of a stepchild, son of wife's elder sister. In such cases, the *Bonga Tala* ceremony would be putting the child's adopting father in an incestuous relation with the child's mother.

[27]See Bodding (1942:157).

[28]O'Malley (1910:122); Kochar, V.K. (1963:59-72). Similarly, according to S.C. Roy (1972:51), among the Oraons, the *khunt-bhuts* are said to become displeased at the instigation or the incantation of a witch or sorcerer.

To honour their *abge bongas* and to ensure their continuing protection, the Santals, once a year, offer sacrifices to these spirits. It is believed that if sacrifices are not offered, the *abges* will grow impatient and cause calamity. The Santals of Pangro sacrifice to their *abges* during the *Erok Sim* or Sowing festival held in the month of *Asar* (June-July). Those who, for some reason or other, do not do so, make it a point to worship their *abges* during the *Sohrae* festival.[29] Though, according to their traditions, the sacrifice is to be performed in an open field close to a white ant-hill[30] the Santals of Pangro now bring a piece of earth from an ant-hill into their cowshed and perform the sacrifice there.[31] Rams and pigs are the animals mostly sacrificed. Women are completely excluded from participating in the sacrificial meal.[32] If the people present are not able to eat everything, the leftovers are burnt. This is done to divert the evil eye of malevolent spirits, powers and witches.

The invocations used, as also the rite of the sacrifice always follow the same pattern. The day prior to the fixed date, the people who are to partake in the sacrifice, go for a purificatory bath. Such ablutions are believed to remove all possible supernatural evil influences. The person chosen to perform the sacrifice must fast, sleep on the ground, and abstain from sexual intercourse. The sexual act is credited with a mysterious power and is consequently tabooed before and during rituals. The following morning his wife, after taking her bath, pounds some flour and some *adwa caole* which she gives to her husband along with two leaf cups, one containing *sindur* (vermilion)

[29]According to O'Malley (1910:122), there is no fixed date on which these sacrifices are to take place, 'each man performing them when it suits his convenience'. Gausdal (1960:25) points out that these sacrifices are offered during the month of *Asar* (June-July) or during the month of *Aghar* (November-December).

[30]See Bodding (1942:157); Gausdal (1960:55, 79, 88, 110, 131, 137, 148).

[31]The fact that *abge* worship is performed outside the *bhitar*, differentiates the *abge bongas* from the other household spirits. According to S.C. Roy, *The Birhor: A Little known Jungle Tribe of Chotanagpur*, op cit., p. 173, among the Birhors, the ant-hill is a symbol of the totem of the clan deities called 'hili buru bonga'. For a further study regarding the belief in white ant-hills, see Crooke (1925:380ff).

[32]Culshaw (1949:84) points out that this same prohibition applies to sons-in-law.

and the other oil. In the meantime her husband goes to a place near a white ant-hill and collects some earth which he carries to the cowshed. Here, all the other members who are to take part in the sacrifice are gathered. The officiating person then prepares the *khond* or sacrificial altar. This he does by first clearing a small patch of ground which he then plasters with cowdung. Marking a circle with flour, he places some *adwa caole* in the centre, making a number of *sindur* marks around it. The animal is then made to eat from the *adwa caole*. The invocation to the *abges* is uttered and the animal is either beheaded or its throat cut. The sacrificial animal is then cooked with rice and eaten on the spot. Once this is over, everyone returns to his respective house.

In his study of the Santal *khuts*, Gausdal (1960) records various names of *abge bongas* from which two major points emerge—(*i*) Certain *khuts* pertaining to the same clan have the same *abge bongas*. This perhaps is most evident in the case of the Soren clan where no less than six different *khuts* have *Acrali* as their *abge bonga*; (*ii*) On the other hand, certain *khuts*, pertaining to various clans also share the same *abge bongas*. Thus, *Campadanagar* is the *abge* of eight *khuts* belonging to four different clans. In fact, of the sixty-one different *abge bongas* mentioned by Gausdal, thirty are shared by *khuts* belonging to more than one clan. Another interesting thing is that certain *khuts* have more than one *abge bonga*. Thus, for example the Nij Hasdaks honour *Campadanagar* and *Katkomkudra* as their *abges*. However, the meat of animals and fowls offered to the *abge bongas* is taboo to people of other subclans. The idea behind this taboo is the belief that although these spirits are helpful to the members of that particular subclan they may be harmful to members of other subclans.

HOUSEHOLD SPIRITS (ORAK BONGAS)

Another class of *bongas* as numerous as the *abge bongas* and as benevolent, are the *orak bongas* or household *bongas*. Like the *abge bongas*, the *orak bongas* are considered to be the most personal spirits of the Santals. In fact, they regard their *orak bongas* in terms of personal relationship and even ownership.

They are assumed to be most intimately related with the household members whom they protect from any malevolent spirits. The names of the *orak bongas* are only known by the head of the household. He tells them to his eldest son when he is dying. The Santals are always careful to keep an amiable relationship with their *orak bongas* whom they hold in great veneration. In the event of disease or any other distress in the household, the Santals appeal to them.[33] As in the case of *abge bonga* worship, very little is known of how the Santals began worshipping their *orak bongas*.[34] Though the names of the *orak bongas* are not divulged to the female members of a household, they do partake of the sacrificial offerings to these spirits.

It is worth noting that after marriage, a woman gains a ritual relationship with a different set of *orak bongas*. This custom ensures that a woman will not be the cause of any calamity to her husband's house, a thing which would have been highly probable were she to continue having dealings with the spirits of her father's *khut* and household. In fact, a married woman is not even allowed to enter the *bhitar* (sacred place) of her father's house (*naihar*). These spirits are inherited patrilineally so that the various domestic groups belonging to the same family line are likely to have the same set of *orak bongas*. Because of this, I prefer using the term *gharonj renko* to signify the body of worshippers in connection with *orak bonga* propitiation. The term *gharonj* can best be translated to mean 'an extended household or a family'.[35] According to Kochar (1963:65), most of the names of the *orak bongas* refer to forests, hills, rivers and sometimes, even to Hindu gods and goddesses. I would go a step further and say that certain Santal households have taken Hindu deities as their *orak bongas*. Thus *Kali*, *Dibi* (*Durga*) and *Mahadev* (*Siva*), are honoured as *orak bongas* by certain households in Pangro.[36]

[33]Among the Mundas, the household gods, *ora bongako*, are the spirits of the deceased ancestors of each Munda household. They are worshipped by the head of every Munda household in the *ading* or sacred place of the house. S.C. Roy, 1970:267.

[34]Kochar, V.K. (1963:59-71).

[35]Skrefsrud (1968) used this term in connection with *abge bonga* worship.

[36]Datta-Majumder (1956:127) is of the opinion that the Santals

The close personal relationship between a Santal household and its *orak bongas* is clearly seen from the fact that in every Santal house, a small place is reserved for the household spirits and the ancestors. It is here that sacrifices are offered to these spirits.[37] This place is called the *bhitar*, an Indo-Aryan word that means 'within'.[78] It is separated from the rest of the main dwelling house by a low mud wall about four feet high. No sacred emblems or symbols are kept in the *bhitar* which, in fact, is often used as a storage place particularly for *bandis* (bundles of reserve rice). Women, other than those belonging to the household, are not permitted to enter. The same restriction holds good for married daughters of the household, for, as we have seen, after marriage, a woman belongs to her husband's household and spirits.

To honour their *orak bongas* and to ensure the continuing welfare of the household in every respect, each Santal householder in Pangro normally sacrifices fowls or pigs during the *Sohrae* or Harvest festival.[39] When, for some reason or other, a householder is not able to do so, then he worships his *orak bongas* during the *Baha* festival. Otherwise, during the *Baha*, only *handi* (rice-beer) libations are made. The various *gharonj* members of Pangro use a rotation system in propitiating their *orak bongas*.[40]

The evening prior to the sacrifice, everyone washes and bathes. The person who is to officiate, fasts and also sleeps on the floor. He is not to have sexual relations with his wife.

belief in *orak bongas* has its counterpart in the Hindu belief in *Griha Lakshmi.*

[37]Bodding (1956:476) remarks that the *orak bongas* are generally propitiated in the cowshed.

[38]S.C. Roy (1970:26) reports that the Mundas also install the spirits of the dead in the *Bhitar* or *Ading* as household deities.

[39]Kochar (1963:64) remarks that although, according to Santal customs, *orak bongas* should be propitiated every year, certain households do so on alternate years.

[40]Thus, in the case of Sona Marandi, Dulari Marandi, Bhattu Murmu and Kapre Kisku and their respective households, since they all belong to one patrilineal family—the Murmus—the annual sacrifice to the *orak bongas* is done in one of the four houses by rotation. The household head in whose house the sacrifice takes place, officiates at the sacrifice and pays for everything.

Outsiders are not allowed to enter the house. In the morning, the wife of the person who is to officiate grinds some *adwa caole* into flour, some of which she uses for making cakes. When this is done, all gather at the *bhitar* and the *khond* is prepared. The animal to be sacrificed is marked with vermilion on its head, chest and forelimb. Then, while it is eating some of the *adwa caole*, the officiating person utters the invocation, addressing the *orak bonga*s by name and invoking it/them to protect all the members present from any sickness or misfortune. Having done so, he beheads the animal. Three libations of *handi* (rice-beer) specially prepared for the occasion are then poured on the *khond* in honour of the *bonga*. The people present then drink *handi* and partake of the victim cooked with rice.

ANCESTRAL SPIRITS (HAPRAMKO BONGAS)

In addition to the household *bongas*, each Santal household worships the spirits of its ancestors called *Hapramko Bongas*.[41] Ancestor worship is a strong factor in Santal social and household solidarity.[42]

The term ancestor worship is sometimes used in a very wide sense to refer to any sort of rituals performed in honour of dead persons including tribal or national heroes and leaders. Here, I will be using the term in the way in which Radcliffe-Brown has used it, limiting the cult group to the 'members of a lineage with reference to the deceased members of the lineage' (Radcliffe-Brown, 1959:164). Ancestors are kin. In most cases they are senior kin and the living behave towards them as towards senior living kin.

[41]Among the Oraons, the spirits of the dead ancestors are venerated as a separate class of spirits. S.C. Roy, (1972:10).

[42]Ancestor worship has played a very important part in the religion of ancient Greece and Rome. It is also a very important feature of traditional Chinese and Japanese societies. Cults of the same kind exist today in many parts of Africa and Asia. The degree of interaction between the dead and the living varies from culture to culture. See Ahern Emily M., *The Cult of the Dead in a Chinese Village*, California: Standford University Press, 1973; Herskovits, M.J., *Dahomey*, Vol. 2, New York: Panther House, 1938; Noss, J.B., *Man's Religions*, New York: Macmillan, 1963; Kuper, H., *The Swazi: A South African Kingdom*, New York: Holt, Rinehart & Winston, Inc., 1963.

The basis behind ancestor worship is the belief that at the death of an individual, his social personality is not annihilated but rather transformed. 'The belief in ancestor spirits', Malinowski points out 'is the result of the belief in immortality . . . which is the result of a deep emotional revelation, standardised by religion rather than a primitive philosophical tradition' (1954:51). The Santals, like most primitive tribes, hold the belief in the survival of the soul after death. According to the original Santal conception, the 'soul' after leaving the body, becomes a *bonga*. The phrases often used when one dies are 'nitok doe hapramena' meaning 'now he has become an ancestor (died)', or, simply, 'bongaenae', meaning 'he has become a *bonga*'. The word *hapram* is nowadays almost exclusively used when referring to the dead.

One however becomes a *hapram bonga* only after his funerary rites have been performed. Those who die an unnatural death or without their *Caco Chatiar* ceremony, those who die from certain infectious diseases such as leprosy, smallpox, etc., and women who die in pregnancy or in childbirth, are not given full funerary rites. They do not achieve full spiritual status and their ghosts are believed to continue hovering around the world as *bhuts* or *curins*. With the *Tel Nahan* ceremony, performed five days after a person's death, the dead person is freed from the enemy that killed him but is not as yet admitted to the realm of the ancestors. He dallies in the household's *bhitar*.[43] It is only once the *Bhandan* ceremony is over that he finally joins his ancestors, along with whom he continues taking active interest in the household affairs. Ancestors are believed to 'live' with the living, assisting at births and weddings, and also in the settling of household problems. In this way, the living and dead of the same lineage stand in a close relationship with each other. The dead are said to be aware of the actions and even the thoughts of their

[43]S.C. Roy (1972:26) reports how, among the Oraons, through the *Ekh-Mankhna* ceremony, the shade of a deceased person is said to be brought back to his former house to remain there till it is admitted into the community of the *Pach-balar* (the pre-deceased relatives) through the *Utur-Khila* ceremony. The Khonds of Orissa and the Gonds of the Central Provinces call back the shades of the dead to their old homes through similar ceremonies.

living relatives. So long as they are remembered, ancestors continue influencing a household's affairs helping out in times of crises. It is almost a duty of the spirits of the departed to see to the welfare of their living relatives.

Ancestor worship serves to keep the memory of the dead alive and welds the community of the living into one with those who have lived in the past. Their welfare is bound up with that of their living relatives. For one generation, at least, they must not be ignored and the conventional tributes must be given to them. Otherwise, though generally benevolent, they would visit the family with sickness and other misfortunes for they are very sensitive to neglect and would make the careless and the forgetful ill. Hence, as with other primitive tribes, the Santals have special rites of veneration for their ancestors. In all festivals, private or public, they are venerated and special offerings are made to them. Their blessings are invoked at every social ceremony. Whenever fresh *handi* is drunk, libations are poured out in their honour. Similarly, the Santals had a custom which is slowly being forgotten, according to which the woman of the house, while preparing the food, used to set aside some uncooked rice grains for the ancestors, making the meal a communion between the dead and the living.[44] This supports Archer's statement that:

> whether it is a time of drinking rice-beer, eating a meal, celebrating a festival, a birth or a wedding or placating the *bongas* the recent dead must be given their small offering (1974:341).

During the *Sohrae*, fowls and rice-beer libations are offered by each family in honour of its ancestors.

Since the Santals believe that their ancestors are still alive as spirits with human qualities and needs, they insist that in their sacrifices there must be the feeling that the ancestors 'are really there'. Thus, during the *Sohrae*, as many relatives as have died from the time of the grandfather and grandmother

[44]S.C. Roy (1972:24) reports a similar custom among the orthodox Oraons.

are each offered a fowl.[45] The name of each person is mentioned.[46] If, due to the lack of fowls, sacrifices to the departed are not made during the *Sohrae*, then these sacrifices are performed during the *Baha* festival. Otherwise, only rice-beer libations are offered in their honour during the *Baha* and the *Erok* or Sowing festival.

Sacrifices to the departed are an extension of filial piety. The eldest male member of the household acts as the officiating priest. If there is no male member of the household qualified to perform the sacrifice, then an agnate of the departed is asked to do so.[47] On the day of the sacrifice the *bhitar* is cleansed and plastered with cowdung. The officiating person does not observe any specific taboos, except that he does not eat anything on the eve of the sacrifice and he takes a purificatory bath. The sacrificial rite is the same as for the *orak bongas*, with the following modifications. No vermilion is used; the sacrificed fowl is not beheaded but it is slain by a blow on the back of the head without any blood being sprinkled on the rice in the *khond*. The ancestral *bongas* are 'made to eat' of the sacrificial meal (*sura daka*) and 'to drink' of the *handi* together with the other living relatives present. In fact, leaf plates containing *sura daka* and leaf cups containing rice-beer are first offered to each of the ancestral spirits prior to anyone present starting to eat and drink.

The social function of the mentioned ritual sacrifices offered to the ancestral spirits is now clear. Their solemnity and collective expression help to reaffirm and strengthen the solidarity of the family. As Radcliffe-Brown (1959:164) observed, they give stability to the social structure by giving solidarity and continuity to the lineage, past, present and future. The Santal is made to feel a certain dependence on his ancestors, who, in turn, watch over him with loving care as long as they are remembered and venerated. Otherwise, they will not only stop sending their blessings but will visit him with illness

[45]Gausdal remarks, 'It is one hen for every one who has died; father, mother, uncle, aunt, brother, sister or children' (1960:192).

[46]The farthest relatives remembered by name among the Santals are the grandfather and grandmother. Very few remember their grandfather's father by name.

[47]See Archer (1974:341).

or other misfortunes. The motives involved in ancestor worship, though not always the same, are chiefly: (*i*) a desire to venerate the dead; (*ii*) a desire for their blessings and protection; (*iii*) a feeling of reverence due to them; (*iv*) a fear of incurring their wrath. In short, we can say that the feelings of the living towards their dead relatives are ambivalent, compounded of affection and fear. The family, represented by the living and the dead, continues to be a focus of powerful sentiments. It is, therefore, unfortunate that those Santals who become Christians are forbidden to make any animal offerings to their ancestors. As Culshaw remarks: 'the Christians are evidently aware of a void in the teaching that they have received in regard to it' (1949:177).

TUTELARY BONGAS OF THE OJHAS (SAKET BONGAS)

We have seen how the *jaher bongas* protect the Santals as a tribe, the *abge bongas* their *khut* members, the *orak bongas* their household members and the *hapram bongas* their patrilineage members. There is still another class of *bongas* whose function is one of beneficence These are the *saket bongas* or the tutelary *bongas* of the *ojhas*, medicine-men who also act as exorcists and diviners.[48]

The *ojha*, who is one of the most respected persons in a village is believed to have special retained *bongas* through whose aid the forces of evil and sorceries are countered. The Santals do acknowledge natural causes of illness. Yet, if the disease is of an unusual character and does not respond to various medicines taken, it is attributed to the displeasure of a *bonga* or to the presence of a malevolent agent. Similarly, when a number of misfortunes occur within a short time in a house, the members suspect the presence of a malevolent agent.

[48]The Santal name for the 'herbal doctors' is *raranic* meaning 'one who administers medicine (*ran*)'. These are different from the *ojhas* in so far that whilst the former give only medicine, the *ojhas* also try to drive away the disease by magic, incantations, etc.

In such cases, an *ojha* is called upon[49] to indicate the cause and nature of the malady or misfortune. He then performs the *Sunum Bonga* ceremony, or the divination by leaves, to discover what spirit has been offended and how to appease it. In doing this, he maintains that his body is simply possessed by one of his tutelary *bongas* who speaks through him. The methods of divination will be described in Chapter VI.

Once a particular *bonga* is divinised on the oil leaf, the *ojha* tries to use one of his tutelary *bongas* against the malevolent *bonga* or mischievous impersonal power, appealing to the knowledge and asking for the help of all his other tutelary *bongas*. He then tells the relatives of the sick person that the malevolent agent is offended and that he should be satisfied through sacrifices and libations. On his part, the *ojha* vows to perform a sacrifice to his tutelary *bongas*, once the patient is cured. Hence, the name *saket bongas*.[50]

These special *bongas* with whom the *ojha* is believed to be in communication and whose power he enlists in time of need are many and different. Bodding (1925:I:64-67), records the names of 104 *saket bongas*. Different *saket bongas* are invoked according to the predilection and faith of the particular *ojha* called upon. Some *ojhas* have a predilection for one, others for another. Besides, certain *bongas* are only invoked for particular diseases. Thus, for example, *Luri Lora* is invoked in the case of smallpox; *Duria Bardo* and *Nason Candi* in cases of madness; *Bhalua Bijai Julumpaika*, *Kapi Karan*, and *Ulumpaika* in the case of women whose labour is protracted; *Gosae Era* against sores, while *Jaher Era* and *Nag Nagin* are invoked for cattle diseases.[51] The *saket bongas* who are specially remembered and invoked are *Kamru guru*

[49]Bodding (1935b:454) reports the following Santal saying: 'Ruak hor ran (t)e bako phariak khan atoren hor ojhako khari ocoyea', which means 'When a sick person does not recover by medicine, the village people will cause an *ojha* to make divination'.

[50]To the Santal, the term *saket*, means a sacrifice vowed to a *bonga* by an *ojha* to be performed when the patient recovers. The term is also used as an adjective meaning the particular *bonga* to whom the *ojha* makes such a vow and whose assistance he is supposed to secure (Bodding 1925:V).

[51]Bodding (1925:64-8).

(from whom, according to Santal traditions the Santal *ojha* have originally learnt their profession), *Serma Sin Thakur*, sometimes also called *Sin Bonga* (the Sun), *Kali Mai* (the Hindu goddess *Kali*), *Dibi Mai* (the Hindu goddess *Durga*), and *Ganga Mai* (the Ganges' goddess). These five *bongas* are invoked by the *ojha* at the opening ceremony of the course during which the young men of the village are taught the fundamentals of *ojha* science (Chapter VI).

Most of the *saket bongas* invoked by the Santal *ojhas* have names of Hindu origin. Many of them also appear to be of a somewhat different nature from the ordinary Santal *bongas*. On the basis of these two factors and also the fact that the work of a Santal *ojha* resembles that of his Hindu counterpart, Bodding expressed the view that the Santal *ojhas* have adopted, or rather received, the 'institution' from the Hindus (Bodding, 1925:IV).

JOM SIM BONGAS

Very little is known about this group of *bongas*. According to their traditions, the Santals had a special feast called *Jom Sim* in honour of *Sin Bonga* (the Sun) and *Maran Buru*. In the course of their wanderings, each Santal subclan acquired a tutelary *bonga* which they used to worship during the *Jom Sim* festival. Hence the collective name of *jom sim bongas*. Gausdal (1960) records the names of forty-four different *jom sim bongas*. It is interesting to note that in the case of twenty-one *khuts* mentioned by Gausdal the *jom sim bonga* was the *khut's* own *abge bonga*.

No definite time was fixed for the *Jom Sim* celebration. It was considered enough to perform it once in one's lifetime. Nowadays, however, this festival is very rarely kept. When I asked an old Santal from Pangro why this festival was not celebrated in the village, he told me that it was a big and costly affair, a heavy drain on their budget. This was so because all male relatives, even those living in other villages, as well as sisters and their families were supposed to be invited, and it was very costly to feed everyone. All that this informant could remember about this feast is that in the evening an animal used to be sacrificed in honour of the *jom sim bonga*. Only men were allowed to partake of the 'sacrificial meal'. The following morning, another animal used to be sacrificed in honour of *Sin Bonga* and *Maran Buru*. Here, everybody partook of the meal. In the evening a village elder used to be invited to narrate the Santal story of creation, their migration, etc.

HINDU DEITIES (DEKO BONGAS).

The pantheon of Santal *bongas*, like that of many other tribes, includes also some Hindu deities.[52] We have already seen how certain Santal households have taken Hindu gods and goddesses as their *orak bongas*. We have also seen how three of the five tutelary *bongas* especially invoked by the Santal *ojhas* are Hindu deities—*Kali*, *Dibi* (*Durga*) and *Ganga Mai*. Most of the other *saket bongas* have names of Hindu origin. In a previous article I have shown how the socio-religious aspect of the Kharwar Movement resulted in the introduction of such Hindu deities as *Lakshmi Mai*, *Mahadev* (*Siva*), *Parvati*, *Rama*, *Kali*, *Durga* and *Krishna* in the Santal pantheon.[53]

In Pangro, many years ago, Choron Murmu, Sunil Murmu's great-grandfather, used to worship the Hindu goddess *Kali* in his house. He also used to celebrate a great feast in honour of this goddess once a year during the month of *Kartik* (October-November) in which not only the people from Pangro but also those from nearby villages took part. Sagram Hasdak's grandfather used to celebrate the *Chata Parab* on the last day of *Bhador* (August-September) in honour of the *chata bongas*. During this festival, the people from the countryside used to attend the *mela* (fair) which was set up near the village *pukri* (water tank). The feast used to last one day. Sagram's parents, being very poor, never celebrated the *Chata Parab* nor does

[52]Fuchs, Stephen, *The Aboriginal Tribes of India*, Delhi: The Macmillan Co. of India, 1973, p. 67, remarks that various Hindu deities like *Vishnu* and *Siva*, play an important part in the religious life of the primitive tribes. Likewise, various rural Hindu castes have adopted tribal gods, giving them a place in their pantheon.

[53]Troisi, J., 'Social Movements among the Santals', *Social Action*, Delhi, 26(3), July-Sept. 1976, pp. 260-5.

Sagram. Cuka Murmu's mother used to worship the *jatra bongas—Sagram Sim*, *Bhan Sim* and *Ubar Sim*. Every three years she used to celebrate the *Jatra Parab*. The feast which was performed in the month of *Magh* (January-February) used to be held near the *jaherthan* where a big *Jatra Khunti* (maypole) used to be erected. Since Cuka's mother's death ten years ago this feast has not been held in Pangro. Though the *Pata Parab* (Hook-swinging festival) was never held in Pangro, there are three families who worship the *pata bongas—Mahadev* (*Siva*) *and Parvati*. They go to offer sacrifices to these spirits at the *Pata Parab* held in Meronda, a village situated between Borio and Banjhi. Those who worship *Dibi* as their *orak bonga*, go to Sahibganj for their *Durga Puja*.

In some cases, the rites and ceremonies associated with these deities among the Hindus are also partially adopted by the Santals along with their traditional form of propitiatory rites. Thus, most of the members of the Kharwar Movement used to take the purificatory bath prior to worshipping *Ram Cando*. Gausdal (1960:100-110) reports that the Poeta Hembroms put on the sacred thread when they are going to sacrifice. The Dhanghara Marandis burn incense like the Hindus before their *bongas*.

MALEVOLENT AND SPITEFUL SPIRITS

The *bongas* we have studied so for are, on the whole, beneficent *bongas*. They are either protective or, at least, well-disposed and intimately concerned with the Santals' welfare and integrity, be it as a tribe, a village, subclan, family or individual. We shall now study those *bongas* who are by nature malevolent and spiteful and from whom inaction is all that can be hoped.

SIMA BONGAS (VILLAGE BOUNDARY SPIRITS) AND BAHRE BONGAS (VILLAGE OUTSKIRTS SPIRITS)

It is a general belief among the Santals that the *sima* and *bahre bongas* are more malevolent than others. *Sima bongas* are particularly feared. They are believed to cause snakes and other animals to attack men in the fields. Sometimes trees, at the end of a village street (*kulhi*), are said to be dedicated to them. Thus, Culshaw (1949:80) points out that in Bankura certain trees are marked by means of a piece of string during the festivals, dedicating them to these *bongas*. Whenever there is a drought in an area, Santal villagers offer sacrifices to their boundary spirits promising further propitiation when rain falls.

The *bahre bongas* are believed to live in the area outside the village, further away from the boundaries. Their favourite abodes are pools, tanks, ponds—places where water is to be found. These *bongas* are said to delude thirsty men with mirages of water reservoirs. When the thirsty men go in search of these imaginary reservoirs, the *bahre bongas* cause the water to vanish, thus tormenting the thirsty men. On vowing to offer sacrifices to the *bahre bongas*, the reservoir is caused to appear in its reality, enabling the men to quench their thirst.

Both the *sima* and *bahre bongas* are said to be very jealous and, if they are in any way hurt, for example, if sacrifices are not offered to them, they become hungry for a sacrifice and cause disease. It is very difficult to propitiate them and not everyone is competent to do so. For this reason, in almost every Santal village, there is a *kudam naeke* whose primary function is to propitiate these spirits through collective sacrifices. This is done twice a year, on the occasion of transplanting and harvesting. Fowls are offered in their honour and all present, with the exception of women, partake of the food. The mode of sacrifice is called *Bul Mayam* since the *kudam naeke* offers some of his blood along with the *adwa caole* given to these *bongas*. If in case of sickness, the *ojha*, through divination, finds out that the *bahre* or *sima bongas* are the cause of the evil, he offers them sacrifices on behalf of the sick man's family. In such cases, the *ojha* also performs the *Bul Mayam* ceremony.

BURU BONGAS (MOUNTAIN AND HILL SPIRITS)

When writing about Santal mountain and hill spirits several authors have unfortunately limited themselves to *Buru Bonga* 'the horrible deity who delights in human blood' as Mukherjea

(1962:278) defines him. To complicate matters certain authors like Hunter (1975:188), have indentified this *bonga* with *Maran Buru* and consequently with the Hindu deity *Siva*. Both views are completely inaccurate. For, besides *Buru Bonga*, to whom human sacrifices used to be offered, the Santals have other mountain or hill spirits. In fact, the Santals believe that their surrounding hills are the residence of some *bonga* or other, who very often derives his name from the mountain or the hill in which he is believed to reside. To try and solve the confusion which the word *Buru Bonga* brings about, Mukherjea (1962:277) uses the word *pats*[54] as a general term to refer to mountain spirits. The Santals of Pangro, however, do not use this term, but refer to these *bongas* as *buru bongas*.

These spirits are believed to be liable to ruin the crops and also to cause accidents of various kinds unless propitiated. Whenever a Santal is going on a long journey, he worships one of these *bongas*, offering sacrifices, mostly of fowls and goats so as not to come to any harm during the journey. Similar offerings are made to these *bongas* in cases of drought, to implore them to send rain and not to let the crops be ruined.

Water Spirits

These female *bongas* are said to reside in hollowed-out water holes and rivers. They are believed to spirit away people, especially young men, to these places with the idea of marrying them. This they do by disguising themselves as beautiful Santal girls. Though a number of Santal folktales describe such romantic encounters in vivid detail, such happenings are said to occur very rarely in actual Santal life.

Rongo Ruji Bonga

It is said that in olden times the Santals used to live merely by their bows and arrows. According to an immemorial custom, the annual hunt, *Disom Sendra*, is a great event in the annual

[54]Among the Oraons, *Pat*, sometimes called *Pat Raja*, is the master of all the village spirits. It protects the villagers from sickness and other misfortunes. S.C. Roy, (1972:33-4).

cycle of the Santals. As there is a village priest (*naeke*) and a priest for the *bahre* and *sima bongas* (*kudam naeke*), so also there is a *dihri* (hunt priest) responsible for the hunt. He sees to it that the necessary sacrificial offerings are made so that no mishap occurs during the hunt. Prior to the actual start of the hunt, and also on each successive day, he sacrifices fowls to various *bongas*, imploring them not to cause any harm to the hunters. One of the *bongas* so propitiated is called *Rongo Ruji*.

This spirit is said to reside in the forest, where a special tree called *Terel* (*diaspyros tomentosa*) is reserved for her. A stone representing this *bonga* is placed at the base of this tree. This spirit is believed to be completely obsessed with sex, as a result of which, it is very important to regale her with obscene songs and stories.[55] The Santals believe that, if she is not satisfied she causes terrible mischief during the hunt. To placate her, the ban on sexual talk is lifted and 'words which if uttered in the village would be visited with fine and disgrace, are not only permitted but enjoyed' (Archer 1974:324).

During the annual hunt, the hunters camp for the night near a place where water is available. After eating, they are entertained by a series of nude jokers (*lanta kora*) to what is called the *Torea*. *Rongo Ruji* is believed to be the patron *bonga* of these nude jokers who must serve her continually by attending as many hunts as possible. Should one of them avoid a hunt, *Rongo Ruji* would be insulted and she would punish him.

This *bonga* is also propitiated along with *Maran Buru* and *Manjhi Bonga* by the *dihri* during a Santal's expulsion from the tribe—*Bitlaha*. Sometimes she also demands menstrual blood by way of offering.[56] In case of impotence or sterility, if medicines have no effect, the woman goes to an *ojha* who divinises whether the *bongas* are interfering. If this is the case *Rongo Ruji* is propitiated.[57]

[55]Archer (1974:309-23) records some of these lewd stories and songs.

[56]Menstrual blood is said to be obnoxious to all the *bongas* except *Rongo Ruji*. The Santals believe that if a girl in her menstrual period comes across a *bonga* then the latter may cause her blood to flow for a month.

[57]S.C. Roy (1972:11), points out that Oraon young unmarried

Baghut Bonga

This spirit, or tiger spirit as the name (*bagh*) indicates, is believed to be the mischievous spirit of a person killed by a tiger or leopard. When irritated, this *bonga* is said to cause disease and to attack people by setting tigers or leopards on them. To keep it pacified and to avert any harm, this *bonga* is propitiated every year during the *Dasae* festival (*Durga Puja*) by one of the youngsters in the village who has undergone training in *ojhaism*. The person who is believed to be possessed by this *bonga* is made to walk on all fours and to pounce upon the sacrificial fowl which is let loose before him and kills it by biting it with his teeth, imitating a tiger.

SPIRITS WHICH HAVE TO BE EXORCISED

Another class of spirits who are particularly feared by the Santals are those who, in cases of sickness or other mischief, have to be exorcised. If this is not done, the disease or mischief which is believed to be caused by these *bongas* will prevail, leading to dire consequences. These *bongas* are *kisar bongas*, *naihar bongas*, *thapna bongas* and the *bonga* husbands of witches.

Kisar Bongas

These spirits are of a rather uncertain character. They are somewhat akin to *nisse*, the hobgoblin mentioned in Norwegian folklore. It is said that they got their name from the belief that they steal from others and bring wealth to their master's house. This is evidenced by a legend which Bompas records.[58]

men propitiate Chandi, a female spirit who is believed to bring success in hunting. She is also the spirit of Oraon bachelors and is represented by a roundish stone. It is interesting to note that there are very close similarities in the way in which both *Rongo Ruji* and *Chandi* are propitiated. See Bodding (1942:120-2) and S.C. Roy (1972:44-5). *Chandi Bonga* is also propitiated by the Mundas prior to their hunting expeditions.

[58]Bompas, C.H., *Folklore of the Santal Parganas*, London: David Nutt, 1909, p. 375.

If, a *kisar bonga* is divinised to be the cause of a disease he must be got rid of immediately otherwise, it is believed, he will 'eat up' everybody in the house. The Santals have the following saying, 'Kisar bongae bhutau akantakoa gujuk kanako', meaning 'the wealth *bonga* has become enraged, they are dying'.

Getting rid of a *kisar bonga* is a costly affair. In Pangro a few years back, a *kisar bonga* was said to have taken up his abode in Sagram Hasdak's house. Everything was going on fine, Sagram was prospering when, all of a sudden, he was not able to turn his neck. No amount of herbal medicine given by Bharat Soren, one of Pangro's *ojhas*, could cure him. Months passed during which two of Sagram's buffaloes mysteriously died. His eldest daughter Gumi also fell sick. Seeing this, Sagram asked Bharat to perform the *Sunum Bonga* divination by leaves to find out the cause of his misfortunes. As a result of the divination, it was found that a *kisar bonga* was present in Sagram's house and he was believed to be the cause of all the mischief. It was then decided to get rid of it immediately. At the *ojha's* command, a man became possessed by the spirit who was entreated to leave Sagram's house. To this, the possessed man answered that the spirit would only leave the house if he was given what belonged to him. A few things were then brought out and placed before the 'spirit'. Whereupon, he entered Sagram's cowshed and selected a cow and a bullock. These were then sacrificed to the *kisar bonga*, everyone present partaking of the sacrificial meal.

NAIHAR BONGA

This spirit, which as the name *naihar* implies, is said to belong to the father-in-law's household. It sometimes accompanies a woman when she joins her husband's house. Also called *Acraele Bonga*, it is a much feared *bonga*.[59] As we have seen, marriage,

[59]'Among the Oraons, *Achrael* and her companion *Joda*, are the special spirits of women, S.C. Roy (1972:47). For the Mundas, *Achrael* presides over married women's interests. If a woman, on her marriage, carries anything from her parents' house to her husband's house, this *bonga* would show his displeasure by bringing sickness to her husband's house.

for a girl, involves a change in her *bongas*. This ensures that she will not be able to bring any calamity to her husband's household. The *naihar bonga*, however, does not belong to her husband's household and is, therefore, an alien spirit. He is believed to have followed the girl because of something which the girl took along with her and from which he did not want to be parted.

When the head of the household comes to know that this 'foreign' *bonga* is in his house, he tries to send the spirit back to its former place since it will not go of itself. To make this possible, however, the head of the household must first return all the things which his wife has brought with her at marriage, from her father's house (*naihar*). Along with these things, he must send two animals which are sacrificed to the spirit in its own house. If these things are not carried out, then it is believed that sickness and death will ravage the house.

THAPNA BONGAS (BURIED SPIRITS)

Sometimes it happens that the *Sunum Bonga* ceremony shows a certain *bonga* to be buried in the house and to be the cause of illness there. Very often, other *ojhas* are consulted to see whether a particular *thapna bonga* is really buried in the house. The Santals believe that witches are the cause of this. One of the methods used by a witch to kill her victim, especially if the latter does not belong to her family, is to localise a *bonga* in a stone over which spells have been pronounced and then bury it in the house or cowshed of the victim.[60] If anyone steps on the stone, he is at once struck with disease or even death. Unless such a *bonga* is disposed of, disease will prevail in the house and very often lead to death.

On the appointed day, the *Tak Taki* or exorcism by sticks is held. I have witnessed this form of exorcism in the house of Kapre Kisku of Manjhi Tola in Pangro. Kapre had been lying sick for more than a year without showing any signs of improvement. Several *ojhas* were called upon and a number of exorcisms carried out, but it was all in vain. Suspicion arose throughout the whole village that a *bonga* had been buried in Kapre's

[60]Bodding (1925:35-6).

house by a witch. The matter became a public affair and Bharat Soren was asked by the village officials to perform the *Tak Taki* exorcism in Kapre's house. On the fixed day, Bharat, accompanied by some villagers, went there and sitting down in the *raca* (courtyard) asked for a large brass cup (*latu bati*) in which he poured some oil from a leaf cup he had brought with him. Looking at the brass cup he explained that the *bonga* was buried in the house. Bharat's assistant then entered the house and he began stamping the ground with a stick (*taini thenga*) until he suddenly stopped. Actually it is believed that the *taini thenga* stops by itself, a sign that it has located the *thapna bonga.* Whereupon, Bharat entered the house and, using a sickle, drew a circle on the spot where the stick had stopped. He then drew a number of marks within the circle and made a hole in the ground. Not finding anything, he spat on the ground and putting his left heel on the circle he rubbed the marks out. His assistant started stamping the ground and the same procedure was repeated a number of times. Nothing, however, was found. I was told that had the *thapna bonga* been found, Bharat would have taken possession of it, and going to the nearest boundary, he would have performed the necessary propitiatory rites.

Thapna Bongas can also be planted in a whole village. This is believed to be the case when a village is struck by a lot of maladies and death, when the cattle die or the crops fail for no known reason.

Bonga Husbands of Witches

The Santals, like many other tribals, firmly believe in the efficacy of witchcraft. While amongst the Mundas, the Oraons and other tribes, a witch can be either a man or a woman, among the Santals only women have a monopoly of witchcraft. Like other malevolent *bongas*, witches can cause a lot of harm, hence they are regarded as very dangerous. We have already seen how witches are said to bury *bongas* in their victim's house, causing him and his family a lot of harm and sometimes even death.

Witches are specially suspected of possessing the power, by their feminine charms to seduce *bongas*, making them swear that they will not appear when divination is performed. As

Bodding (1934:218) points out, 'dando bongako kobojetkoa' which means 'The witches master the *bongas* (bring them under their influence)'. Bompas remarks how as part of her initiation into witchcraft, a girl:

> is conducted to the great *bongas*, one of whom approves of her and when all have agreed she is married to that *bonga*. The *bonga* pays the usual bride price and applies *sindur* to her forehead.[61]

Archer goes a step further, saying 'A witch must not only be married to a *bonga* but must learn from him the art of killing' (1974:106).

Though a witch may herself do the 'killing', it is said that she can only do so through the powers given her by her 'husband *bonga*' and only after obtaining his approval. In certain cases, the witch herself does not 'eat' the victim but only strikes through a *bonga* instigating him to do so. Thus, *bongas* may be used by, or, themselves use witches as mediums of destruction. When an illness persists in spite of all attempts to cure it, the suspicion of witchcraft arises. Before consensus that a witch is at work is reached, more *ojhas* are consulted. The matter becomes a public affair and the assistance of the village community is sought. Vigorous action is taken to try and localise the witch and to get rid of her presence as fast as possible. I shall deal with this in Chapter VI.

IMPERSONAL SPIRITS AND POWERS

We now come to a class of mischievous impersonal spirits and powers which are not objects of worship nor require sacrifices but which have to be exorcised mainly through magic. The spirits of persons who die in childbirth or die an unnatural death, mischievous beings who devour people, and stray

[61]Bompas, C.H., *Folklore of the Santal Parganas*, London: David Nutt, 1909, pp. 423-4.

powers residing in or connected with various objects fall in this category.[62]

CURINS

These are the spirits of women who die in pregnancy or childbirth. They form a special class of female goblins with terrifying appearance reported to have heads like spinning wheels. They are said to waylay and suck the blood of people whenever they find them alone. As a result, the Santals fear them very much and take a number of precautions not to let such goblins move about and harm the villagers. Elwin observes, 'The unusual is always risky . . . and so when a lady dies in childbirth, taboos are observed to protect those who are still alive' (1955:395). Thus, even in those places where the Santals used to cremate their dead, it was always the custom to bury the body of a woman dying in pregnancy or childbirth, deep in the ground. To make sure that she would not escape from her burial place, the Santals insert an iron nail in the sole of her foot and also put thorns over her body.[63]

BHUTS (GHOSTS)

Children who die in their mothers' womb are believed to become *bhuts*. So also do those who die before they are

[62]The Santals share the belief in these spirits and powers with the peasantry of northern India. Refer to William Crooke (1925: Chapter VII).

[63]Culshaw (1949:92) mentions another precaution to be taken, according to which the husband cuts open his wife's body and removing the foetus buries it separately. Among the Oraons, S.C. Roy (1972:69, 70-136), the ghost of a woman dying in pregnancy or childbirth is called *churil*, *churel* or *malech*. These ghosts are believed to carry loads of coal on their head imagining them to be their babies. They are said to attack men teasing them and tormenting them till they fall down in a swoon. Like the Santals, the Oraons bury their *churils* outside the village. As a further precaution, their eyes are sewn up with thorns and their hands and legs broken. The corpse is laid in a grave with its face downwards. The Mundas, S.C. Roy (1970:267), believe that the *churins* occasionally haunt their old places causing mischief. In such cases they are propitiated by the ghost finders who very often are not Mundaris.

The Santals are also known to look upon their ansestor spirits with filial love and intimacy. In fact, veneration for their ancestors is so profound that in almost every sacrifice, the ancestors are remembered and their intercession sought. In short, we can say that they are the allies of the Santals in their struggle against adverse circumstances and untoward happenings. They relate to these *bongas* with reverential awe, submission, hope, affection and trust.

One, however, cannot deny the fact that a certain type of terrifying fear does characterise the Santals' attitudes towards the malignant *bongas* such as the *sima* and *bahre bongas*, the water *bongas*, *Rongo Ruji* and *Baghut Bonga* and towards the impersonal powers. These, in fact, outnumber the benevolent *bongas* and most of the mischief is attributed to them. As noted earlier, these impersonal powers are not directly connected with Santal religion, but rather with Santal magic. Here, the attitude of the Santals is mainly one of defiance, control and domination over these impersonal powers. In view of all this, I think that what fits the facts best is to say that Santal religion is one of both fear and trust, which, though they may be opposites are not contraries. By facing facts and accepting life as it is, Santal religion is able to provide a certain feeling of security or, at least, of hope.

Beliefs and rituals are invariant factors in all religions. There is a mutual interaction between the two, in the sense that while belief is made expressive and dynamic in ritual, ritual is rationalised and made effective by belief. It is only by considering religion as a mode of action as well as a system of belief that the living meaning of both ritual and belief becomes evident. Ritual activities are the best expressions of the religious life of human groups. As expressive actions of behaviour, rituals are symbolic and as such are not arbitrary but appropriate to a given culture. These symbolic actions as Goode (1964:49) noted, help men to enter into alliance and reassert their social relationships with the supernatural world.

The Santals firmly believe that it is very important for every household, subclan, and village community to cultivate friendly relations with their spirits. To do this, it is essential to provide the *bongas* with offerings and sacrifices. It is through these that the Santals believe that they can enter into communion with their spirits. The intimate inter-relationship between the Santals and their spirits is perhaps most clearly evident in the seasonal rites and festivals which mark the agricultural cycle and also the life-cycle of an individual.

As we shall see in the next chapter, though the religious rites and festivals connected with the agricultural cycle, are mainly concerned with the immediate practical interests of life, namely, to appease the malignant *bongas* and to beseech the benevolent ones to continue showering their blessings and protection for the safety and prosperity of the village community as a whole, they evoke an emotion that goes beyond mere response to practical needs. Even in pursuing his materialistic desires the Santal does not lose his deep-rooted spirituality. These rites and festivals bind the community members together in their beliefs and give them a sense of the sacred. Collective ritual and rejoicing during these rites and festivals serve to intensify the emotional appeal of religion. In short, we can say that they are symbols of their beliefs in communal settings.

Chapter IV

Religious Culture: Seasonal Rites and Festivals[1]

One would be mistaken in believing that there could be a religion which has no external manifestation of its beliefs. 'As with society, so with religion, external form is the condition of its existence. As a social animal, man is a ritual animal' states Mary Douglas (1966:78). Similarly, Berger points out that 'The farther back one goes historically, the more does one find religious ideation (typically in mythological form) embedded in ritual activity' (1969:40). The conception of religion as embedded in ritual is strongly emphasised in Durkheim's assertion that all religious phenomena are naturally arranged in two fundamental categories, beliefs and rites. Beliefs are states of opinion and consist in representations, while rites are determined modes of action (1967:51).[2]

In his analysis of the interrelation between religious beliefs and practices, Durkheim assets that:

> In principle, the cult is derived from the beliefs, yet it reacts upon them. . . . On the other hand, there are

[1]The term 'rite' is used to denote a prescribed form of religious activity having reference to beliefs in invisible spirits and powers. It consists of sacrificial offerings, libations and invocations. The term 'festival' is a wider term referring to a community celebration. It is usually a combination of social, economic and religious elements.

[2]See Radcliffe-Brown (1959:155-60) and Goode (1964:49-50).

> beliefs which are clearly manifested only through the rites which express them (1967:121).

In order to incorporate religious experience into the traditional dichotomy of religious phenomena into beliefs and practices, it is necessary to elucidate briefly the complementary dialectic between ritual and experience, on the one band, and between belief and experience, on the other.

Collective rites, as Durkheim observed, give rise to collective effervescence. 'They put the group into action.... their thoughts are centred upon their common beliefs ... the collective ideal of which they are the incarnation; in a word, upon social things' (1967:389-90). The opposite view that religious experiences give rise to religious ritual is equally valid. Such an argument has been put forward by Wach (1962: Ch. 2) who, starting with a definition of religion based on Otto's theory of the Holy, treated beliefs and rituals as objectifications of man's experience of the Holy. It is not my intention here to discuss whether or not the origin of Santal ritual is in religious experience or vice versa.[3] What is sure however, is that ritual is by definition a highly traditional form of behaviour. Public rites are handed down already constructed and hedged with prescriptions. Various rites are celebrated by the Santals because their ancestors did so. It is in this sense that rituals are objectifications. They are elements of an external social reality which exercise a constraint over the individual. Participation in ritual provides the individual with a sense of social solidarity and personal security. While ritual fosters religious experience, it also channels religious experience into controlled and acceptable forms.

Durkheim was well aware that the effect of religious rituals was to create and control experience. It was his main occupation to analyse how religious rituals manifest to men their social selves, thus creating their society. Radcliffe-Brown treated rituals as part of a theory of action rather than a theory of knowledge as Durkheim did. According to Radcliffe-Brown, rituals express and focus attention on common values. Thus, he asserts that rituals are regulated symbolic expressions of

[3]For a study on this point refer to Radcliffe-Brown (1959:155-60), (1964:233ff); Evans-Pritchard (1956); and Berger (1969).

certain collective sentiments which are necessary for the existence and maintenance of an orderly social life (1959:157). Lienhardt, on the other hand, follows up Durkheim's theory and devotes his whole discussion of Dinka religion to showing how rituals create and control experience.[4]

Santal religious beliefs represent an attempt to make sense of the world in which they live. They stimulate certain types of experiential response. Yet, it can also be said that religious experiences react back upon beliefs. One important function of all religious experiences is to provide evidence for the reality of the non-empirical domain which lies behind religious belief. While religious experience has this crucial role to play in supporting the plausibility of belief, there is a tendency for belief and experience to become separated over time. And it is exactly then that the relationship between ritual and experience comes into play.[5] Men forget, remarks Berger (1969:40), and so they must be constantly reminded. Religious ritual has been a crucial instrument of this 'reminding' process.

In the last chapter, I have given an extended account of the supernatural spirits and powers which are the objects of Santal worship or propitiation. In this chapter I shall describe the seasonal rites and festivals which Santal society has organised to ensure safety and prosperity to the village community at each new stage in the annual cycle of its economic life. These constitute the Santals' Public Worship.[6]

As already mentioned, agriculture, especially paddy cultivation, is the chief source of livelihood of the Santals in Pangro. It keeps them engaged for the greater part of the year, namely from the middle of April till January, in different agricultural operations like ploughing, sowing, transplanting, weeding, harvesting, threshing, etc. (see Table 2.8, Chapter II).

[4]Lienhardt, G., *Divinity and Experience· The Religion of the Dinka*, Oxford: Clarendon Press, 1961.

[5]See B. Turner, 'Belief, Ritual and Experience: The Case of Methodism', *Social Campus*, Louvain, 18(2), 1971, pp. 187-201.

[6]By public worship, I mean those rituals in which the village community as a whole takes part. They are to be distinguished from other rituals such as the worship of *orak* and *abge bongas* which are performed by a particular household or subclan. Here, only the members of that households or subclan take part.

Agriculture gives the full rhythm and measure of the seasonal sequence of the year. To the Santals, the annual revolution of the seasons is defined by the cycle of agricultural activities. Yet, for them, as for other tribals, agriculture is something more than just a means of livelihood. It is a whole way of life. It unites an entire family, even a village, into a single task. It is of primary importance in village life and enters either directly or indirectly into almost every activity. In other words, it permeates the whole Santal life.

One aspect of Santal agriculture is very prominent and raises problems of wider implication. This is the relation between the purely economic work on the one hand, and religion and magic, on the other. The association between the agricultural cycle and its belief and ritual counterpart is so intimate that, for the success in an agricultural enterprise, religious and magical beliefs and rituals are as indispensable as the manual activity itself. The manner in which the Santals cultivate rice, their primary means of sustenance, store it and handle it, and the way in which they surround it with religious and magical beliefs, are clear signs of the intimate relationship between the two. The sequence of agricultural stages, on the one hand, and the beliefs and rites, on the other, run parallel. In other words, Santal religion is a social force intimately connected with the economic organisation of agriculture.[7]

The Santals know the variety of dangers involved in their agricultural tasks. They are well aware that a drought or a destructive blight on the crops inevitably means hunger for all, while a good harvest means prosperity. These aspects of the material life of the Santal are sought to be guarded by appropriate ceremonials and rituals in honour of the *bongas*. Thus, the Santals have a series of seasonal rites and festivals which mark the different stages of their agricultural year. They perform inaugurative rites and concluding rites before and after their main agricultural activities. Through these rites, the village priest acting in the name of the whole community, beseeches the benevolent *bongas* to continue showering their blessings and care. The *kudam naeke* appeases the malignant *bongas* so as to avert any natural calamities.

[7]Malinowski (1965) emphasises this point in his study of the Trobriand Islanders.

The Santals believe that, should they fail to perform these annual rituals, their *bongas* would be displeased and visit the village with calamities. On the other hand, the Santals also rejoice with their spirits over a bumper crop. This is manifested by the feasting, rejoicing and social reunion that accompany the successful termination of an agricultural event.

GENERAL CHARACTERISTICS OF RITES AND FESTIVALS

The annual community festivals of the Santals—*Baha, Erok Sim, Hariar Sim, Iri-Gundli-Nawai, Janthar, Sohrae* and *Magh Sim*—are all connected with agricultural operations.

TABLE 4.1: ANNUAL CYCLE OF SANTAL FESTIVALS SHOWING THEIR CONNECTION WITH AGRICULTURAL OPERATIONS AND THE MONTH WHEN PERFORMED

Festival	*Month*		*Agricultural Operation*
Baha	*Phagun*	(February-March)	Offering of the 'first fruits' of *matkom* and other wild fruits and flowers.
Erok Sim	*Asar*	(June-July)	Sowing of rice seeds.
Hariar Sim	*San*	(July-August)	Sprouting of the rice seeds.
Iri-Gundli-Nawai	*Bhador*	(August-September)	Offering of the first fruits of the millet crops.
Janthar	*Aghar*	(November-December)	Offering of the first fruits of the winter rice crop.
Sohrae	*Pus*	(December-January)	After the paddy has been harvested.
Magh Sim	*Magh*	(January-February)	Cutting of the thatching grass.

The annual hunt is also a festive occasion for the Santals. In addition to these agricultural festivals, which are celebrated every year, the Santals also have other festivals which are neither performed regularly nor associated with agricultural activities. The most important of these are *Karam*, *Jom Sim* and *Mak More*. Before describing the seasonal rites and festivals performed by the Santals of Pangro, I shall describe some general characteristics of Santal seasonal rites and festivals.

The Santals' religious worship is mainly congregational. There is no individual approach to the *bongas*, but fellowship with them is maintained through sacrifices, offerings and libations made on behalf of a particular social unit, be it the village, the subclan or the household. Likewise, the celebrations which accompany such collective rituals, in which people participate for the welfare of the entire group, are truly occasions for collective action. They function as channels through which cultural traditions are expressed and affirmed.

It is generally on the occasion of such collective seasonal rites and the dances and festivals associated with them that the Santal experiences a religious feeling. He sees in these festivals an occasion to forget the worries, stresses and strains of his day-to-day life. Under the mutual stimulation of collective public worship, the Santals feel or imagine themselves to be in touch with their spirits upon whom they depend. In this way they are inspired with confidence and hope and with a certain sense of security amidst the uncertainties of life. Similarly, as a result of such communal worship, the feeling of community-belonging is intensified, thus strengthening also social solidarity.

Santal seasonal rites and festivals contain two strands—the religious and the secular. The two are intimately interwoven yet analytically distinct. I shall briefly describe each separately. The Santals being agriculturalists, their religious rites have the social urge of fertility, fecundity, generation and all that is connscted with their very existence. The Santals are a highly ritualistic people. They rarely doubt the efficacy of their rituals, being convinced that these must produce the expected results. If the expected results are not achieved, they believe that the lack of success is either due to some hostile forces or that the ritual prescriptions were not properly observed. They are thus very particular about the time and place of the sacrifice and about the person who is to officiate at the rite. They also pay great attention to the things that have to be said. The officiating

Baha or Flower festival: The *naeke* and his assistant offering sacrifices beneath the shed set up in honour of *Maran Buru*, *Jaher Era* and *Moreko-Turuiko.*

Disom Sendra: The *dihri* or hunt priest propitiating *Rongo Ruji Bonga* and the other spirits of the hunt and forest.

The *kudam naeke* performing the *Bul Mayam* ceremony in honour of the *bahre* and *sima bongas.*

Menfolk dancing in front of the headman's house on *Daka Hilok* - the second day of the *Sohrae* or Harvest Festival.

person has to submit to certain ceremonial interdictions and there is a prescribed content of invocations.

The sacrificial offering is clearly at the centre of every Santal ritual. Much has been written about the nature of sacrifice. Loisy defined sacrifice as the combination of a magic rite and a ritual gift. Tylor's view of sacrifice as being pre-eminently a gift to a supernatural being, was modified by Frazer's theory of sympathetic and contagious magic. The work of Robertson Smith brought about a revolution in the traditional theory of sacrifice.[8] He was the first to point out that sacrifice is a meal in which the worshippers who offer it share it along with the god to whom it is offered. According to him, sacrificial banquets have the object of making the worshipper and his god share the same sacrificial meal so as to form a kinship bond between them. Where he went wrong was in his considering the communion aspect as the unique element of the sacrifice but leaving out the notion of oblation. In fact, he claimed to find in the very notion of oblation an absurdity so revolting that it could never have been the fundamental reason for such an institution. Durkheim (1967: 384) emphasised both the essential elements of sacrifice—communion and oblation.[9]

In the Santal sacrifices connected with their agricultural activities, both the communion and oblation elements are intimately interconnected. The sacrificial communion symbolises a sense of presence and of fellowship with the spirits. Though the major portion of the victim is consumed by the people present, a portion is set aside for the spirit or spirits in whose honour the sacrifice is made. The communion element is also manifest when rice-beer libations are made to the spirits. After each libation made in honour of a spirit, the worshippers also drink. Through this process of sharing in the sacrificial food and drink, the Santals share in the beneficial power of their providence. Moreover, according to Santal beliefs, the invisible world is considered to be an extension of the visible one. As a

[8]Loisy, A., *Essai historique sur le sacrifice*, Paris: Nourry, 1920; Robertson Smith, *The Religion of the Semites*, Lectures VI-XI , London, 1907, and 'Sacrifice' in *Encyclopaedia Brittanica*, 9th edition.

[9]See also Hubert, Henri, and Marcel Mauss, *Sacrifice: Its Nature and Function*, Chicago: University of Chicago Press, 1964.

result, the spirits are believed to be driven by the same fundamental desires as humans are. They are believed to take pleasure in eating and drinking. As Kolean reports, 'As we have got fresh crops we also fill our *bongas*' (Bodding, 1942: 137). The oblation element symbolises, in an emphatic manner, the Santals' acknowledgement of their spirits as the real lords of their fields to whom tribute must be paid. It also manifests the Santals' dependence on these spirits who, as in the case of the Trobriand Islanders, must receive 'their share sacrificed from the general plenty' (Malinowski, 1954:43).

As we have seen, the purpose of Santal sacrifices is twofold —to seek protection and prosperity from the benevolent *bongas* and to control the malevolent *bongas* of their malign influence. Thus, on the one hand, through their sacrificial offerings, the Santals make a kind of bargain with the spirits so that they may be protected. On the other hand, the malevolent spirits are persuaded to turn away from the Santals and not to trouble them any more.

A series of preliminary operations, purifications, anointings and invocations precede the actual immolation of the sacrificial offering which, in the case of these seasonal rites and festivals, consists mainly of fowls. The *naeke*, who performs the sacrifice in the name of the whole village community, has to submit to certain ceremonial interdictions. The evening prior to the actual sacrifice he, like all the other villagers, takes a purificatory bath. Such ablutions are believed to remove all supernatural evil influences. During the night, he fasts and sleeps on the floor. He is required not to have sexual relations with his wife. Prior to the sacrifice itself, he once again bathes and then goes to the place of sacrifice. There he prepares the sacrificial altar called the *khond*. He puts small handfuls of *adwa caole* in many places making three marks of *sindur* near each small heap. He then sprinkles water on the sacrificial fowl and applies *sindur* on its forehead, legs and wings. The fowl is made to eat from the *adwa caole* during which the *naeke*, turning his mouth directly on the fowl, pronounces the invocation. Thereupon, the fowl is beheaded and the blood is allowed to drip on to the *khond*. The other fowls, if there are any, are sacrificed in the same way.

It is interesting to note that *sindur* is the Santali word for vermilion which, apart from its fertility significance, has a special relevance to the *bongas* and is, in fact, a kind of a blood covenant with them. The *naeke* puts *sindur* on the *khond* because, as village priest, he is the channel through which the spirits can be approached. Similarly, *sindur* is put on sacrificial animals and fowls in order to attach them to the spirits. These practices illustrate the application of the principle of alliance. Another interesting aspect is the sprinkling of the victim's blood on and before the altar. In the book of Exodus (29:12), we read of Yahweh telling Moses:

> and you shall take part of the blood of the bull and put it upon the horns of the altar with your finger, and the rest of the blood you shall pour out at the base of the altar.

This signified the sealing of the covenant between Yahweh and the Israelites, his chosen people. Similarly, Durkheim (1967: 371) reported that the Arunta and the Dieri Australian tribes sprinkled the sacred rock or the totemic design with blood. These effusions of blood are veritable oblations.

One cannot deny the instrumental efficacy believed to be inherent in the rituals. Thus the Santals, do hope that rain rituals for example will cause rain and that harvest rituals will produce crops. But instrumental efficacy, as we have seen, is not the only kind of efficacy to be derived from these ritual actions. They help the Santals to enter and reassert their relationships with the invisible world. In so doing, they fill themselves with confidence and harmony. Although a spirit may have accepted his token gift or dedicated animal, there is no certainty that he will fulfil his part of the bargain. It is true that he is expected to do this owing to the belief that, if he is treated well, he would respond. However, the Santals are aware that the unseen world is as incalculable as the visible world. Hence, the most they can do is to invest wisely and hope for the best.

The secular aspects of the Santal seasonal rites and festivals provide entertainment and diversion to the Santals. Culshaw remarks that 'the word *raska* meaning 'pleasure' is often on the lips of the Santals, and it is dear to their hearts' (1949:39). Their behaviour is characterised by a carefree, uninhibited attitude and a joyous frame of mind. Men and women, adults and children all gather together for the occasion to indulge themselves and to meet their friends and relatives. Dancing and singing hold a very important role in almost all these festive occasions. A social feature of Santal dancing and singing, as that of other tribals, is their social character. From the time a girl can toddle, she joins the line of dancers, while little boys ape the antics of the drummers. The Santals have a large number of different dances according to the special seasons and festivals. According to Mukherjea, 'these dances . . . are a part and parcel of the tribal religious life' (1962:365). Bodding (1934:331) mentions thirty-one types of dances, most of which are performed by men and women together though some are reserved for either of the sexes.[10]

Drumming plays a very important part during dancing since the rhythm and style of the latter depends very much on the way in which the drums are played. The Santals use two types of drums during their dancing—the *tamak* or kettle drum which is made of iron and is shaped like a big bowl and covered with buffalo or bullock hide, and the *tumdak* or dancing drum made of burnt clay and conical in shape, the narrow end being covered with goat's skin and the broad end with bullock, buffalo or goat's hide. The *tumdak* which is played with the hands sets the rhythm while the *tamak*, played with small sticks, echoes and adds to the rhythm.

Dancing is often connected with singing. Thus, Raha remarks, 'when any new event is marked by the Santals they at once give it a poetic expression and sing spontaneously on their way to or during any festival'.[11] As the Santals have different

[10]The *lagre* is the most common of the Santal dances and may be danced at any time, though preferably during moonlight. *Don* is usually danced during marriage festivals. *Jatur* is performed during the *Sohrae* and the *Baha* festivals. *Danta* is also danced during the *Sohrae*. Women generally do not join in this dance. On the other hand, only women dance the *Baha* dance which, as the name implies, is performed during the *Baha* festival. During the *Karam* festival, the Annual Hunt and *Bitlaha*, the menfolk perform special dances.

[11]Raha, Manis Kumar, 'Folk Songs of the Tribals of West Bengal: An Analytical Study of Continuity and Change', in Hemango Biswas

dances for different festive occasions, so also they have elaborate song cycles for various festivals. Bhattacharya reports that the Santals have more than twenty different tunes.[12] Though most of these songs are ancestral,[13] it is also part of the vitality of Santal poetry to compose songs on the spur of the moment. These songs reflect certain feelings, emotions and sentiments of the Santals.[14]

The festivals of the Santals would appear lifeless if no reference is made to the practice of drinking rice-beer on these occasions. 'Give me rice-beer (*handi*) or give me death' may be the summary of a Santal's instinctive craving for rice-beer which can be rightly called their 'national' intoxicating drink. So important is the drinking of rice-beer that nothing of a public character can be ratified without the drinking of *handi*. In fact, as we have seen, the Santals elect a *handi manjhi* when the headman of their village is not a Santal. It is compulsory to offer *handi* libations to the major spirits, the ancestors, and other spirits during worship. Santal tradition stresses the divine origin of *handi*. Nobody drinks of freshly brewed rice-beer before offering libations to *Maran Buru*, the first couple *Pilcu Haram* and *Pilcu Budhi* and other ancestors. Presentation

(ed.), *Folk Music and Folk-lore. An Anthology*, Vol. I, Calcutta: Folk Music and Folk-lore Research Institute, 1967, p. 58.

[12]Bhattacharya, Subhendu Sekhar, 'Santal Songs: Different Types', *Bulletin of the Cultural Research Institute*, Calcutta, 1(2), 1962, pp. 54-61. The different tunes are named after the occasion on which they are sung or after the dances in connection with which they are used. Thus, Bodding (1936:242) mentions nine different types of songs connected with different occasions and fourteen melodies connected with dancing.

[13]Culshaw (1946:66-7) shows how by means of songs, the Santals keep alive the memory of past events. Many of them also contain the Santal philosophy of life.

[14]For a further study of Santal songs and poetry refer to Archer, W.G., 'Santal Poetry', *Man in India*, Ranchi, 23(2), June 1943, pp. 98-105; 'Festival Songs: The Santal Sohrae', *Man in India*, 24(2), June 1944, pp. 72-4; 'Santal Transplantation Songs', *Man in India*, 26(1), March 1946, pp. 6-7; Sinha, Sunity Kumar, 'Santal Folk Songs', *Journal of the Bihar and Orissa Research Society*, Patna, 32(2), June 1946, pp. 184-8; Mukherjea, Charulal, 'Santal Folk Poetry', *The New Review*, Calcutta, 4, July-Dec. 1936, pp. 220-6.

of pots of *handi* on ceremonial occasions is also an important social custom.[15]

AGRICULTURAL RITES AND FESTIVALS

SOHRAE

Though traditionally the Santals have seven annual festivals connected with agriculture, the Santals of Pangro and the adjoining villages celebrate five of these—*Sohrae, Baha, Erok Sim, Hariar Sim* and *Janthar*. The *Sohrae* or Harvest Festival is the principal and most important public event among the Santals. It is also their largest and merriest annual event when the villagers are given to general dancing and relaxation. This festival is held in the month of *Pus* (December-January), after the paddy has been reaped, threshed, and stored.[16] Formerly, the festival was held on different dates in each village. This gave villagers from neighbouring villages an opportunity to participate in each other's festivities with the result that there was debauchery and drunkenness for weeks. To prevent this, the Government has exerted pressure on all villages to celebrate the *Sohrae* at the same time. If a death or birth occurs in a particular village, however, the dates of the *Sohrae* are changed. Whatever be the case, all the festivities connected with the *Sohrae* must be over by the full-moon night of *Pus* (December-January).[17]

In Pangro, the festival continues for six days and nights, each day having a distinctive name to indicate the proceedings

[15]Mukherji, Sankarananda, 'The Recipe of Rice-Beer', *Bulletin of the Cultural Research Institute*, Calcutta, 6(1-2), 1967, pp. 116-8, shows how the Santals distinguish a dozen different types of rice-beer in accordance with the name of the cereal used. Nearly fifty prefixes are used in accordance with the social or festival events when rice-beer has to be used.

[16]According to Culshaw (1949:110), the Santals of Sarenga in the Bankura district of West Bengal, celebrate the *Sohrae* at the time when the Hindus in the area celebrate *Kali Puja*.

[17]The Oraons and the Mundas have a feast bearing a similar name —*Sohorai*. This feast celebrated in the month of *Kartik* (October-November) is not their harvest festival but is connected with cattle. Roy, S.C., (1970:275), (1972:169).

of the day. Among other things, the *Sohrae* includes the blessing and baiting of cattle, a fishing expedition and a village hunt. The spirits are not forgotten for the *Sohrae* offers the Santals an occasion to thank their spirits. The rituals performed include sacrifices of fowls to the village spirits, and the ancestral spirits. Kinsmen from other villages are invited; married daughters are expected to return to their father's household for the occasion; relatives bring gifts along with them. In this manner, the village community is bound together; all—human and divine, living and dead—partake of the festivities.

'It has frequently been remarked that popular feasts lead to excesses, and cause men to lose sight of the distinction separating the licit from the illicit' (Durkheim, 1967:428). Sexual licence is frequent. Thus, Spencer and Gillen speak of what is called a *corrobbori* among the native and northern tribes of Central Australia. During this ceremony, the effervescence often reaches such a stage where it causes unheard of actions. Similarly, during the *Sohrae*, the Santal code of sexual conduct is deliberately relaxed and the Santals indulge themselves in a veritable saturnalia of sexual licence.[18] In fact, on the eve of the first day of the *Sohrae*, the young men of the village go to the *jog manjhi* and ask him, in formal language, to turn a blind eye to any of the faults they commit during this time. A village elder of Pangro told me that during the *Sohrae*, one must close one's ears with cotton-wool and put clay on one's eyes, so that one may not hear nor see what a neighbour says or does. This is to say that during the *Sohrae* the Santals' moral code is in abeyance and everyone does what he likes.[19]

Because of this licence, the Protestant and Catholic churches encourage their followers not to take part in the dancing. The *Sohrae* has always been looked upon by the missionaries as something evil, sinful and thus to be avoided. By being prohibited from taking part in the gaiety, the Santal Christians are alienated from their village community. As Culshaw points out:

[18]This licence, however, does not extend to adultery nor does it sanction clan endogamy. If the rule of clan exogamy is breached during the *Sohrae*, the punishment is less severe than at other times.

[19]When the festival is over, offerings are made to atone for the misconduct that has taken place.

> It is impossible to live in a village at the time of the . . . Harvest festival without becoming acutely aware of the gulf which divides the Christians from their neighbours and without realising that the Christians are themselves deeply conscious of the gulf (1949:176).

As a substitute, the Santal Christians are encouraged to celebrate Christmas Week as their Harvest Festival. The Santal Christians of Pangro and of the adjoining villages of Adro and Nirepara celebrate the Christmas season on a grand scale. On Christmas day itself all Christians from the three villages gather at the chapel in Pangro. The courtyard in front of the chapel is decorated and so is the chapel itself. They are all dressed in new clothes. The service, conducted by the Protestant pastor from Mahadevganj, begins in the afternoon. This consists predominantly of singing and praying. The Christmas songs that they sing are set to *Sohrae* tunes although some are translations of ancient Christian hymns set to western melodies. Once the service is over, they all share tea and *taben khajari* (puffed and parched rice mixed together) and some Indian sweets. These are also given to the other villagers. In the evening, the young Christian boys and girls go along the *kulhi*, singing and dancing to the accompaniment of the violin, harmonium, cymbals and *kabkubi* (a kind of stringed musical instrument). They visit every house and continue dancing and singing throughout the night.

During that week, anyone who visits the Santal Christian houses is given tea and *taben khajari*. Then, on New Year's day, another big religious celebration is held in the chapel. This is preceded by a big meal in which all the Christians partake. During the religious service, the first fruits of paddy are offered, each household offering a *khaclak* (basket) filled with paddy.[20] This is then sold and the money is used to cover the expenses incurred in organising the festivities. After the service, a sports festival is organised by the Christian households in an open field on the outskirts of the village. Various events are held and these attract large number of villagers from

[20]The Santal Christians of Pangro and the neighbouring villages celebrate the *Janthar* Festival on this day.

neighbouring villages, many of whom also try out their skill in the hope of winning some prize or other. This is followed by singing and dancing along the village *kulhi*. These festivities help to unite the Christian households together. They, however, do not appear to be a functional substitute for the cultural, traditional and communal rejoicing which takes place during the *Sohrae*. In this way, they are being estranged from the village community and from the tribe at large. I shall now describe how the Santal non-Christians of Pangro celebrate the *Sohrae*.

The day of the *Sohrae* is decided upon by the villagers themselves in conjunction with their officials. A *Kulhi Durup* is convoked for this matter. All households prepare rice-beer and, on the eve of the first day, the *godet* goes from house to house to collect sacrificial offerings which, in Pangro, consist of a fowl, half a seer of rice, some onions, pepper, salt and turmeric.[21] These he keeps in the house of the village priest. The first day is called *Um Hilok* (the word *um* means 'to bathe' and *hilok* means 'day'). On this day, all the villagers take a purificatory bath. They clean their houses and courtyards.

Towards the afternoon the priest, the *kudam naeke* and the *godet*, followed by a number of male members of the village, go to a rice field beyond the village houses.[22] This place is called *Got Tandi* and the ritual performed is called *Got Puja*. Here the priest prepares the *khond*, puts some *adwa caole* heaps in the *khond* and makes five *sindur* marks in front of each. The odd number of marks is considered an ominous sign. He places an egg in the centre of the *khond* which he also marks with *sindur*. He then marks the fowl with *sindur* and makes it partake of the rice. Meanwhile, he addresses the major *bongas*, asking them to bless the festival and tokeep it

[21]The contributions of rice collected from each household are called *got caole*. The fowls collected are called *got sim*. *Got* is another name for the *Sohrae*.

[22]The *naeke* carries in his right hand a winnowing fan containing all the materials needed for worship (cowdung, *adwa caole*, *sindur* and flour). In his left hand he carries a pot of water. The *godet* carries the fowls to be sacrificed and the *kudam naeke* carries a *tukuc* (earthenware pot) filled with *handi*.

free from any harm. Thereupon, he saws off the fowl's head with a sickle or axe, letting the blood drip on the egg and rice heaps. He also places the fowl's head on the *khond.* The same is done with all the fowls collected from the village. The *naeke* then fills three leaf cups with rice-beer, which he pours over the *khond,* repeating the same invocation as before. Then the people present drink *handi.*

Meanwhile, the *kudam naeke* takes a black fowl, and, making a separate *khond,* offers the fowl, in the name of the *bahre* and *sima bongas,* by twisting its neck. He also performs the *Bul Mayam* ceremony, mixing his own blood with the *adwa caole* which he then scatters over the place beseeching all the *bongas* to accept the offering and cause no harm. The *kudam naeke's* sacrificial blood is believed to possess the greatest potency. When this is over, he singes the fowls for plucking on a small fire, and rolling them in flour, bakes them on the fire in a skin of leaves. The heads are cooked separately. Once cooked, the priest eats the flesh of the heads while the other villagers eat the *sure jel* (hash) made from the rest of the flesh. Everyone is given rice-beer to drink.

While everyone is drinking, the headman delivers a speech reminding the people present of the taboo on clan exogamy, apart from which they are free to do as they like. He then announces the form the *Sohrae* festivities should take. There is a great difference in the social character of the proceedings and in the mental outlook of the villagers. This depends on whether there had been a good harvest or not, and whether the village had been free from any maladies and deaths or not. In the case of the former, the *manjhi* declares the *Sohrae* to be a *sari Sohrae* meaning that it is a full *Sohrae.* Otherwise, the *Sohrae* is declared to be a *nase Sohrae,* a poor one. During my sixteen months of fieldwork in Pangro, I witnessed two *Sohraes.* One was a *sari Sohrae,* while the other, due to four deaths having taken place during the year in the village which was also ravished by sickness, was termed a *nase Sohrae.* In the case of the latter, the *Kada Khuntau* ceremony was not performed. The festivities were also more restrained. I shall now describe the *sari Sohrae* festivities as witnessed in Pangro.

Once the announcement regarding the nature of the *Sohrae* is made by the *manjhi,* the *Got Lebet* (trial of luck) ceremony takes place. The *gupis* (cowherd boys) are invited to bring their cattle which they drive to the *khond* to the drumming of the *tamak* and the *tumdak*. The cow which treads on and breaks the egg in the centre of the *khond* is caught. Her feet are washed and after anointing her horns with oil they are smeared with *sindur*. The Santals believe that the owner of the cow is assured of good fortune for the following year. It is the luckiest possible omen to befall a person. The breaking up of the egg according to one Santal saying signifies the breaking of the "teeth and the mouth" of the evil powers thus depriving them of their nefarious potencies. The victorious *gupi* is carried over the *godet's* shoulders for everyone to see. Everyone then is invited to visit the village officials' houses starting with that of the *manjhi* where they are given rice-beer to drink.

Later in the evening, the young men of the village conduct the ceremony known as 'waking the cattle' starting from the *manjhi's* cowshed, drumming and singing as they go along. After this, the girls perform the *Cumaura* or 'blessing of the cows' ceremony. This they do with *adwa caole, dhubi ghas* and a small lit lamp. Starting from the *manjhi's* cowshed, they throw some *adwa caole* and *dhubi ghas* towards the cattle-shed and the cows at the same time pronouncing the blessing. Then they visit every house in the village. The purpose of this 'blessing ceremony' is to make the cows fruitful and to protect them from any disease and witchcraft. The cattle are garlanded and their horns rubbed with oil and smeared with vermilion.

The second day is called *Daka Hilok* which literally means 'food day'. The day starts with the ceremony known as *Gadoe*. The menfolk of the village collect in front of the headman's house where, to the accompaniment of flutes and drums, they perform various dances starting with the *danta*,[23] and refresh themselves with rice-beer, provided by the *godet*. They visit every house going about begging for fun and depositing whatever they collect with the *jog manjhi*. Then they all go to bathe, taking with them their plough yokes and hunting implements. While the menfolk are away, the women dance and sing all along the *kulhi*.

[23]Other dances performed are: *gunjar, matwar mucet kher, don, lagre* and *dhurumjak*.

When the men return to their houses, sacrifices are offered by the heads of the households to *Maran Buru*, the *orak bongas* and the ancestors. Here, it is interesting to note that the fowls offered to *Maran Buru* and the *orak bongas* are decapitated and blood is allowed to drip on the *khond*. On the other hand, those offered to the ancestors are killed by a blow on the back of the neck without any blood being shed. Rice-beer libations are also offered to all the spirits. The flesh of the fowls sacrificed is cooked separately from the rice with which it is eaten. Every member of the household partakes of the meal. In the evening, the 'blessing of the cows' ceremony is once more repeated. The rest of the day is spent in community feasting and drinking on a large scale.

In the early morning of the next day called *Khuntau Hilok*, the *jog manjhi* orders some youngsters to help the *paranik* and *jog paranik* put up poles (*khunti*) in front of those houses where buffalo bulls are to be found. A circle is made in front of each pole on top of which a *circaudal* or ornamental mimic roof is placed. The household elder puts gifts, either in the form of money, clothes or food, on it. Gifts are also placed within the circle itself. The buffalo bulls are washed and rubbed with oil. *Sindur* is put on their foreheads and they are garlanded.

In the afternoon, the buffalo bulls are led to the posts to which they are securely tied. The people who gather around begin to bait the animals. Doms are also invited to come and play the *rahar* and the *dhol*,[24] thus adding to the excitement. Baited in this manner, the bulls do not let anyone enter the circle to take away the gifts, let alone to climb and take the gifts on the *circaudal*. This pastime continues for several hours till late at night when dancing and singing along the *kulhi* start again and continue unabated till early morning.

The fourth day is called *Jale Hilok*. The youngsters who, the day before, had put up the poles now remove them. For their work they receive from each house half a seer of rice and any vegetables they can scrounge from the *barge*. All the things collected are taken to the *jog manjhi's* house where they prepare

[24]These are two kinds of big drums. The Doms are given one winnowing fan of paddy and half a seer of rice by each household to whom they render their services.

a meal for themselves and drink what is called *sisir handi* (dew-beer). The young boys and girls of the village dance and sing *dahar* songs. They then spend the rest of the night at the *jog manjhi's* house.

The fifth day, called *Hako Katkom Hilok* (*hako* means 'fish' and *katkom* means 'crabs'), is devoted to fishing. The Santals believe that if one catches and eats fish on this day, his life-span will be prolonged.

On the last day called *Sakrat*,[25] an early meal is cooked, after which the menfolk go for a hunt which begins with the beating of the *tamak* by the *godet*. On their way to and from the hunt, they sing various forest songs (*bir seren*). A plantain stump (*kaera*) is brought by the *godet* from the forest. On their return from the hunt, the menfolk bathe and then offer rice-beer libations to the ancestors and to *Maran Buru*. The *naeke*, on behalf of the headman, offers rice-beer libations to *Manjhi Haram* at the *manjhithan*. In the afternoon, everybody gathers in an open field at the end of the *kulhi* for the *Bijha* or archery competition. The *naeke* helped by the *kudam naeke* fix the plantain stump in the ground. The *naeke* makes a *khond* around the stump and marks it with vermilion. He also puts three *sindur* marks on the stump. Then he libates the spirits with three leaf cups full of *handi*. Some flour cakes (*pitha*) are put on the stump. Thereupon, all the villagers taking part in the archery competition start shooting at the stump from a distance of about a hundred feet. The person who succeeds in hitting the target is regarded as the hero of the day. He is carried around on the *jog manjhi's* shoulders.[26] The *jog manjhi* then cuts the plantain stump into three pieces giving one to the headman, another to the *naeke* and the third he keeps for himself. The flour cakes are eaten by those who can lay their hands on them first. A sports festival is organised for all the villagers, after which everyone returns to the village. Here, once more, the villagers begin dancing and singing along the *kulhi*, starting from the *manjhi's* house where they are also offered rice-beer.

[25]In some places, this is also called *Mokor*.

[26]In Pangro, if a person hits the stump five years in succession, he is given a *dhoti*, a shirt and a turban by the headman.

The following morning, the *jog manjhi* goes around the village informing everyone that the *Sohrae* is over and thus all licentiousness is to stop and no one is to sing *Sohrae* songs or dance the *Sohrae* dances. A week later, the *jog manjhi* gathers all the people of the village in his house. He gives them rice-beer to drink. This they call *chatiar handi* which means 'social cleansing beer'. It signifies the cleansing of the young people and of the villagers in general from the liberties they took during the *Sohrae*.

BAHA

The second great festival of the Santals is the *Baha Parab* or Flower festival held after the full moon in the month of *Phagun* (February-March), when the *sal* (*shorea robusta*) and the *matkom* or *mahua* (*bassia latifolia*) trees begin to blossom. This feast, which lasts for two days, marks the beginning of the Santal year.[27] Until this festival has taken place, no Santal will gather the *matkom* blossoms which provide them with both food and drink.[28] Though the feast is characterised by drinking, dancing and eating, it is 'a righteous festival not licentious like the *Sohrae*', remarks Kolean (Bodding, 1942: 151). The feast is held on different days in dfferent villages so that people may visit their relatives and friends. The festival is a massive propitiation of the major *bongas* who are asked to keep the village free from any sickness or witchcraft and to preserve the crops and cattle. It is also considered a fertility feast.[29]

Like the *Sohrae*, the *Baha* starts with a day of purification called *Um*. The *naeke*, *kudam naeke* and the *godet* go to the *jaherthan* where, with the help of some villagers, they set up two sheds with *sal* branches and thatching grass. One of these sheds is for *Maran Buru*, *Jaher Era* and *Moreko-Turuiko*. The second shed, in honour of *Gosae Era*, is put up beneath the *mahua* tree. The *naeke* then plasters the floor of the sheds with

[27]Some authors also consider this feast as a Spring festival of the Santals.

[28]The Santals brew *paura* from the *matkom* flowers. *Sal* wood is used for rafters and for fuel and the leaves for making plates.

[29]The major *bongas* are propitiated to ensure children as well as to promote prosperity.

cowdung and also smears some cowdung on the ground in front of the *sarjom* tree representing *Pargana Bonga.* When this is over they go for the purificatory bath. The *naeke* takes with him the articles that are to be used at the celebration—three winnowing fans, a flat basket, a bow and an arrow, a battle-axe, a broom, bangles, a necklace and two buffalo horns. After cleansing all these and smearing them with oil, the *naeke* returns to his house where he presents rice-beer to those who helped him set up the sheds. He himself breaks his fast.

In the evening, the *godet* calls the villagers to assemble at the *naeke's* house for the *Bonga Lagao* or 'spirit-possession' ceremony. The articles for the celebration are placed in the courtyard. Everyone starts singing *Baha* songs. Three young men of the village enter into a trance and impersonate *Jaher Era*, *Maran Buru* and *Moreko-Turuiko* respectively. The winnowing fans are placed in front of them. Then, the person believed to be possessed by *Jaher Era* puts on the necklace and bangles and takes the flat basket on his head and the broom in his hand. *Maran Buru* takes the battle axe and *Moreko-Turuiko* takes the bow and arrow. They run to the *jaherthan* where *Jaher Era* sweeps the sheds. When this is over, they return to the *naeke's* house and he washes their feet. Each of them in return washes the *naeke's* feet. After imploring each one of them to take care of the village and ward off any disorder, the *naeke* applies *sindur* on their foreheads and bids them to return to the *jaherthan.* Thereupon, the three mediums regain consciousness. Rice-beer is drunk by all present, dancing and singing starts and continues till early morning.

The following morning, the *godet* visits every house in the village, collecting fowls and other things to be offered by the *naeke* to the *bongas.*[30] The *naeke* and *kudam naeke* go for their purificatory bath, after which they go to the *jaherthan* taking with them the materials necessary for the sacrifice. The *naeke* wears a new white *dhoti* given to him by the *manjhi.* Everyone assembles at the *jaherthan*, and the *naeke* prepares the *khond* in each shed. The three young men become possessed again and

[30]The same things given during the *Sohrae* are offered during the *Baha.*

dash off to the fields. After some time, they return laden with *sal* and *mahua* flowers which are put on the two *khonds*. The mediums sit in front of one of the *khonds* and the *naeke* sacrifices the fowls first on one *khond* then on the other, each time imploring the mediums to protect the village. Then the *kudam naeke* takes a black hen which he sacrifices, after performing the *Bul Mayam* ceremony, a little further away from the sheds. There is a mutual washing of feet by the *naeke* and the mediums, who are then released. The fowls are cooked with rice. The *naeke* and his wife are given the heads and one fowl to eat while the rest is consumed by the other villagers. Rice-beer libations are offered to the spirits after which everyone present drinks. Each girl or woman present receives some *sal* and *mahua* blossoms from the *naeke*. Thereupon, everyone, with the exception of the *naeke* and his wife, returns to his respective home where sacrifices are offered.

In the late afternoon, the *tumdak* is played, announcing the return of the *naeke*. Young boys and girls go to the *jaherthan* where they dance and sing and return in procession to the village with the *naeke* in their midst. On entering the village, the priest visits every house. His feet are washed by a girl of the house, in return for which she receives some blossoms. The presentation of *mahua* blossoms by the *naeke* is another case of imitative magic emphasising fertility. Once all the houses have been visited, the *naeke* returns to his house where he pours the remaining water of the pot on his roof and offers rice-beer to all present. The water festival follows, in which men and women throw water on each other. It is interesting to note that certain persons due to avoidance relationships are tabooed from sprinkling water on each other. Thus, it is not considered proper for a person to throw water on his younger brother's wife (*bokot bahu*) or on his wife's elder sisters (*ajhnar*). Both of them are held in great respect.[31] When the water festival is over the whole village joins in dancing and singing well into the night.[32]

[31]Various other taboos exist between a person and his *bokot bahu* and *ajhnar*. Among others, they cannot mention each other's name. They cannot touch each other nor can they sit near each other.

[32]There is a great similarity between the way in which the Santals and the Mundas celebrate this feast. S.C. Roy (1970:272).

Erok Sim

Another agricultural festival of the Santals is called *Erok Sim.* Fowls (*sim*) are offered on the occasion of sowing the winter paddy (*erok*). The feast is celebrated in the month of *Asar* (June-July). The exact date when the feast is to be held is decided by the village council. The *godet* visits each house collecting fowls and other materials for the sacrificial offering. In the afternoon, after taking the purificatory bath, the *naeke*, accompanied by the *kudam naeke*, the *godet* and some villagers, goes to the *jaherthan* where the *naeke* sacrifices the fowls. He offers one fowl each to the *jaher bongas* and another to *Manjhi Haram*, invoking each one of them to make the earth fertile to let the rains come down and to give them a bumper crop. These spirits are also implored to ward off any disease and evil influences and to let the cattle increase in number. A black fowl is then offered to the *sima bongas* and another to the *bahre bongas* by the *kudam naeke* in the manner mentioned earlier.

Once the offerings are over, the fowls are cooked along with rice and the people present eat of the *sure jel.* The fowls offered to *Jaher Era* and to *Moreko-Turuiko* are cooked separately and eaten only by the *naeke*. That day, or the following day, each household head sacrifices fowls in honour of the *abge bongas*, the *orak bongas*, *Maran Buru* and the spirits of the dead ancestors. The festival is concluded by singing and dancing along the *kulhi*. It is only then that the sowing of the winter paddy starts. No one dares to do this before the *Erok Sim* festival, for the Santals believe that he who does so, will bring ruin not only upon himself but also upon the whole village. They are, therefore, more than careful to see to it that nobody breaks this custom and displeases the spirits.

Hariar Sim

In the month of *San* (July-August) when the paddy seeds have germinated and pushed out new shoots, the Santals perform the *Hariar Sim* festival. On this occasion, the Santals offer sacrifices to the village spirits so that the paddy may grow green, i.e., for a luxuriant growth of paddy.[33] On the night preceding the appointed day, the *naeke* fasts and observes the usual taboos. In the morning, after taking the purificatory bath, he goes to the *jaherthan*, carrying with him a winnowing fan (*hatak*) containing some flour, *adwa caole*, *sindur*, some paddy seedlings and two fowls. He sacrifices, on behalf of the whole village, the fowls to the *bongas* of the village, namely, *Maran Buru*, *Jaher Era*, *Gosae Era*, *Moreko-Turuiko*, *Pargana Bonga*, *Manjhi Haram Bonga* and also to the *sima bongas*. On his return home, he offers rice-beer to all the villagers who visit his house. Unless this public worship is performed, no one in the village may start transplanting the paddy seedlings..

JANTHAR

It is a general rule that the first fruits of the harvest are regarded as sacred. According to Durkheim, 'by their very aspect the first fruits of the harvest manifest the energy which they contain' (1967:379).[34] It is strictly taboo for anyone to eat of the first fruits until ceremonial rituals have been performed to the spirits on behalf of the whole village. The spirits are honoured by being offered the first fruits of the land. The ceremonial rituals performed are an acknowledgement of the spirits' lordship over the land and crops. We have already seen how the Santals do not gather the *sal* and *matkom* blossoms which provide them with both food and drink, prior to the *Baha* festival being performed. Similarly, according to their tradition, the Santals have three festivals connected with the offering of first fruits to their *bongas*. The first, called *Iri-Gundli-Nawai*, is celebrated in the month of *Bhador* (August-September). As the name indicates, it is connected with the offering of the first fruits (*nawai*) of millets called *iri* and *gundli*. The Santals of Pangro do not perform this festival, since millet is not sown during this time.

[33]*Hariar* is the Santali word for 'green' and the word *sim* means 'fowl'.

[34]According to Hebrew and Jewish beliefs, all the products of nature, such as grain, fruits, domestic animals etc., were created by God and so in principle belonged to Him.

The second festival called *Janthar* or *Baihar-Horo-Nawai* is celebrated in the month of *Aghar* (November-December) when the lowland winter paddy crop has ripened. This is the way the festival is celebrated by the Santals of Pangro. The day for the festival is fixed by the village council. A few days before, the *godet* visits every house collecting money to buy a goat or ṛam to be offered in sacrifice. Early in the morning of the appointed day, the *kuḋam naeke*, wearing a new *dhoti* given to him by the headman, goes to a field where the crop has ripened and takes some *horo gele* (ears of paddy) which he puts on the winnowing fan containing the other materials for sacrifice. It is interesting to note that these articles for worship, along with the rice for cooking the hash are supplied by the *kudam naeke* himself. Accompanied by the menfolk of the village, he goes to the *jaherthan*, stopping in front of the *sarjom* tree representing *Pargana Bonga*. After saluting the tree, he prepares the *khond* in front of the sṭone at the foot of the tree. He then places the ears of paddy on the *khond* and puts *sindur* marks on them. He also applies *sindur* on the forehead of the ram and makes it eat of the *adwa caole* at the centre of the *khond*, uttering the following invocation:

> We salute thee *Pargana*. In the name of the *Janthar* we are offering you this ram and these first ears of winter paddy. We exhort you not to let us suffer from any stomach trouble while eating it. Multiply the paddy as we harvest and thresh it. Protect the crop from rats or other pestilence.

The ram is then beheaded and the blood is allowed to drip on the *khond*. The ram is then cooked with rice and eaten by all the men present. The head of the sacrificed animal is taken by the *kudam naeke* to his house. Similar offerings of the first fruits to the *orak bongas* and to the ancestors are made in every household. Once this festival is over, the taboo on the eating of winter paddy is lifted.

MAGH SIM

Another festival connected with first fruits is called *Magh Sim.*

It is celebrated in the month of *Magh* (January-February) prior to the reaping of the thatching grass (*sauri*). It marks the end of the Santal year. Since the Santals of Pangro do not cultivate any thatching grass, they do not celebrate this feast. However, I was informed by a Santal whose family had settled in Pangro and in whose village they celebrate this feast, that on the day fixed for the feast, the *godet* collects one fowl, half a seer of rice, some salt and turmeric from every house in the village. These are sacrificed by the *naeke* to the village *bongas* invoking them to multiply the *sauri* crop. The villagers then partake of the meal.

Besides its religious aspect, the feast has, according to Santal tradition, a socio-political aspect. Formerly, the Santals used to symbolically give up their land to the headman.[35] Similarly, the village officials used to pretend as if they had resigned their posts. After some days, however, the officials were 're-appointed' and the villagers got their land back.

OCCASIONAL RITES AND FESTIVALS

JOM SIM AND MAK MORE

Besides the annual festivals connected with agriculture, the Santals have other festivals which are neither associated with agricultural activities nor performed annually. The most important are *Jom Sim*, *Mak More* and *Karam*. The *Jom Sim* is a clan celebration. It is a sacrifice in honour of the Sun-God *Sin Bonga*. No definite time is fixed for the celebration but, according to tradition, each household should strive to observe it at least once in a life-time. Nowadays, however, it is rarely performed. In fact, in Pangro no one remembers of it having ever been celebrated. When I asked the reason for this, I was told that financially they could not pay for the sacrificial animals necessary for performing this festival. The same can be said of the *Mak More* festival which, according to tradition, and as the term *more* meaning 'five' denotes, used to be

[35] It should be clear from these traditions that, in the olden days, the Santal households shared in the village land on equal basis.

observed at intervals of five years. A white goat was sacrificed by the *naeke* on behalf of the village community to *Moreko-Turuiko* in thanksgiving for the village having been rid of sickness.

KARAM

In the absence of written documents, the traditional lore of the Santals is handed down orally, as we have seen, from generation to generation. The Santal story of the origin of man and the division of the tribe into clans and subclans is recited by village elders in villages on certain occasions, one of which is the *Karam* festival. It is not an annual ceremony, nor one that the village as a whole must perform regularly. In fact, the festival is sponsored by an individual household and the villagers are free to assist. Whenever it takes place, it is observed in the month of *Asin* (September-October).[36] This feast was not originally a Santal festival but it is believed to have been borrowed (by the Santals) from their neighbours.[37] According to Culshaw (1949:114), many of the songs sung during this festival contain references to various heroes of the Ramayana. The aim of this festival is to seek an increase in wealth and progeny and to ward off any evil through the worship of the *karam* tree (*adina cordifolia*). This festival is also celebrated by other tribals such as the Oraons, the Mundas and the Hill Kharias.[38]

Among the Santals, no sacrifices are offered during this festival but rice-beer libations are poured out to *Manjhi Haram* and *Maran Buru*. The villagers give themselves up to merry-making, dancing and singing. The festival starts after dark when two unmarried men of the village bathe and go to the nearby forest from where they bring two branches of the *Karam* tree (*adina cordifolia*) and 'plant' them in the *kulhi*

[36] *Archer* reports that, 'the standard ceremony with slight modifications is also performed on six further occasions' (1974:256).

[37] Culshaw (1949:114) is of the opinion that this festival has been borrowed from the Mahatos.

[38] S.C. Roy (1972:273), (1970:176-81), (1937:341-3). According to Mukhopadhyay (1975:80), this festival is common to the Austric tribes and the lower Hindu castes in the Chotanagpur plateau.

outside the house where the festival is to be celebrated. The villagers accompany the youths to and from the forest, dancing and singing *dhurumjak* tunes to the accompaniment of drums. Dancing and singing continues around the two branches. Then the household elder, at whose instance the festival is performed, approaches the branches. He sprinkles the tree with water, puts a piece of cloth over the branches and a small light in front of them. Thereupon, he marks the branches with *sindur* and pours three rice-beer libations in front of them, each time invoking *Manjhi Haram* and *Maran Buru* to bring prosperity to his household. The villagers present are also given rice-beer to drink. Whereupon a village elder starts reciting the *Karam Binti*, that is the history of creation, the origin of man, and the division of the tribe into clans and subclans. When the recital is over, those present start dancing and singing again, till about sunrise, when the branches are taken and immersed in the village water tank. Then everyone returns to his house.

According to Santal tradition, young unmarried people of the same sex who want to enter into a friendship alliance formalise this life-long friendship during this festival. The alliance between boys is called *Karmu Dharmu* and among girls *Karamdar*.[39] It is brought about by the parties concerned exchanging *karam* buds and fixing them in each other's hair in the presence of the villagers gathered for the festival. Besides linking two friends who promise each other mutual economic assistance, especially in times of crisis, the alliance also puts each one of them into a new relationship with the other's family. Thus, in the case of boys who address each other as Karmu and Dharmu, the alliance gives each one of them the status of brothers while girls become sisters. As a result, incest taboo relationships are created between each other's families.[40]

[39]Parallel to this type of friendship there is the *Phul* type of friendship which is usually solemnised at Sibrat Melas. Another type of friendship is called *Baha Phul* among girls and *Jom-nu Gate* among boys. In this latter type of friendship relation, there is no obligation of economic aid nor do the parties enter into any kinship relation.

[40]In this manner the parties concerned are liable to the same penalties imposed on those who are guilty of breaching a prohibited incest relation.

HINDU RITES AND FESTIVALS

The pantheon of Santal *bongas*, like that of many tribes, includes, as we have seen, certain Hindu deities. Similarly, in addition to the festivals mentioned here, the Santals also have certain festivals which are said to be of Hindu origin like the *Chata*, *Pata* and *Jatra*. These three festivals are not village festivals but are sponsored by individual households. There is no public worship but as Kolean puts it, 'only the man who celebrates it, worships, and we go to look at it, we do not worship' (Bodding, 1942:158). The Santals are aware that these festivals are not their own. As Kolean remarks 'but as these festivals do not belong to us, Santals do not act rightly offering to *bongas* of other races. On account of this our *bongas* are angry with us' (ibid).

CHATA

As we have seen, two Santal families of Pangro formerly used to celebrate the *Chata* and *Jatra* respectively. Thus, Sagram Hasdak's grandfather used to celebrate the *Chata Parab* or Umbrella Festival during the month of *Bhador* (August-September) in honour of the *chata bongas*.[41] The following is an account of the *Chata* festival held in Pangro as told to me by a village elder.

On the day on which the festival was to be held, the household elder, at whose instance the *Chata* was held, worshipped the *chata bongas* through sacrificial offerings. Two poles were erected in an open field. On these poles, another pole was placed horizontally. In the middle of the latter, there was a big iron pivot in which another pole was put vertically. A small decorated umbrella was tied to the top of this revolving pole. A lot of shouting accompanied the erection of this pole. Then all the people present gathered mud and dust from the ground, and threw them at the umbrella. People then engaged in dancing, singing and merry-making. Big crowds—Santals, other tribals and even non-tribals—used to flock to see this festival

[41]Various accounts are given regarding the origin of this festival. See Mukherjea (1962:29); Man (1867).

and to attend the *mela* which was set up in the vicinity. After Sagram's grandfather's death, nobody from his family or from the village ever celebrated this festival. Nowadays, boys and girls from Pangro often visit villages where this festival is organised.

JATRA

Formerly, Cuka Murmu's mother used to celebrate the *Jatra Parab* every three years in honour of the *jatra bongas*. The feast, which was performed in the month of *Magh* (January-February), used to be held near the *jaherthan* where a big merry-go-round was set up.[42] A fair attended by many people used to be organised. During the sacrificial offering of a ram and a pigeon, three persons acted as *chatyas* or oracles of the *jatra bongas* by whom they were said to be possessed. It was believed that, if consulted, these *chatyas* were able to foretell the future. Quite a number of Santals used to consult them.

PATA

Though there are three families in Pangro who worship the *pata bongas—Mahadev* (*Siva*) and *Parvati*—the *Pata Parab*, or Hook-Swinging Festival, was never held in Pangro. I have witnessed this festival at Meronda, a village situated between Banjhi and Borio where I had gone with one of the three families mentioned. The festival, which is held in the month of *Baisak* (April-May), is said to be a corrupt form of the festival called *Charak Puja* in which the Hindus worship *Siva*.[43] The devotees who take part in the ritual sacrifice must have abstained for three days from eating any salt or oil. Besides this sacrifice, the main feature of the festival is the swinging ceremony. A thick mast is placed in the ground on top of which a revolving cross bar is fixed. Ropes are tied at either end of the cross bar and hanging on these ropes two devotees swing themselves while the others shout '*Mahadev, Mahadev*'. Formerly people used to be suspended by iron hooks hooked under certain back

[42]According to O'Malley (1910:129), the Santals borrowed this feast from the Bhuiyas.

[43]See Archer (1974:133).

muscles and swung round and round very fast.[44] As a result of accidents, the Government has prohibited the use of hooks. The festival concludes with special songs and dances.[45]

Although these three festivals are not of Santal origin, they are attended by large numbers of Santals wherever they are held. Everyone puts on his best dress, and anoints himself with oil. Santal girls decorate their hair with flowers and their neck with a *hasli* or chain. The boys wear turbans on their heads and most of them carry staves in their hands. These festivals serve as occasions for Santal girls and boys from different villages to meet one another. Sometimes, marriages are negotiated as a result of these meetings.

If these three festivals attract a number of Santals from all over the area, the same can be said of *Durga Puja* and of the various fairs or *melas* held each year in various parts of the district. The Santals of Pangro and of the neighbouring villages go to Sahibganj to take part in the *Durga Puja* festival or as they call it *Dasae Parab*. This feast, as we shall see in Chapter VI, is of special significance to the disciples of the *ojha*. It marks the end of the course in *ojhaism*. On the last day of the festival, the village goes as a body to see the various shrines of *Durga* whom the Santals call *Dibi*, set up in different parts of Sahibganj Town. For this occasion the Santals, like the Hindus, buy new clothes for themselves and their servants. Late at night, on their way home from Sahibganj, many of the villagers, especially young boys and girls, dance and sing to the accompaniment of flutes. In Pangro, *Dibi* is worshipped by the three Karmakar families.

One of the largest fairs which the Santals of Pangro and the neighbouring villages attend is the one held at Moti Jharna near Maharajpur railway station on the loop line, fourteen kilometres from Sahibganj Junction. This fair is held on *Shiva Ratri* which symbolises the marriage of *Mahadev* with *Parvati*. Booths are set up where sweets and other things are sold. A number of amusements are also organised to attract the crowds. The place is full of tribals, especially Santals and Pahariyas who flock to the place in large numbers.

[44]This gave rise to the English name of this festival.
[45]See Man (1857).

ANNUAL HUNT

The communal worship of the village *bongas* during their annual festival cycle does not exhaust the Santals' expression of their ritual unity. Another important festive occasion which manifests the intimate inter-relationship between the Santals and their *bongas* is the *Disom Sendra* or Annual Hunt. Although, hunting has, for a long time, been substituted by agriculture as the principal mode of living, the Santals still take an intense delight in hunting. Nothing pleases them more than going after game with bows and arrows. They also use hunting spears and axes. Santal hunting expeditions are of two types, one called the *Disom Sendra* or Annual Hunt which lasts for three days, and the other called *Por Sendra* which is an informal one-day hunt organised at the village level. Hunting is done only by the menfolk and if anyone, unless excused by sickness, does not partake in the hunt, he is considered to be a coward. The Santals have a saying that while a woman's peril is childbirth, a man's peril is the hunt.

The *Disom Sendra,* which is the most important hunting occasion of the Santals takes place during the month of *Phagun* (February-March) after the *Baha* festival. As there is a village priest and a priest of the outskirts, there is similarly an annual hunt priest called *dihri.* He is chosen because of his knowledge of the appropriate sacrifices and the incantations uttered to the *bongas* of the forest and hunt so as to assure the success of the hunt and to ward off any harm befalling the hunters.[46] Each *dihri* is thus the spiritual and secular leader of a hunt. For the *Disom Sendra,* the hills and forests are divided into sections, each under the jurisdiction of a *dihri.*

As the name itself indicates—*disom* means 'country'—the *Disom Sendra* involves a number of villages. If festivals, as we have seen, bring people from various villages together, the same can be said, and perhaps to an even greater extent, of the Annual Hunt which is open to all the local tribals and non-tribals. The Santals, however, form the main bulk of the participants. The *dihri* decides on which day the hunt is to

[46]In Pangro, two persons act as *dihris* on different occasions. Both of them are also *ojhas.*

commence and the places where the hunters are to pass the nights. He then sends a man carrying a *dharwak* (a small *sarjom* branch with leaves on it) to the various markets around, informing everyone of the hunt. When people see the *dharwak* they ascertain the day on which the hunt will comm nce, the place of meeting, where the nights are to be spent, and the name of the *dihri*.[47] Meanwhile, the hunters prepare their hunting implements, sharpening their spears, axes and iron-tipped arrows.

On the eve of the hunt, the *naeke* of every village partaking in the hunt sacrifices five fowls for the safety of the villagers belonging to his village and to ensure a good catch. These fowls are given by the *naeke* himself. In return, as we have seen, he receives a strip of flesh cut from the backbone of every big animal killed by his co-villagers. The *dihri* also prepares himself. For a few days before the hunt, he refrains from sexual intercourse and sleeps on the ground. On the eve of the hunt, he fasts. That same evening, he puts two *sal* twigs on a brass water vessel. If, on the following morning, these twigs are still found to be fresh then it is considered a good omen. Early in the morning before the hunters begin to assemble, he goes for a purificatory bath.

Though the menfolk of Pangro, like other villagers, take part in more than one *Disom Sendra* organised by different *dihris* on different days and in different areas, locality-wise, Pangro forms part of the *Disom Sendra* organised by the *dihri* of Kodma, a village about thirty miles away from Pangro, situated in Banjhi *Bungalow*.[48] All the people taking part in this particular hunt gather on the outskirts of this village. Persons from the same village usually go together. Each person carries a bow and some arrows, and has a hunting dog on a leash.[49] In addition to this, some carry axes or spears. All carry their own food on their backs.

[47]Formerly, the number of *sal* leaves on the *dharwak* used to indicate the number of days left before the hunt.

[48]Of the various *Disom Sendras* organised in Borio Community Development Block, the one organised by the Mandro *dihri* is considered to be the biggest.

[49]It is considered essential to have a hunting dog. In every Santal house one finds two or three hunting dogs.

Once everyone has gathered at the place decided upon (*dupurup*—from the word *durup* meaning 'to sit'), the *dihri* performs the sacrificial ritual to the *bongas* imploring them to ensure success and safety during the hunt. After preparing the *khond*, he places three arrows in the ground around the *khond* and encircles them with a cotton thread. Then, he makes several small circles with flour on the *khond* and puts some *adwa caole* and molasses into each. Thereupon, he makes five *sindur* marks in front of each *adwa caole* heap and sprinkles milk over the whole *khond*. Taking a fowl, he sprinkles it with water and applies *sindur* on its forehead, wings and legs, letting it eat of the *adwa caole*. Meanwhile, he invokes the spirit in whose honour the fowl is being sacrificed. He beheads the fowl with an axe and lets the blood drip on the *khond*. In the same manner, he sacrifices five fowls, one to *Rongo Ruji Bonga*—the patroness of the hunt, one to his own special *bonga*, and the other three to other *bongas* of the forest. He then performs the *Bul Mayam* ceremony, letting his own blood run down on some *adwa caole* which he offers to the spirits of the hills and valleys. The fowls are then cooked together with rice and the *dihri* breaks his fast.

As soon as the sacrifice is over, the *tamak* is played by one of the *dihri's* assistants. This serves as a sign for the hunt to start. It is considered very improper for anyone to enter the forest before the sacrifices have been performed. It is believed that such an action incurs the displeasure of *Rongo Ruji* who, being a very jealous spirit, brings misfortune in the form of physical injury or poor game on the whole village to which the culprits belong. The hunters chase any game available. While formerly, as Kolean (1942:120) points out, 'our ancestors have fought tigers and bears', nowadays due to de-forestation in the area, the game available consists mainly of wild pigs, peacocks, hares and foxes.

While hunting, certain customary rules are supposed to be observed. Thus, when a person hits small game like hares, peacocks, foxes or any kind of bird, he shouts the name of the animal or bird he has shot. In the case of big animals, the fictitious name of the village is shouted so that his co-villagers will know that he has either shot an animal with an arrow or killed it with a spear. In this way, other villagers are informed. In the case of wild pigs, the person who hits a pig with an arrow gets a *mandal*—a hind quarter of the animal for himself. He who kills it with a spear or axe is entitled to a *phari*—a forequarter which he immediately cuts off. A distinction is made here. If the person who spears or axes the pig belongs to the same village as the one who shot it with an arrow, then the former gets a *cagat phari*—the foreleg with the shoulder. If they belong to different villages, the one who spears or axes the animal gets a *tota phari*, that is, the forequarter and the neck part. The rest of the pig belongs to the village of the person who shot it with an arrow. In the case of small game, the person who kills the animal is entitled to the *mandal* while the person who shoots it gets the rest of the animal for his village, keeping the *phari* for himself. In the case of a pig which is speared or axed without having been previously hit with an arrow, the person who spears it or axes it first is entitled to the whole animal if it is killed. If, however, in spite of being speared, the animal escapes, then the person who kills it is entitled to a *tota phari* of that animal which he immediately cuts off.

Since huge crowds take part in the *Disom Sendra*, it is virtually impossible to validate claims as to who shot, speared or axed the animal. A lot of bitter inter-village quarrelling takes place since each village supports and defends its own claimants. All these disputes are settled by the *Lo Bir* Council presided over by the *dihri* himself.[50] It meets during the nights of every *Disom Sendra*.[51] Besides settling hunt disputes, the *Lo Bir* Council also arbitrates in other social disputes which are brought to its notice, making it the Santals' highest court of appeal. In these social disputes, however, non-Santals are debarred from taking any active part.[52] In the case of certain hunt disputes remaining unsolved, once the hunt is over, the *dihri* calls together the villagers concerned and they try to settle

[50]Some *dihris* keep a police licence which enables them to judge in the same capacity as a *daroga* or police superintendent.

[51]Because of this connection, the *Disom Sendra* is also known as *Lo Bir Sendra*.

[52]See S.R. Sarkar, 'The Hunting Festival of the Tribals of Bankura District', *Bulletin of the Cultural Research Institute*, Calcutta, 1(2), 1962, pp. 29-31.

the matter together. This is called *Phuta Phuti* which literally means 'to disperse'.

At dusk, the hunters gather near the Karampura village water tank. Here they spend the night. Such places, decided beforehand by the *dihri*, are called *gipitic* from the word *gitic* meaning 'to sleep'. Here, the members of each village assemble in one place. Spears are placed in the ground in the form of a tripod and the hunted game is suspended on them. While the food is being cooked, some cut off the *dihri's* portion of every big animal killed during the day's hunt. This consists of a piece of flesh about three fingers' broad cut off from the animal's neck, *serom*.

When everyone has eaten, those who do not attend the *Lo Bir* Council meeting, gather village-wise in small arenas to watch the night's entertainment called *Torea*. In each arena, two men dressed up for the occasion, often in women's garb and with flowers in their hair, play the flute. They are followed by a nude joker, *lanta kora*. As we have already mentioned, *Rongo Ruji Bonga* is believed to be the patroness of these nude jokers who must serve her continually by attending as many hunts as possible and exhibiting their nakedness. The *Torea* consists in the two flute players singing songs and telling stories about sex marked with bawdy humour, obscenity and coarse ribaldry. Most of these songs and stories exult in forbidden sexual relationships. It is the joker's part to mime what the flute players sing or recite. Like the English ballad system, these songs and stories are, now and then, interrupted by the playing of the flute by the two players, while the joker makes a lot of funny sounds and gestures. This continues until dawn, when the hunters prepare and eat their morning meal.

Meanwhile, early in the morning, the *dihri* goes for his purificatory bath, after which he sacrifices some fowls to the spirits following the same ritual already mentioned. Once the sacrifices are performed, the *tamak* is played and the hunt resumed. The second day and night are passed as the first. For the night, the hunters stop near Pangro water-tank. The hunt ends on the third day in the afternoon when the weary hunters return to their respective villages taking along with them the game.

When the hunters reach their homes, they are welcomed

by their wives who wash their feet and anoint them with oil, after which they are given food to eat. Having eaten, the hunters of Pangro gather near the village tank where they singe and cut up all the killed animals. The portions for the *manjhi* and the *naeke* are set aside. So are the portions reserved for the persons who had shot or killed the animals. The remaining flesh is divided equally among all the hunters. According to custom, the *manjhi* gives two and a half seers of rice as a hunt-bounty. This is cooked together with the flesh of the heads, into a kind of hash. All those present receive a portion which they eat or take home along with the other portion of uncooked meat.

Although the ritual meaning of the hunt has been obscured in the minds of many Santals, it is implicit in much that accompanies it. The divination by *sal* twigs performed by the *dihri* on the eve of the hunt, the various precautions taken by the *dihri* and the sacrifices to *Rongo Ruji Bonga*, the presiding spirit of the hunt, and to other forest *bongas*, are the principal magico-religious rites connected with the hunt. The *Torea* is an efficient means of placating and keeping *Rongo Ruji Bonga* happy. Various magical precautions are also adopted to ward off the evil eye. It is because of the belief in the evil eye that the hunters do not mention the names of their villages but refer to them by using other 'fictitious' names. To the Santals as to most tribals a name is an integral part of its owner and consequently offers a suitable means to the sorcerer for his evil operations.

Though women are not permitted to take part, certain taboos must be observed by them while the men are away hunting. These taboos serve to avert the evil eye and other dangers. Thus no married woman may wear flowers in her hair or iron bangles in her hands. The *dihri's* wife is also held responsible for placating the malevolent influences residing in the forest and hills. She is to remain at home and must not approach the forest or village outskirts lest mischief befalls the hunters. No animal or fowl must be killed in the village so long as the hunters have not returned. Such an infringement is believed to prevent success in the hunt.

Such are the various rites and festivals observed by the Santals to ensure the safety and prosperity of their village communities at each stage in the annual cycle of their economic life. They also serve to express the community rejoicings at the safe and successful termination of each stage.

As mentioned earlier, rituals are symbolic expressions of certain collective sentiments of a particular society. In the course of this chapter, it has been made evident that there are certain common symbols repeated in various forms and under various circumstances in the different rites and festivals described. A study of this symbolism provides us with an understanding of the meanings and values prevalent in Santal society.

The first symbolic value is a sense of presence and of fellowship with the spirits. This is expressed in the libations and sacrificial offerings which are shared by the people and the spirits. The villagers get together for the worship of their village *bongas* and each household donates part of the sacrificial offerings. The collective sacrificial eating and drinking with the spirits symbolises also the sealing of a compact of alliance and friendship. The sacred places, namely, the *jaherthan*, *manjhithan* and *bhitar* where these rituals are celebrated, as well as the sheds erected during the *Baha* festival, the possession by *Maran Buru*, *Jaher Era* and *Moreko-Turuiko*, and the sacred altar (*khond*) indicate a sense of special presence of the spirits and of their intervention.

These rituals also symbolise in an emphatic manner the Santals' dependence on their spirits. The oblation aspect of the sacrificial offerings, the dripping of the victim's blood on the *khond*, and the invocations uttered by the *naeke* on behalf of the whole village, symbolise the Santals' acknowledgement of their spirits as their lords and masters. The applying of *sindur* on the sacrificial animals symbolises that the animals are set apart for the spirits. During the *Erok Sim* and *Hariar Sim* festivals, the Santals invoke in a special manner their benevolent *bongas*, seeking their protection and active help, realising that without their help they can do nothing. The spirits' lordship is perhaps most evident in the offerings of first fruits like the *sal* and *matkom* blossoms and the winter paddy crop to the *bongas* during the *Janthar* and the *Baha* festivals. Prior to such offerings, no one can even harvest the crop, let alone eat it. The spirits' lordship is also manifested in the fact that the rejoicing and festivities of the *Sohrae* can only start once the *jaher bongas* have been propitiated. Similarly, if these *bongas* have been defiled either through a birth or death in a village, no festivities can take place unless they are first propitiated.

Another symbolic element that comes to the fore is a sense of new life and of harmony with nature. The *Baha* is a symbol of new life when nature is blossoming. It marks the Santal New Year. Similarly, the *Sohrae* and the *Janthar* festivals are symbols of new life and of abundance. The *Hariar Sim* symbolises the germination of the paddy seeds. The theme of new life is also manifested in the purificatory bath which is taken by all the villagers prior to every rite and festival. This newness is also extended to the surroundings. Thus, we have the cleansing and white-washing of the houses, courtyards and cowsheds, and of the sacred places and *kulhi* (village street). The *naeke* and the *kudam naeke* put on white *dhotis* prior to the sacrificial offerings. The place where the *khond* is to be made is cleared of grass and purified with cowdung. The harmony with nature is manifested in the fact that most of the village feasts are connected with the agricultural and seasonal cycles of nature.

The idea of community solidarity is expressed in collective feasting, drinking, singing, dancing, mutual visits and exchange of gifts. The whole village community, young and old, males and females, join in these manifestations of joy and exaltation. Each individual member is aware of his fellowship with his community. He experiences and expresses his joy and exaltation not merely as an individual but as a member of a community. These festivals are also occasions for the reunion of relatives and friends.

The mutual stimulation of collective public worship gives. and enhances meanings to the Santals' complex and varied lives. They become conscious of their unity and at the same time dependence on their spirits. Shorn of this religious element, these festivals would lose their special character. These expressions of social religion are techniques for entering into, continuing and reasserting social relationships with the invisible world. The collective celebrations are an affirmation of all the values that the community holds dear. They are the creative self-expression of the community's life and identity. As one delegate to the four-day All India Santal Social Assembly held at Asansol declared: 'We have sacrificed a lot to the changing times. But such festivals are sacrosanct. They are rooted in our tradition and we must cling to them'.[53]

The dependence of the Santals on their spirits is also manifested in each stage of the individual's life-cycle. As we shall see in the following chapter, various rituals and ceremonies accompany the birth, initiation, marriage and death of every Santal.

[53]*The Statesman*, Calcutta, 28 April 1978, p. 7.

Chapter V

The Santal Life-cycle: Rites and Ceremonies

In the last chapter, we have described the various seasonal rites and festivals by which Santal society seeks to ensure safety and prosperity to the village community as a whole at each new stage in its annual agricultural cycle and the feasting, social reunion and rejoicing that mark their successful termination. In this chapter, we shall study the various religious rites and ceremonies[1] by which Santal society marks the physiological phases of human life and above all its crises and transitions.

These rites and ceremonies are mainly concerned with securing the active help of the benevolent spirits and the passive forbearance of the malignant ones, so as to ensure the safety and well-being of the individual and his family at the different turning-points in his life-cycle. They are also public and collective occasions which emphasise the relations of mutual harmony and solidarity between the individual and society and the dependence of the former on the latter.

The turning-points in the life-cycle of an individual Santal are the critical occasions of birth, initiation, marriage and death. The Santals believe that these critical junctures of an individual's life are replete with danger both for the individual

[1]The term 'ceremony' is used in a wider sense than the term 'rite'. It includes not only the sacrificial offerings, libations and invocations which make up a 'rite', but also the secular elements of behaviour which accompany the rite but are not exclusively part of the rite.

himself and also for the others. As O'Dea points out, 'In such crises men are potentially exposed to the dangers involved in the contingency and powerlessness inherent in the human condition' (1969:40). To control these dangers, guard against any external harm, and satisfy the emotional need of restoring hope and confidence, these life-crises moments are set off by elaborate socio-religious rituals involving the help of the benevolent *bongas*. These rites of passage, as Van Gennep (1960) called them, are practised universally though their number and the stages of life selected vary from society to society.[2] They 'consecrate the crises and marginal situations in individual and collective life' (Wach, 1962:42). The gravity of these events is also marked by a whole repertoire of ideas regarding pollution and purification.[3]

Van Gennep argued that alterations of status or movements into new statuses, such as in pregnancy, child-birth, at initiation, betrothals, marriage and funerals, disturb both the life of the individual and that of the society in which he lives. Danger lies in transitional states because transition is indefinable. It is neither one state nor the next. The person who passes from one state to another is himself in danger and emanates danger to others. The function of the rites of passage is to reduce the harmful effects of these disturbances.

BIRTH CEREMONIES

One of the greatest things a Santal married couple dreads is to have no offspring. They will secure adult respect only when they beget a child. Besides, children are also considered very important because of their potential working ability. So important is a child, especially a son, that a husband can lawfully divorce his wife if she is found to be barren and, vice versa, a

[2]Van Gennep argued that the rituals dealing with movements of people and groups, and of persons between groups; with movements into new statuses; changes of seasons and moon phases; sowing, first fruits and harvest; all these exhibited three common phases: a separation by a marginal period, an aggregation to a new condition or re-aggregation to old. These phases are described by Van Gennep's translators as rites of separation, transition and incorporation.

[3]Mary Douglas (1966).

wife can divorce her husband if he is found to be sterile. In some cases, the husband is persuaded to take a second wife. This, however, is done only with the consent of the first wife. Normally if a couple cannot beget any children, they consult a *raranic* who prescribes various medicines.[4] If these prove to be of no effect, recourse is had to supernatural aids. The woman approaches an *ojha* who divinises whether *bongas* are 'blocking the way'. If this is so, the *bonga* is said to be transferred into a fowl. If, however, all these means of securing the birth of a child prove of no avail, the couple, as a last resort, approaches the *bonga* or *bongas* that are said to be latent in certain Hindu shrines.[5]

The Santals believe that at no time of life is a human being more exposed to supernatural evil influences than while still in the mother's womb and at birth. Because of this, as Malinowski in his study of the Trobriand Islanders points out, 'the very beginnings of human life are surrounded by an inextricably mixed-up medley of beliefs and practices' (1954:37). Added to this, there are many precautions which have to be observed so as to protect the mother and the child in her womb.

The various precautions which a pregnant Santal mother must observe may be broadly divided into two categories: (*i*) those meant to protect the mother and child from the unsatisfied souls of the dead, and (*ii*) those enjoined because of their effect on the physical appearance or the character of the child. Among the precautions in the first category, we find that a pregnant woman must not take any life, nor must she look upon or touch a human corpse. Contact with a corpse is believed to transmit danger. She must not weep when a death occurs. She must never go near rivers and streams where *curins* are supposed to dwell. She must not walk over the straw rope (*bor*) used for binding *bandis* (bundles for storing grain). She must not lie down in the courtyard or any other open space lest *bongas*, and a particular type of bird called *Puni-cere*, 'might fly across her body'. She must not put a flower of the *kanthar* tree

[4]Archer, W.G. (1974:273-4) and Bodding, P.O., 'Santal Medicine', *Memoirs of the Asiatic Society of Bengal*, Calcutta, 10(2), 1927, pp. 133-426.

[5]Culshaw, W.J. (1949:120).

(jackfruit) in her hair, lest the child should shrivel in the womb as a *kanthar* flower does when it dries.

Among the precautions in the second category, we find that during a thunderstorm a pregnant woman must keep indoors and put her fingers in her ears so that the child will not hear the noise and be born a coward. She is not to make bread, lest her child's ears be wrinkled, nor must she plant or break turmeric roots, lest the fingers of her child be forked, or the child gets an extra finger. She must not make leaf cups lest the child be born with a split lip, nor look upon an elephant, lest her child's tongue be very long and his ears be large and floppy. Certain restrictions are also imposed on the child's father. Thus, for example, he must strictly observe the rule against taking any life and must avoid all contact with dead bodies. He is to refrain from eating the flesh from the head of an animal offered in sacrifice or slain in the hunt.[6]

Provided these precautions are observed, the Santals believe that a birth is rarely attended with any difficulty. In case of a difficult delivery, an *ojha* is called upon to divinise whether a *bonga* is present. If this is asserted, a vow is taken to make the proper sacrifices in the case of a speedy delivery. Midwives are engaged for the delivery. Though there are two Santal midwives in Pangro, certain households call upon a midwife from a neighbouring village. She is a Dom by caste. Several married women of the village, especially the older ones, gather in the house where the birth is to take place, to give courage to the mother, as they say. No men are allowed in the house as their presence is believed to hinder delivery.

When the child is born, the umbilical cord is severed by the midwife using a sharp iron arrow. The placenta and the afterbirth are then buried near the main door of the room where the delivery had taken place. The Santals assert that the reason for burying the afterbirth is because should it be eaten by a dog or any other animal, the mother will become sick and die. They also believe that if the afterbirth is buried deep in the ground, the difference in age between the present child and the next will be long. If it is, however, buried near the surface, another birth

[6]Radcliffe-Brown (1959:150) points out that among the Andamanese, these taboos are symbolic expressions of the expectant father's concern.

may be expected after a short time. It is also interesting to note that the Santals do not talk of their 'birthplace' but refer to it as 'the village where their afterbirth was buried'. As soon as the child is born, the women present cry out the news to the husband who, taking a large stick, repeatedly beats the roof of the house so as to drive any lurking *bhuts* or *curins*. When the other villagers hear that a birth has taken place in their village, they ask 'Dipil se bharia?' which means, 'Does it carry on the shoulder (a boy) or does it carry on the head (a girl)'.[7]

When a child is born, the house is considered ritually unclean. This ritual uncleanness is shared by the whole village. The *bongas* of the sacred grove are said to become defiled. No festival or any *bonga* worship is held in the village, and nobody drinks or dines in the house where the child has been born, till the purification ceremony is observed. One ceremony, performed on the day of birth, is meant to protect the mother and the child. This ceremony is known as *Met Halan* which literally means 'lifting the eye'. The mother and the midwife sit facing each other on the floor of the house. The mother then fills a leaf cup with rice-beer and gives it to the midwife who throws away its contents on her left side. This is repeated three times and is believed to render both the child and the mother immune from any imminent danger.

The cleansing ceremony after birth, is called *Janam Chatiar*. *Janam* means 'birth' and *chatiar* is a word connected with the Hindi word *chut* which means 'polluting'. This ceremony may be said to have a three-fold function: (*i*) it purifies the house and the village from the defilement caused by the birth of a child; (*ii*) it gives a child a name, thus formally admitting it into its father's clan and subclan, also giving it the protection of its father's spirits; (*iii*) it incorporates the child into the tribe.

As we have seen in Chapter II, normally the *Janam Chatiar* ceremony is held on the third day after the birth of a girl and on the fifth day after the birth of a boy. Since, until this purifying ceremony is performed, the whole village remains polluted and no festivals, weddings or sacrifices can take place, the

[7]This alludes to the way in which men and women carry water pots.

time rule mentioned is abruptly rescinded and the ceremony is anticipated if a festival is imminent. This is also the case if a birth occurs on the eve of a wedding or on the day before a new moon.[8] The reason for the latter is that the Santals believe it is not propitious to name a child in a different month from that in which it is born. Misfortune may befall the child especially after his or her marriage.

Blood relatives on the father's side are invited for the ceremony. They generally bring gifts of bead necklaces, cloth, bangles (in the case of a girl), rice, etc., for the newborn child. The villagers also gather in the courtyard. Two essential elements in the removal of the defilement are shaving and bathing.[9] The barber shaves the male members of the village starting with the village priest and ending with the child's father. Thereupon, the newborn child is brought out in the courtyard by the midwife. The barber then cuts some locks from the child's hair, which he puts in a leaf-cup. He pours some oil in the leaf-cup and gives it to the midwife who rubs the child's head with oil mixed with turmeric. Then the men go to the water tank to bathe. While they are away, the midwife winds two pieces of cotton thread around the arrow with which she had cut the child's umbilical cord, and collects the child's hair in a small bundle. On the return of the menfolk from their purificatory bath, the midwife, carrying the child, takes the mother and all the women present to bathe. Reaching the spot, she takes one of the strings from around the arrow and ties the bundle of hair. After invoking *Maran Buru* and the ancestral spirits of the child's father to take care of the child, letting it prosper in life and free from any disease, she lets the bundle float on the water.

When everyone has returned to the child's house, the child's mother is made to sit down in the veranda with the baby in her lap. The midwife takes the other string wound around the arrow, soaks it in oil and turmeric and ties it round the child's waist as a loin string (*dora*). She mixes some cowdung with

[8]Even when postponed, the celebration must always be observed on uneven days after birth.

[9]Shaving of the child and of its father, symbolises the passing of the child from one stage to another in his life-cycle.

water and lets it trickle into the left hand of the child's mother, who dabs it on her head and also sips a little. This concoction is credited with beneficent powers with the aid of which the mischievous influences of evil powers may be neutralised. The midwife, then, takes the child and entering into the house, puts it on the *parkom* (stringed bed) on which the mother lay when she had her labour pains. Making a mixture of *adwa coale* flour and water, the midwife sprinkles some of it on the four legs of the *parkom*, and on the child. She then brings the child out in the courtyard and sprinkles the mother and the assembled people. Once this is over, the midwife, taking the child in her arms, goes round the courtyard formally announcing the child's name.[10]

The name-giving is an essential part of the *Janam Chatiar* ceremony, for, as we have already seen in Chapter III, the giving of a name to a child, formally admits it into its father's clan and subclan. In so doing, the child is given the protection of its father's *bongas*. In giving it a name, the father removes all traces of illegitimacy, if any, recognising the child as his own. The child thus acquires a definite status in the village and among its kinsfolk. It is considered to be a Santal. The name-giving also emphasises the social obligations of the household to its new addition.

The name is chosen by the parents of the child. In assigning a name, however, they follow a traditional formula. Provided the marriage is not in the *ghar jawae* or *ghardi jawae* form, the first-born son is named after his paternal grandfather, the second after his maternal grandfather, the third receives the name of his paternal grandfather's eldest brother, while the name of the maternal grandfather's eldest brother is given to the fourth son. Other male offspring, if any, consecutively receive the name of their paternal grandfather's brothers and maternal grandmother's brothers. Daughters receive the name of the equivalent female relatives in the same order. In the case of the father being a *ghar jawae* or *ghardi jawae*, the naming order is

[10]Culshaw (1949:127) remarks that in the area around Sarenga, a village in Bankura district in West Bengal, this name-giving ceremony is sometimes performed on a separate day from that on which the shaving and the bathing take place.

reversed, that is, names on the maternal side come first.[11] By following these traditionally established practices in naming their children, the Santals perpetuate the memories of their ancestors. In the case of twins, the names are drawn from Hindu mythology. Thus, if both the twins are male, they are named Ram and Lokhon, and if female, Chita and Khapra. If one is male and the other female, they are named Ram and Chita.[12]

It is interesting to note that most Santals are given two names. One is called *mul* or *bhitri nutum* which literally means 'inner' or 'private' name, and the other is called *bahna* or *cetan nutum* which literally means 'upper' or 'outer' name. The *bhitri nutum* of the child must correspond to that of the relative after whom it is called. The *cetan nutum* is a kind of nickname. These nicknames, given in early childhood, are often replaced by others as the child grows up. This second name is important, because, on the whole, the Santals are reluctant to call someone by his real name fearing it may cause him harm. As already mentioned a name is said to be an integral part of its owner and consequently presents a very potent means to the sorcerer for his magical operations. The second name is also necessary as a result of the prohibition which the Santals attach to the use of the *bhitri nutum* by certain categories.[13]

The conclusion of the ceremony is marked by the drinking of gruel made out of boiled rice-water (*dak mandi*) with *nim* leaves. This is why this ceremony is also called *Nim Dak Mandi*. Though very bitter, this beverage is said to have a purificatory

[11]If the child's mother had taken any medicine, either from the *raranic* or *ojha*, or visited any Hindu shrine, so as to become pregnant, then the child receives the name of the man from whom medicine or advice has been obtained.

[12]Other names for male twins are: Sidhu and Kanhu; Bhim and Arjun; and Bharat and Chatur. In the case of female twins, they are named: Hisi and Dhumni; Dargi and Pargi.

[13]Thus, if a boy has been named after one of his grandfathers, then all those who, due to kinship relations are prohibited from pronouncing the grandfather's name, like the grandmother, are equally prohibited from applying that name to anyone else. Brothers and sisters-in-law, husbands and wives are also prohibited from mentioning each other's names. Besides, to avoid confusion, the child is not called by its grandfather's name, while the latter is still alive.

effect.[14] The household head offers some of the gruel to *Maran Buru* and the ancestor spirits, invoking them to give the baby a long and healthy life. All the people present are then offered *nim dak mandi*, after which everyone returns to his house. If the family can afford to do so, they give a meal to all the relatives. With the end of the ceremony, the village *bongas* are purified and the village and the house where the birth has taken place are cleansed.

Three factors stand out as being of prime importance in the *Janam Chatiar* ceremony: (*i*) The religious role of the father who provides the child with *abge* and *orak bongas* (subclan and household spirits); (*ii*) The intimate connection between the removing of the childbirth pollution and the admission of the child into the tribe and the *bongas*; (*iii*) The Santals' reluctance to lose one of their progeny. Because of these three factors the illegitimate child is almost unknown in the Santal community. The ingenuity of the Santals has evolved a system whereby all children of Santal parentage are legitimatised.[15]

When a child is born to a Santal girl out of wedlock, the girl's father and household are semi-outcasted (*Pante-Begar*) and they can only return to the tribe by arranging a father for the child. This can be done in two ways. First, if a person is proved to be the *genitor*, whether he accepts the paternity or not, he either has to marry the girl or pay for a 'bought husband'. Second, if the village cannot prove who the real father is, then a substitute father is arranged. In both instances, the *Nim Dak Mandi* ceremony removes all traces of illegitimacy and the child takes the *bongas* of his father.[16]

INITIATION

The second critical stage in the life-cycle of a Santal is marked

[14]For its connection with disease godlings, see Crooke (1925:119).

[15]Campbell, A., 'Rules of Succession and Partition of Property as observed by the Santals', *Journal of the Bihar and Orissa Research Society*, Patna 1(1) Mar. 1915, pp. 21-5. If a child is born to a Santal girl from a man of another tribe, or vice-versa, both the child and its Santal parent are outcasted for life.

[16]For further details about this, refer to Archer (1974:162-9); Bodding (1942:25) and A. Campbell (1915:21-5).

by a purificatory rite called *Caco Chatiar.* Though the word *caco* literally means 'a toddler', the ceremony is not performed until the child has grown up. In fact, there is no fixed time when the *Caco Chatiar* is to be held as long as it is observed before marriage. While the *Janam Chatiar* ceremony admits a child 'to the outer fringes of the tribe', the *Caco Chatiar* ceremony is believed to give an individual all the responsibilities and privileges of a full-fledged member of the tribe. Through this ceremony, an individual enters into a new relationship with the *bongas* whom he can now approach with sacrificial offerings and also share in the sacrificial meal.[17]

In Pangro and the neighbouring Santal villages, the performance of this ceremony is of an extremely casual nature. It is, however, considered important by Santals because of the dire consequences that would follow if it is not observed. Thus, no Santal boy can get married unless he has undergone this ceremony.[18] The ceremony used to be rather expensive since the whole village had to be feasted. It has, therefore, now become customary for a family to wait until the ceremony can be performed for several children at the same time.

On the day appointed by the headman, the villagers are summoned by the *godet* to the house where the ceremony is to take place. When all have assembled, the midwife, who had presided at the birth of the children, or, if this is not possible, any other elderly village woman, bathes the children to be initiated by pouring water over them. Then three girls from the village anoint all those present with oil and turmeric, starting with the priest and his wife. Rice-beer, brewed for the occasion, is served to all present, after which they sing and dance in honour of the household in whose honour the ceremony is to be performed. An old man of the village, then recites the Santali account of creation, the wanderings of the Santal ancestors and how they came to occupy the present habitat in the village, making allusions to the household which has sponsored the ceremony. This is an essential aspect of the ceremony since it is considered very important for a Santal young man to be instructed

[17]For a similar view among the Trobriand Islanders, see Malinowski (1954:39).

[18]See Datta-Majumder (1956:87); Archer (1974:58).

in the tribal tradition and made to realise what being accepted as an adult Santal implies. The recitation also serves to transmit the Santal tribal lore, ensuring a certain continuity in the tradition.

After serving rice-beer to all, the *jogmanjhi* of the village, stresses that by participating in the drinking of rice-beer, the village community has expressed its acceptance of these young persons as full participants in the village affairs. If the family can afford the expense, a meal is given to all those present. Otherwise, it is considered sufficient to feed the relatives and the village officials. Through this ceremony, the initiated persons are, as it were, reborn in society. The rebirth is signified by the presence of the midwife. No sacrifices are offered and the people's part consists mainly in approving the proceedings by drinking rice-beer.

The universal custom, among the Santals, of cicatrization of boys and the tattooing among girls, has been connected by Hunter (1975:204) with the ceremony of initiation. There is, however, no evidence of such connection in the past and it certainly does not exist now. In fact, there is no ceremony to accompany this custom and Santal boys usually brand themselves when they are herding their cattle in the fields.[19] The branded marks remain for life. Each boy can brand himself as often as he wishes, though the scars must always be odd in number. Odd numbers are considered as ominous signs. They are said to signify life, *jion*, while even numbers mean death, *moron*. The term for each mark is known as *sika*. The Santal believes that the *sika* is an indication of his Santal identity. It is very important to show these marks to the guardians of the next world, for otherwise, huge worms in the form of *tumdaks*, will sit on his lap and slowly torment him till they eat him up. An individual is proud of his scars which are also considered as a mark of his endurance.

A similar belief leads the girls to be tattooed. There seems to be no special connection between the designs tattooed, called

[19]A rag is rolled like a cigar to a thickness of about an inch and set alight. Each boy then presses the burning rag on to the skin of his left arm, midway between the wrist and the elbow. When the skin is burnt out, ashes are pressed on the scar.

khoda, and the Santal traditional history, as is the case among the Kharias. There is also no specific time when the girls are tattooed. The custom is that a girl must have her left arm, shoulder and breast tattooed prior to her marriage. A girl without these tattoo marks will not be accepted by her mother-in-law as a daughter of the house. After marriage, a woman gets her right arm, shoulder and breast tattooed. In Pangro, the work of tattooing is usually done during the cold season by a Karmakar woman from another village, who visits Pangro for this purpose. As in the case of Santal boys, if a woman dies before being tattooed, *Jom Raja* (the *bonga* of death) will consider her to be impure and will send her straight to the underworld.

The Santals consider cicatrization of boys and tattooing of girls as having a social and religious importance. Through these magico-religious customs, the Santals protect themselves against any calamities at the hands of the malignant spirits in their future life. Commenting on a similar custom to be found among the Andaman Islanders, Radcliffe-Brown (1964:315-20) remarks that this custom marks a special relation between the adult Andaman Islander and that system of powers on which the welfare of the society and of the individual depends.[20]

MARRIAGE

Judging by the complexity of the ceremonies and the long period of time during which the complete procedure for contracting a marriage is gone through, it is obvious that marriage is the most important stage in a Santal's life-cycle. It is considered indispensable for every Santal, whose tribe members cannot visualise how a normal man or woman can remain unmarried. Bachelors and spinsters are looked upon as unhappy wretches.

[20]Cicatrization and tattooing are also to be found among many tribes of India as for example the Oraons, S.C. Roy (1972:96-7); the Kharias, S.C. Roy, (1937:218-9); the Mundas, S.C. Roy, (1970:213-4); the Bhils, S.L. Doshi, *Bhils: Between Societal Self-awareness and Cultural Synthesis*, New Delhi: Sterling Publishers (P), Ltd., 1971); the Mikirs, the Juangs, the Gonds, etc. The custom is also prevalent among various castes (W. Crooke, 1925:296-8).

The groom's party (*bariatko*) arriving at the bride's village.

Gidi Cumaura - 'second waving' ceremony. The *manjhi* saluting the married couple prior to their leaving the village.

Tarware Dak or 'sword water' ceremony.

Bahu Um - bathing of the bride.

As a result of this attitude, unmarried people are very rarely found.

The general custom prevalent among the Santals is to contract monogamous unions. Polygamy is not favoured unless the wife is barren, in which case, as we have seen, the husband can either divorce his wife or take a second wife with the former's consent. Otherwise, Santal opinion is against polygamy. Santals consider that only a fool can live happily with more than one wife for, as the proverb goes, 'A co-wife pricks like spear grass'. Adult marriage is normally the accepted norm among all the Santals. It is considered more appropriate for the bride to be younger than the groom. The average marriage age of a boy is twenty and that of a girl sixteen.

To protect their tribal solidarity, the Santals have very stringent marriage laws. As mentioned in Chapter II, a Santal cannot marry a non-Santal or a member of his own clan. The former is considered as a threat to the tribe's integrity, while the latter is considered incestuous. Formerly, a Santal was barred from marrying into his mother's subclan. Strictly speaking, the only forbidden degree of consanguinity in relation to marriage are brothers and sisters, cross cousins or children of siblings of the opposite sex, and parallel cousins or children of siblings of the same sex. In practice, however, the Santals recognise relationship up to three generations as a bar to marriage. Though senior levirate and sororate are tabooed, there is no restriction on junior levirate and sororate. Thus, a man, on the death of his wife, may marry her younger but not her elder sister. Similarly, a woman, on the death of her husband, may marry his younger but not his elder brother. This, however, is not compulsory, though levirate marriage is sometimes contracted so as to keep the family property intact.

Residence is normally patrilocal. After marriage, the bride goes to live in her father-in-law's house. It is only in the *ghardi jawae* or *ghar jawae* types of marriage, as we shall see, that this custom is reversed. If the house is not big enough to harbour more than one married son and his household, then some build their own house, usually close to their father's house. There also exists a certain social reluctance towards intra-village marriage, for, as the proverb says, 'A hen and a bride from the same village run to their homes'. A girl also often marries outside her native village. According to another saying, 'Parents-in-law in the same village are like broken pipes. The fire falls out. They hear each other's quarrels'. As can be seen from Table 5.1, out of sixty-seven married men from Pangro, twelve married locally, the other fifty-five, of whom eleven are now deceased, married girls from other villages. Out of thirty-six married women from Pangro, twenty married boys from other villages. This includes two widows and two divorcees who are now living in the village. The other sixteen, including four who are widows, married locally. Through marriage alone, the people of Pangro are socially related to people from forty-four other villages.

TABLE 5.1: MARRIAGE PATTERNS IN PANGRO

Total population of married males and females		*Married within village*	*Married outside and settled inside*	*Married outside and settled outside*	*Married outside and returned to village after divorce/husband's death*
Males	67	12	53*	2	
Females	36	16**	5	11	2 (divorced) 2 (widowed)

*This includes 11 married males who are now deceased. Their widows continued to live in Pangro.
**This includes 4 widows.

Divorce was formerly rather rare among the Santals, although the following three reasons did justify a divorce: (*i*) adultery; (*ii*) the suspicion that the wife practised witchcraft; and (*iii*) sterility or barreness. Nowadays, a couple can also be divorced if they cannot live peacefully together. A man may also seek divorce if his wife is too extravagant and wastes the family resources; if she is permanently ill, or if she is very lazy. A woman may be granted a divorce if her husband cannot supply her with the necessities of life or if he wants to get a second wife against her consent.

If a divorce is requested as a result of their not living in peace, the guilty person has to pay a fine called *chadaodi* or divorce money. In Pangro, this amounts to seven rupees. If the husband asks for the divorce, he pays the *chadaodi* and gives a saree to his wife. He cannot claim back the bride-price. If it is the wife who asks for the divorce, her father must return the bride-price and pay the *chadaodi*. If a divorce is granted on account of the woman's fault, her father must return the money received as bride-price. In the case of the husband being at fault, the bride-price is forfeited. When a wife demands a divorce because of her husband taking a co-wife against her consent, the bride-price will not be paid back, but, on the contrary, she will receive some remuneration from her husband. In the case of a widow marriage, should there be a divorce owing to the husband's fault, the woman can claim half of her husband's household property. On a divorce being granted, the father gets the custody of the children. No divorced woman is allowed to take her children with her.[21]

A simple ceremony called *Sakam Orec* or 'the tearing of the leaves' symbolises the breaking of relations between husband and wife. This is performed in the following manner. On the day appointed by the headman, all the villagers of both parties, if they belong to different villages, assemble in the husband's village.[22] The husband and wife are made to stand facing each other and a *lota* filled with water is placed in their midst. The headman of the husband's village then addresses the gathering, invoking the village *jaher* spirits to bear witness to the occasion. If the divorce has been approved, the customary payments are made. The party wanting the divorce is then made to stand on the left leg and given three *sal* leaves which he/she tears along the mid-rib. Thereupon, he/she kicks the *lota* with the right foot. The *manjhi* then declares that, having torn the leaves, they are now separated. First the man and then the woman go round bowing to those present, starting with the headman.[23]

[21]In the case of a baby at the breast, it must also be returned to the father, after it has been weaned. The mother, however, is paid for suckling the child and for any other expenses incurred.

[22]All divorce cases are adjudged by the village council in which all the villagers stand witness.

[23]Though this ceremony appears rather simple, its consequences are

If divorce is granted as a result of witchcraft, the *Sakam Orec* ceremony is not performed, but the woman is simply handed over to her parents or near relatives. It is interesting to note that divorce among the Santals applies only to this life. According to Santal belief, a man and a woman who have been married as bachelor and spinster, will continue belonging to each other in the next world. Thus, if a divorced woman called *chadui,* marries again, she still will belong to her first husband in her after-life.

The generic Santal word for marriage is *bapla.* Among the Santals there are seven traditional forms of marriage.

1. *Kirin Bahu bapla* which takes place when a man brings his son a bride (*bahu*) for whom he has paid (*kirin*) the bride-price.

2. *Kirin Jawae bapla,* when a husband is acquired/bought for a girl made pregnant by a man who, either does not want to marry her, or, cannot marry her because he belongs to her clan. Here the cost of acquiring/buying (*kirin*) a husband (*jawae*) is borne by the offender.

3. *Tunki Dipil bapla* or the poor man's marriage. This is resorted to by persons who cannot bear the expenses of a regular marriage. No bride-price is paid. The bride gathers all her belongings in a small bamboo basket (*tunki*) and she is brought to the groom's house with the basket on her head (*dipil*).

4. *Sanga bapla* contracted by a widow or a divorced woman, and a widower or a divorced man. The bride-price is half of that given in the case of *kirin bahu bapla.* This is due to the belief that, after death, a woman will eventually rejoin her first husband. Her first *sindur* has given her a special relation to her first husband's *bongas.* If, however, a widower wants to marry an unmarried girl, he has to pay the full bride-price plus another amount called *randi bakhra* or 'widowhood allowance' which, in Pangro, amounts to seven rupees. This serves as an incentive to the girl's parents who believe that their daughter will be risking a premature death in marrying a man whose first wife has died. While in the case of a widower marrying a

far from trivial. A divorced man is considered less eligible for marriage than a bachelor. Similarly, a divorced woman faces still greater difficulties in getting re-married.

widow, there is no *Sindradan* (applying of vermilion on the bride's forehead), when a widower marries an unmarried girl, the *Sindradan* ceremony is done privately.

5. *Ghardi Jawae bapla* is resorted to by the parents of a household in which there are grown up daughters and, either no sons or, if any, minor sons. In such cases a *ghardi jawae* is brought in to help in the work of the household. This type of marriage is also arranged in the case of an only daughter or, of one who, for some reason or other, such as ugliness or deformity, has not been sought in marriage by anyone. All marriage expenses are borne by the bride's parents. The groom pays no bride-price but instead works for five years for his father-in-law, for which he gets no wages but food and clothing. Because of this form of serving-son in-law, normally only boys from the poorer households agree to becoming *ghardi jawaes*. At the time of marriage, the girl's parents choose a calf for the boy. This calf becomes his personal property and, should he decide to leave the house after the five years are over, he takes it with him. Though the marriage ceremony takes place in the girl's house, as in the case of *kirin bahu bapla*, the girl's father and some villagers go to the boy's village, instead of the boy's party coming to fetch the bride. This signifies the fact that the groom comes to live with the bride's household. As we have noted, in the case of a *ghardi jawae* marriage, the custom of naming the first boy after his paternal grandfather and the second after his maternal grandfather, is reversed. The maternal relations come first.

Another form of negotiation marriage in which the groom takes up matrilocal residence is called *ghar jawae bapla*, in which case the boy lives permanently in his in-laws' house. This type of marriage is usually resorted to by a father who has no male offspring but only daughters. By bringing a *ghar jawae* into his household, the father ensures that his property and land will be inherited by his grandsons, through his daughter, to the exclusion of all other relatives. Because of this, nominating a person as *ghar jawae* requires the approval of the family's other relatives who, quite often, object since they will be losing a share in the property. The villagers' consent is also essential.

On the day following the wedding, the girl's father, followed by the village officials and other villagers, takes the groom to show him the family fields. This inspection signifies the boy's status. He, however, acquires no right of inheritance in his father-in-law's lands and property. He continues to retain his rights in his father's land and property. He cannot sacrifice to his father-in-law's *bongas* but keeps his father's *bongas*. His children, though they take his clan and subclan, are named first after their mother's relatives. In the case of his wife's death, he is allowed the *usufruct* of the land and the property if he does not remarry, in which case he loses everything. On her part, the girl's rights in her parents' property continue as long as she remains in her father's house. If, on her husband's death, she were to take up residence outside, then she loses her rights of inheritance.[24]

6 and 7. The last two forms of traditional Santal marriages, namely *itut bapla* and *nir bolok bapla*, can be classified as marriages by force and are rather rare. In the case of *itut bapla*, it is the boy who takes the initiative. When the boy is not sure whether the girl he loves will accept him as her husband, or when the parents refuse to give their consent, the boy, choosing a public place such as a fair or a market, forcibly applies *sindur* to the girl's forehead claiming her as his wife. *Itut* is a Santali word meaning 'to mark with paint'. In the case of *nir bolok bapla*, it is the girl who takes the matter in her hands. By intruding (*nir bolok*) into the house of the boy who, after having had sexual relations with her, refuses to marry her, she forces him into marriage. These two types of marriage are usually followed by regular marriage. In the case of *itut bapla*, since the girl's parents and co-villagers consider themselves insulted by the boy's behaviour the boy's father has to pay a sum of money called *jobrani* 'for doing it by force', to the girl's father, a fine to the *manjhi* as *bohok bancao* 'for saving his head', and a smaller sum to the villagers. If there is any objection to the marriage, the girl must first be formally divorced. Should she remarry, she does so as a divorced woman.[25]

[24]She still keeps her rights, however, if she were to take another *ghar jawae* as her new husband.

[25]The custom of marrying a girl by forcibly smearing *sindur* on her forehead has been recorded of other Chotanagpur tribes, such as the Birhors and the Dudh and Dhelki sections of the Kharias. For a more elaborate picture of 'marriage by force' among the Santals, see

Of all the forms of Santal marriage mentioned here, five are found at Pangro. These are *kirin bahu bapla*, *sanga bapla*, *ghardi jawae/ghar jawae bapla*, *tunki dipil bapla* and *hirom cetan bapla*. Of the seventeen widows in Pangro, two had remarried a second time in the *sanga bapla* form. There are also two cases of divorced men from Pangro marrying divorced women from outside, in the *sanga bapla* form. Two men from Pangro are married outside as *ghar jawaes*. Bajal Soren was brought in as *ghar jawae* by Salhai Murmu who has only two daughters. As we have noted, though in the headman's house there are no sons, Gangaram Marandi was not accepted by the headman's relatives as *ghar jawae*. He is only married in *ghardi jawae* form. The only case of *hirom cetan bapla* is that of Sagram Hasdak who took Simoti Besra as a co-wife to Delho Soren. The first wife, called *batki*, remains the mistress of the house. The second wife is called *chutki*. There are seven cases of marriage in *tunki dipil bapla* form. The greatest number of marriages are in *kirin bahu bapla* form. This is the most common and most respectable form of marriage among all the Santals, and is only possible with young men and women who have not been married before.

We shall now give a brief account of the main procedures and customary ceremonies observed in a *kirin bahu bapla*. Special attention will be given to the rituals that have symbolic value, so that we may be able to evaluate their religious significance. In this form of marriage, the boy's parents start the proceedings by commissioning a *raebaric* or a match-maker to try and find a suitable bride for their son. The *raebaric* begins by making inquiries as to where an eligible maiden is to be found. Once this is done, he has to make a number of

Campbell A., 'Santal Marriage Customs', *Journal of the Bihar and Orissa Research Society*, Patna, 2(3), Sept. 1916, pp. 329-30; and Archer (1974: 149-57). Other forms of marriage among the Santals, which, though irregular, are valid unions, include *hirom cetan bapla* where a man takes a co-wife; *apangir bapla* or marriage after elopement; *raja raji bapla* and *baha dor bapla*, both of which are love marriages; and *golaeti bapla* when two families intermarry, a son in each family marries a daughter in the other. See Uma Chowdhury, 'Marriage Customs of the Santals', *Bulletin of the Department of Anthropology*, Calcutta, 1(1) Jan. 1952, pp. 86-116; Mukherjea (1962:212-5); Campbell A., 'Santal Marriage Customs', op. cit., pp. 304-37.

trips between the boy's and the girl's villages, meeting and discussing with the parents of both parties.[26] Because of the important role played by the *raebaric*, this form of marriage is sometimes called *raebar bapla*.

Once the boy and girl are regarded as a suitable match, arrangements are made for them and their relatives to meet one another. This first meeting, called *Nepel*, meaning 'to see one another' takes place in a public place, either at a fair, in a market place, or, in an open field. This is the first occasion on which relatives on both sides see one another and critically scrutinise the prospective couple. Neither side commits itself but, if after deliberate discussion, both parties agree, a day is fixed for an informal inspection of the boy's house, *Orak Duar Nel*.

On the fixed day, the *raebaric* accompanies the girl's father, village headman and other relatives to the boy's village. On the way, ominous signs are strictly noted. Thus, should the party on their leaving their own village or on entering the girl's village, see a man carrying an axe, a snake or a jackal crossing the path from left to right, or a woman carrying firewood on her head, they consider this as a bad omen. They return home and stop the proceedings. If, however, they see a full water pot, a cow, a pack bullock or a jackal crossing the path from right to left, these are considered as favourable omens. If all goes well, they proceed to the boy's house accompanied by the *manjhi* and *jog manjhi* of the boy's village. After the usual ceremonial greetings, which include the washing and anointing of feet, rice-beer is given to all the guests. Before anyone drinks, the *manjhis* of both parties offer libations to the ancestral spirits of the girl and the boy invoking their blessings. The girl's party then inquires from the boy's headman and *jog manjhi* whether the boy and his family have ever been guilty of any social offence or neglect of social duty. If all is well, the guests are treated to a meal and all retire to bed.

The following morning, the girl's party is shown the boy's house and fields, after which they discuss details regarding the

[26] Archer, 'Betrothal Dialogues', *Man in India*, Ranchi, 23(2), June 1943, pp. 151-3, records the various dialogues which take place between the *raebaric* and the parents of both parties.

bride-price. The Santals use two words, both of which are of Indo-Aryan origin, to denote the bride-price—*gonon* which is derived from a root meaning to 'count' or 'calculate' and *pon* which means 'earnest money' or 'pledge'. In Pangro, the sum of fourteen rupees has been fixed as the amount to be paid by the groom's father as bride-price. Besides the giving of the bride-price, other gifts are mutually given by both parties.[27] They also decide when the marriage is to take place.[28] Sometimes, a similar return visit by the groom's party to see the bride's house is made. Similar formalities are followed, but the fields are not inspected. If both parties are pleased, they fix a day for the betrothal ceremony known as *Horok Cikhna*, the 'putting on of a sign' to ratify the agreement. This usually takes place first in the groom's house (*Jawae Dhuti*) and later in the bride's (*Bahu Bande*). If an early wedding is desired, then only the *Jawae Dhuti* ceremony is performed.

For the *Jawae Dhuti*, the bride's party consisting of the *raebaric*, the girl's father, her uncles, the headman, *paranik*, *jog manjhi* and some other villagers, go to the groom's village. There they are received by the headman and the *jog manjhi* who escort them to the boy's house. After having their feet washed and massaged with oil, they are given parched rice with molasses to eat and rice-beer to drink. The washing of the guests' feet besides being a sign of Santal hospitality also symbolises the removing of all possible evil influences which might have been gathered on the way. Then the groom, carrying a *lota* of water in his hand, is brought out of the house by a married relative, either a maternal uncle or a sister's husband (*tinyan*), to pay his respects to the visitors. Placing the *lota* in front of the bride's father, the groom (*jawae*) sits on his thigh. Some rice-beer is offered to the bride's father who, after drinking, rinses

[27]Thus, in addition to the bride-price, the groom's family gives the following gifts (*itat*): a saree each to the bride's mother (*enga itat*), her father's eldest sister (*hatom itat*), her maternal (*here jia itat*) and paternal (*bonga jia itat*) grandmothers, and a cloth to the bride's eldest brother (*bare itat*). A cow or a goat is given to the bride's father and some money to her maternal uncle. In return, the bride's parents present the cloth to be worn by the groom during the *Sindradan* ceremony, one pot of *handi* and a cow or goat to the groom's father.

[28]This depends very much on whether the families have had a good crop or not.

his mouth with water. He then invests the groom with the 'sign', a new dhoti (*dhuti*); and some money; and then kisses him. Hence the name *Jawae Dhuti*.

This ceremony is performed by all the guests present. Some give money, dhotis, shirts or pieces of cloth. The *paranik* counts the money and the number of gifts received and announces the amount to all. These are divided among the boy's family members. A goat is then sacrificed by the *jog manjhi* of the boy's village in honour of the family's ancestral spirits and the *jaher bongas* invoking them to protect the couple from all misfortune. A pig is also killed for the occasion. After partaking of the meal, the girl's party and the boy's party proclaim to each other full access to their homes.

If the marriage is not to take place soon, the groom's party in the same manner go and give the bride the sign of the betrothal. This is called *Bahu Bandi*. An expression used at the time of this ceremony is *sutam tolakadea* meaning 'he has tied her with a thread'. Various gifts are made to the bride by the groom's party.[29] These two ceremonies, *Jawae Dhuti* and *Bahu Bandi* constitute the formal betrothal of the boy (*jawae*) and the girl (*bahu*). The gifts presented are regarded as a seal on the contract entered into by the two families. Both the boy and the girl are prevented from running away with somebody else or from being given to someone else by the parents without the previous consent of the other family, in which case the gifts received have to be returned. This explains why all the gifts are counted and the exact amount is publicly announced by the *paranik*

The ceremony connected with the paying of the bride-price is called *Taka cal*. For this purpose the groom's father, headman, *jog manjhi* and other relatives go to the bride's house. After the usual salutations and welcoming ceremonies, rice-beer is drunk and the bride-price is paid. The payment of money is intended as proof of legal possession. They then decide on the actual date of the marriage (*gira tol*). A meal is served to all present. Before anyone starts eating, the respective

[29]In her *Bahu Bandi*, Minoti Murmu received three sarees, four petticoats, five blouses, four necklaces, various bangles and thirteen rupees. These were divided among her family members.

ancestor spirits of both families are invoked for the future welfare of the boy and girl.

The Santals have a time and season for everything. So also marriage ceremonies, and here I refer more to the *kirin bahu bapla*, have their appointed season. The most popular months are March to June when the work-load is light and food abundant. It is interesting to note that among the Santals of Pangro and the neighbouring villages, no marriage is performed before the Moti Jharna Mela which symbolises the marriage of *Parvati* and *Mahadev*. It is also considered inauspicious to perform the marriage in the month in which either the bride or groom was born. When the time is approaching, the *raebaric* goes to the bride's house carrying the *gira*, a cotton string dyed yellow with turmeric and containing various knots, the number of which indicates the number of days to pass before the actual wedding.

Two or three days before the wedding, the *jog manjhi* and the *jog paranik* ask some villagers to come and help in setting up the *mandwa* or marriage shed in the girl's house. Before the actual work starts, the girl's father gives three fowls (*mandwa sim*), some rice and a pot of rice-beer to the village priest which he sacrifices to *Jaher Era*, *Maran Buru* and *Moreko-Turuiko* invoking them to ward off any evil. In the centre of the *mandwa*, a *mahua* branch called *mandwa khunti* is fixed in the ground.[30] A *mandwa* which signifies the villagers' co-operation in the marriage ceremony is also built in the boy's house.

On the day before the bridegroom's party (*bariatko*) sets out for the bride's house, the *Dak Bapla* or 'water marriage' ceremony is performed. The ceremony starts with the *tetrekuri* anointing all the people assembled beneath the *mandwa*, with oil and turmeric (*sasan sunum*) starting with the priest and his wife and the other village officials and their wives. The groom's parents and the groom are the last to be anointed. Meanwhile, danicing and singing go on, to the drumming by the Doms. The

[30]The posts of the *mandwa* are made out of *matkom* branches. The canopy is made of *sal* and mango branches. Beneath the *mandwa khunti*, are placed some *adwa caole* mixed with turmeric, five cowrie shells and some *dhubi ghas*. The Santals believe that if the grain were to sprout during the marriage ceremonies, the couple will have a happy life.

jog manjhi carrying a *lota* filled with rice-beer and accompanied by some people from the girl's house, goes to fetch the ceremonial water. Two girls carry two small earthenware pots which are called ominous pots (*sagun thili*) on their heads having covered them with a yellow cloth, *sasan kicric,* which is later used to clothe the bride. The groom's mother carries a flat basket on which there is *adwa caole, dhubi ghas,* oil, vermilion and three cowrie shells. Two paternal aunts of the groom in turn carry a sword and a bow and arrows.

On reaching the spot, the *babrekora* or groom's bestman, usually the groom's eldest sister's husband, digs a small hole at the water-side, letting the water seep through. The *jog manjhi* then plants three arrows around the hole. He winds a thread five times around the arrows and puts a cowrie shell at the base of each arrow. The cowrie shells are believed to be symbols of fertility.[31] They are also meant to divert the attention of the evil spirits and malicious powers. Marking the arrows and cowrie shells with *sindur,* he then offers rice-beer libations to *Maran Buru,* the *Manjhi* and *Pargana Bonga* and the ancestor spirits. The *sindur* is a reminiscence of a covenant with the benevolent spirits. The tying of the thread around the arrows symbolises the bond of friendship thus formed.

After emptying the *sagun thili* from the *taben khajari,* the *jog manjhi* fills them with water which is believed to contain special powers bringing good luck to those washed in it. Then the *tetrekuri,* the groom's mother and paternal aunts dance thrice round the hole. One of the women 'shoots' at the water while the other 'strikes' with a sword. These gestures are said to simulate sexual intercourse and thus to promote fertility. After this, all return to the marriage shed where the *babrekora* digs a hole in the ground by the side of the house and places two yokes on either side of the hole. The groom is made to squat on the yokes facing the East, while the groom's father stands in front holding a sword letting its point rest on his son's head. The mother stands behind her son. The *jog manjhi* then pours water from the *sagun thili* over the sword, letting it drip down on to the groom. This is known as *Tarware Dak* or

[31]The Oraons put cowrie shells round the necks or waists of their children and round the necks of their cattle so as to protect them from any harm.

'sword water' ceremony. After this, the groom is given a bath, (*Jawae Um*) and anointed with oil and turmeric. The yokes of the plough are said to bring the groom and the bride prosperity in agriculture. Through a similar process of imitative magic the sword is meant to chase away any evil spirits lurking around.

Everyone goes near the *mandwa khunti* for the *Jawae Kora Ul Sakam Tol* or 'the binding of the groom to the mango leaf' ceremony. The *jog manjhi*, taking a piece of thread, passes it round the groom's left ear, to his left foot toe, back to the left ear and round the *mandwa khunti*. The *tetrekuri* are similarly tied to the post by a thread fastened to the little finger of their left hand. Each has to husk five grains of paddy with their little fingers without breaking them. Whereupon, all are set free by the *jog manjhi* who puts the husked rice grains on three mango leaves, adding also some pieces of turmeric and some *dhubi ghas*. All these are wrapped in a small bundle and tied to the groom's left wrist. The groom is allowed to unloosen this bundle only after returning to his parents' house. The Santals regard the mango tree sacred and possessing the property of scaring away evil spirits and influences.[32] *Dhubi ghas* was, according to tradition, the second grass that *Thakur* sowed after the creation of the earth. The husked grains of paddy are calculated to bless the couple with agricultural prosperity.

While these ceremonies are going on at the groom's village, similar ceremonies are held at the bride's place. Before the groom's party (*bariatko*) leaves for the girl's house, the *Nunu Taka* or 'sucking money' ceremony is performed. The groom's mother arranges a *lota* with water and molasses in a leaf cup and his father ties up money in his clothes. They go to the *manjhithan* where they spread out a mat on which the groom's mother sits, letting her son sit on her thigh. He is given molasses

[32]S.C. Mitra, 'The Mango Tree in the Marriage-Ritual of the Aborigines of Chota Nagpur and Santalia', *Journal of the Bihar and Orissa Research Society*, Patna, 5(2), June 1919, pp. 259-71, analyses the part played by the mango tree in the marriage rituals of the Santals, Mundas, Birhors and Bhumij. T.C. Hodson, 'Tree Marriage', *Man in India*, Ranchi, 1(3), Sept. 1921, pp. 202-21, considers tree marriage among the Santals, Hos and other members of the Munda linguistic group, as a fertility rite.

to eat. After rinsing his mouth with water, he places a rupee note between his lips and puts it in his mother's lap. Rice-beer libations are then offered to *Manjhi Haram* invoking his protection during their trip to the girl's house. The procession then starts towards the girl's village to the accompaniment of merry music. The groom and his *lumti kora*[33] are carried in a *rahi* or palanquin. The *raebaric's* wife carries the *daura*, marriage basket.[34]

When the groom's party reaches the girl's village, they stop at the west side of the *kulhi*. The *raebaric* informs the bride's party who, along with the *godet* and *jog manjhi*, go to welcome the groom and his party. They are accompanied by some young people who dance and sing, shouting insulting remarks about the groom and the village from which he comes. All then proceed to the *manjhithan* where the *jog manjhi* sacrifices two pigeons to *Manjhi Haram*. Rice-beer libations are also offered, invoking *Manjhi Haram* and the *jaher bongas* for the success of the wedding ceremony. Once the sacrifice is over, the groom is made to sit on the bride's mother's thigh, who after washing his mouth, gives him molasses to eat. She does the same to the *lumti kora*. Close relatives of the bride repeat the same ceremony. This welcoming ceremony is called *Daram Dak*.

The *Balaea Johar*, or salutation ceremony among in-laws, follows. This manifests the social bond entered into by the two families. The relatives from each family form two lines facing one another. Then the relatives, starting with the father, male relatives and finally female relatives, salute the girl's relatives in the same order. This is followed by the *Gurjom* ceremony or 'eating of molasses' which consists in the visiting of every house in the village from where the groom and his *lumti kora* receive molasses to eat. It signifies the solidarity of the girl's village.

On arriving at the bride's house, some of her friends pretend that the groom is not very clean. They proceed to 'shave' him again using a leaf as a mirror and a piece of wood for a razor. The groom is then washed, anointed, and dressed in a saffron cloth. Soon after, the groom is lifted on the shoulders of his best man (*babre kora*) while the bride's younger brother is carried on the

[33]A young man, preferably a cousin.

[34]This is given by the groom's parents. After the wedding it is returned to them.

shoulders of his *gumtet* (brother-in-law). A white cloth is placed between them. Each is given a mango twig with five mango leaves by their respective *jog manjhis*. Dipping this in water, they sprinkle each other five times, after which they blow some chewed rice on each other. The odd number of mango leaves and sprinklings is said to be very auspicious. The groom is then given a saffron turban. While this is going on, men from the boy's and the girl's parties dance in mock combat with their staves held high. The Doms employed by each party add to the excitement.

Meanwhile, the bride is anointed with oil and turmeric and dressed in a saffron cloth completely covering her face and head. She is placed in the *daura* and brought out of the house by members of the groom's party. Then follows the most important part in the whole marriage ceremony, namely the *Sindradan*, or 'the smearing of the bride's forehead with vermilion'. The groom, carried on his best man's shoulders, faces East opposite the bride.[35] Both, using a mango twig with five leaves dipped in water, sprinkle each other for five times, after which, the groom uncovers the bride's face. He takes a leaf containing *sindur* and using his right-hand thumb and little finger applies vermilion on the bride's forehead.[36] This he does five times, after which he smears the remaining vermilion on the bride's neck and covers her face with the saffron cloth.[37] This is loudly acclaimed by shouts of 'Haribol' and the rattle of drums. The shouting and drumming is said to scare away any evil spirits loitering in the area, thus making the marriage truly auspicious. Then one of the bride's maternal aunts ties together the ends of the clothes of the new husband and wife and leads them into the house.[38]

[35]Sometimes the groom is carried in a *rahi* instead of on the best-man's shoulders. After the *Sindradan*, the bride is put in the *rahi* and they are taken around the *kulhi* before coming to the girl's house for the *Cumaura* and *Parchau* ceremonies.

[36]This leaf is returned to the *babre kora* who ties it up safely in the edge of the groom's cloth. It is not to be thrown away, otherwise the groom's party is fined for its negligence.

[37]The covering of the bride's face is meant to protect her from the evil eye.

[38]The tying of clothes of bride and groom symbolises the precept that one must always follow the other.

Before entering the house, two other ceremonies are performed—*Cumaura* or 'waving ceremony' and *Parchau* or 'purifying ceremony'. The bride's mother holds a winnowing fan (*hatak*) containing some *dhubi ghas*, paddy and *adwa caole*. She waves this winnowing fan three times over the heads of the couple, best man, *lumti kora* and *lumti kuri*, scattering the *dhubi ghas*, paddy and *adwa coale* behind their backs.[39] Two younger sisters of the bride's mother, come out of the house each carrying a brass plate, one containing two leaf cups filled with molasses and two filled with oil, the other containing two leaf cups with turmeric, five cowdung balls and five flour balls. The bride's mother, taking some oil, anoints the couple giving them molasses to eat and water to drink, after which she smears some turmeric on both their cheeks. They reciprocate the latter action. Then, taking the five cowdung and five flour balls, she scatters them over the couple's heads. Other female relatives repeat this ceremony. The significance of this ceremony called *Cumaura*, is to drive away any evil spirits and thus let the married couple lead a happy and peaceful life.

The two younger sisters of the bride's mother, then go into the house and bring a wooden pestle (*tok*)[40] and an earthenware lid containing some glowing embers which are placed in front of the couple. Taking the pestle in her right hand, the bride's mother waves it over the glowing embers, at the same time saluting the embers with her left hand. She repeats this three times, interchanging the pestle from her left to her right hand, while saluting the embers with the other. Other in-laws repeat this performance. The last person pounds the embers into ashes and takes the pestle quickly inside the house. The aim of this ceremony called *Parchau*, is to 'break' the evil spirits so that they will not be able to cause any harm.

[39]The scattering of rice is believed to be auspicious to the couple's fertility.

[40]The *tok* is used for pounding and husking grain in a large wooden mortar (*ukhur*). For the Santals, the *tok* signifies the male genital organs, while the *ukhur* signifies the female genital organs. An expression sometimes still used by the Santals when enquiring into the number of children existing in a house, is 'tinak do tok ar tinak do ukhur', which literally means 'How many are pestles (boys) and how many are mortars (girls). The *ukhur* and *tok* are used as symbols for fertility during the *Parchau* ceremony.

The couple is then led inside the house and served food which they eat from the same plate signifying the spirit of mutual help and co-operation which should exist between husband and wife till the end of their lives. Outside, while the villagers and guests are eating and drinking, the headmen of the two villages, the *raebaric* and the bride and groom's relatives meet. Presents (*itat*) from the groom's family are handed over by their headman to the bride's headman. Gifts are also given to the village officials, thus acknowledging their special duties.[41]

The following morning, the bride and groom are brought into the courtyard for the *Gidi Cumaura* or 'second waving ceremony'. The couple are made to sit on a mat. To the right of the groom sit his *lumti kora* and *babre kora* while the girl's *lumti kuri* and *babre kuri* sit on her left. Each one is then anointed by the bride's mother followed by her maternal aunts. The couple is then carried around the *mandwa khunti*, after which the girl's female relatives and village officials' wives come forward to perform the *Gidi Cumaura* to the couple and their companions, starting with the bride's mother. Each in turn takes the *daura* containing some *adwa caole* and *dhubi ghas* and waves it three times before each one, sprinkling a few grains of *adwa caole* and *dhubi ghas* on their heads. As each woman finishes the *Gidi Cumaura*, she puts some money known as *Cumaura paisa* into a brass plate placed before each one. The elder sisters and cousins of the bride are the last to perform the *Gidi Cumaura*. Each one of them asks the groom what his *bhitri nutum* is and, in return, they mention theirs. After that, they will never utter each other's name, nor talk together except on urgent matters and, even then, from a respectful distance. The object of the *Gidi Cumaura* is that the girl may not take away all the prosperity from her parents' house.

Everyone then goes to the *manjhithan* where the *jog manjhi* pours out rice-beer libations to *Manjhi Haram*, invoking his protection over the couple both during their return journey home and also throughout their life-time. Thereupon, all go to

[41]The headmen receive one rupee each, the *godet* and *tetrekuri* also receive some money, while cloth presents are given to the *jog manjhi* and the *jog paranik*.

the eastern end of the village for the *Bida* or 'parting ceremony'. A mat is spread and the bride's mother sits on it. Then the groom sits on her thigh and he is given molasses to eat and water to drink, after which she kisses him. The same thing is done to the bride. This ceremony is repeated by the bride's maternal aunts and the wives of the village officials. Thereupon, the in-laws of both parties stand in two rows facing each other for the *Balaea Johar* salutations which, as we have already noted, manifest the social bond entered into by the two families. Finally, the farewell addresses are delivered by the bride's headman and by the *jog manjhi* of the groom.[42]

In both speeches, the union of the two villages, as a result of the marriage, is stressed as the following words indicate:

> . . . from today our two villages have become as one . . . . Formerly you were strangers and you used to pass by our village. Now if any of your people is passing this way . . . he must stop and ask for a drink.

They also reveal the social and moral teaching which the Santals emphasise in marriage. The bride's headman also emphasises the fact that the 'pot', as the bride is symbolically called, had been chosen after careful deliberation and good omens and that *Maran Buru*, the *jaher* spirits and the ancestral spirits have borne witness to this union. 'The groom has secured the family of the bride, the bride has received the house of the groom'. Then the bride is presented by her *jog manjhi* to the groom's headman who, along with the groom's party, start on the return journey. Some male relatives of the bride and an elderly female relative accompany the *bariatko* to the groom's village. One of the bride's male relatives carries the *mandwa khunti* to protect the couple from any evil spirits on the way.

On their arrival, the *Daram Dak* and *Gurjom* ceremonies are performed in the way already described. Other ceremonies like *Cumaura* and *Parchau* are performed in the groom's house. After staying for about two days, the girl's brother is given a cow or a goat to take back home. A few days later, the bride

[42]Archer, 'An Anthology of Marriage Sermons', *Man in India*, Ranchi, 23(2), June 1943, pp. 106-7.

and groom return to the girl's parents' house. On this occasion, the goat left behind by the groom's party at the time of marriage is offered by the bride's father in honour of the ancestor spirits, invoking their protection. Rice-beer libations are also made and all present are offered food and drink. The bride does not partake of the food for it is believed, that if she does so, some ancestor spirits will follow her and cause her illness.

In the Santal marriage rites and customs we have described, we notice clearly two fundamental attitudes: (*i*) the new social involvement of the couple, (*ii*) the consciousness of the Santals' relation and dependence on their spirits. We shall now examine these two points in some detail.

Marriage is as much a union of two villages and two families as it is of two persons. It is not a mere arrangement entered into by two individuals or even two families. Both village communities are vitally involved in the wedding celebrations. This is not only emphasised during the parting speeches but, more strongly, by the role of the village officials and the village community itself. The prominent role played by the headman and the *jog manjhi* of each village is an indication of the degree to which the community is vitally concerned in the matter. As we have seen, once the two families are satisfied with the *raebaric's* reports, the village headmen are called in. They have to be present when the *Orak Duar Nel* ceremony takes place, at the betrothal ceremony, the *Taka cal* ceremony and, of course, the *Sindradan*. In other words, the headman is present in all the important ceremonies. Moreover, the headmen of both the villages are consulted regarding suitable dates for the marriage. Important also is the part played by the *jog manjhi* who acts as the master of ceremonies.

The role of the villagers themselves is also evident. They assist in the setting up of the *mandwa*. They take an active part in the wedding ceremonies, the dancing and singing, and in the partaking of the marriage food and drink. Every Santal ritual and ceremony is ratified by the collective drinking of rice-beer. The *Gurjom* ceremony also shows the solidarity of the village. The anointing with oil and turmeric signifies the acceptance of the couple as part of the village. By marriage, the bride is taken into the groom's community. As the groom's headman, on the return of the couple to the groom's house, says 'You bride, this here is your house and home'. In the same address he says, 'She did not come of her own accord; we have brought her here'. In spite of being integrated in her new household and village community, a woman does not lose contact with her natal village which is her last refuge in the event of divorce or widowhood. Every family in a village is an integral part of the village community.

The intimate relationship between the Santals and their *bongas* is concretely manifested in the various rituals performed throughout many of the marriage ceremonies. Right from the *Orak Duar Nel* ceremony, invocations and libations abound in practically every ceremony. Various sacrifices are also offered during the *Jawae Dhuti*, *Bahu Bandi*, *mandwa* building, *Daram Dak*, after the *Sindradan* and on the return of the bride and groom to the bride's natal house. The anxiety for the future welfare of the married couple, the warding off of evil spirits, is revealed in the sacrificial offerings to *Maran Buru* and the other *jaher bongas*, *Manjhi Haram* and the ancestor spirits. This is also manifested in various ceremonies like the *Cumaura*, *Parchau*, *Gidi Cumaura* and the frequent use of ominous water and ominous pots. Three times during the marriage celebrations, water is poured from these pots. This water is believed to contain special powers to ward off any evil powers and to bring luck. Another sign of their preoccupation with the unseen world is the importance given to ominous signs. As we have noted, if the girl's party, on their way to the boy's house, see a man carrying an axe, or a woman carrying firewood, these are taken as bad omens since they are believed to be connected with death. References to omens are also made in the farewell speeches during the *Bida* ceremony. At the basis of such omens is the belief that a future event sometimes casts its shadow before it in the shape of another analogous event.

Perhaps the intimate relationship between the Santals and their *bongas* during the marriage rituals is most evident in the *Sindradan* ceremony itself which, as we have noted, is the main ceremony. In Santal society, *sindur* has a special relevance to the *bongas* and is in fact a kind of mystic link or way of access to them. As already mentioned, the village priest puts *sindur* on the *khond* because he is the channel through which the community approaches the *bongas*. The applications of *sindur* on the sacrificial animals and fowls is also considered a means of attaching them to the *bongas*. The use of *sindur* in a marriage has a similar purpose. As long as a girl is unmarried, she is in touch with her father's *bongas*. She can also clean the *bhitar*. Once *sindur* is applied on her forehead, her own *bongas* are replaced by those of her husband. She is now qualified to help her husband in the service of his *bongas* and is allowed to clean the *bhitar* in her husband's house. She is debarred, however, from entering the *bhitar* in her father's house. This she is forbidden to do, lest she may have any connection with the spirits of both houses, and thereby bring evil consequences.[43] Even if a girl were to remarry, in the next world she will always continue to belong to her first husband, since he was first person to apply *sindur* on her forehead.

In Pangro and the neighbouring villages, the Christian form of *kirin bahu bapla* is slightly different from the one described here. The main difference is that no *Sindradan* ceremony is performed. Instead, the bride and groom exchange rings. Three weeks prior to the actual wedding, bans are read in a church. The musical instruments used also differ. No Doms are employed, and violins, cymbals and *kabkubi* (a stringed instrument) take the place of the *tamak* and the *tumdak*. No sacrifices or libations are made to the spirits.

The Santals are very strict about their marriage traditions, especially those regarding their tribal endogamy and clan exogamy. According to their traditions, the ancestors twice ran away from the country in which they were, rather than submit to the disgrace of marrying the *Dekus* or persons not of the tribe. All breaches provoke intense and angry disapproval and carry with them strict penalties. The village *bongas* are believed to be polluted by such actions and have, therefore, to be purified and propitiated. So also must the whole village which is considered polluted.

A curious form of social ostracism named *Bitlaha* was formerly much resorted to by the Santals. It is a form of tribal purification and of extreme punishment meted to those who transgress the tribal code, as for example, when a Santal woman

[43]If she marries in a manner without *sindur*, then she remains attached to her father's *bongas*.

indulges in sexual intercourse with a non-Santal, the worst kind of offence, or with a person of the same clan. According to various authors, *Bitlaha* was analogous to a hunt , in which the culprits were the hunted and the villagers were the hunters. The lewd songs and actions demonstrated the bestiality of the culprits. As Archer points out, 'It is the exposure to collective shame that is the essence of the ritual and which makes it far more dreaded than physical torture or confinement in a jail' (1974:98). In certain cases of permanent outcasting, the offenders suffer social death—they cease to exist for the community as such. They are not allowed to take food with others, get water from the village well, join in any festival, hunt or village council, nor give their children in marriage within the Santal community. In the case of sickness or death, nobody visits them. Anyone having any dealing with an outcaste was considered liable to being punished. So great was this punishment, that it could only be given by the Santal supreme council or court of appeal, the *Lo Bir*.

The incidence of *Bitlaha* is difinitely declining.[44] The Government has stopped recognising this form of sanction. In Pangro, nobody remembers any such event. This, however, does not mean that the Santals are becoming lax regarding their code of tribal endogamy or clan exogamy. The participants of the All-India Santal Social Assembly which took place at Asansol from 13-16 April 1978, recognised the threat to their tribal integrity in inter-community marriages. Nowadays, heavy fines are imposed on the offenders. Thus, for example in 1974, a Jolha from Bara Madansahi was fined 450 rupees for having had sexual relations with a Santal girl from Pangro. The case was finally judged by the *Mukhia* and the *Sarpanch* of the *Gram Panchayat*. The culprit was barred from entering the village A 150 rupees of the fine imposed, were used to offer sacrifices to the *jaher bongas* for the ritual cleansing of the village. The girl's parents were also fined. They were temporarily outcasted (*Pante Begar*) and were readmitted only after paying the fine and undergoing the *Jom Jati* ceremony. Because

[44]Roy Chaudhury (1965: 881) remarks that in the decade 1953-63, only eight *Bitlahas* were performed and these only in Dnmka and Pakur sub-divisions.

of the social ostracism which *Pante Begar* implies, the fine is usually paid at once.

During the course of my fieldwork, the village council of Pangro judged four breaches of clan exogamy and one case of kin incest.[45] In all the cases, heavy fines were imposed on both the boy and the girl. Thus, for example, in the case of Sunil Murmu, who impregnated Ester Murmu, he was fined 150 rupees, plus a big pig, a castrated goat and half a maund of rice. Ester's family had to pay seventy-five rupees and a maund of rice. Both the families were temporarily ostracised till the *Jom Jati* ceremony was performed by both families. In the case of Matal Hasdak, he not only had to pay a heavy fine, but had also to procure a father for Kinka Hasdak's daughter whom she got through him. All these fines serve to cleanse the village and the families of the grave offence committed. It can rightly be said that the Santals' social code of morality helps the tribe to maintain its solidarity. It also manifests the Santal preoccupation with the stability of the marital union.

DEATH

The final rites of passage are related to the rituals performed on the death of a person. The Santals do not recognise the possibility of a natural death. They are also of the opinion that death is never due to accident, but like other tribals, generally attribute death to the malignancy of certain *bongas*, impersonal powers and witchcraft. They believe that these malignant agencies against whom an individual has to counteract throughout his life-time, put an end to his life.[46]

Their ideas about life in the future world (*hanapuri*) as opposed to this world (*noapuri*) are rather confused. One thing is certain—the belief in the survival of the soul after death.

[45]In Santal society, any sexual relation between two members of the same clan amounts to kin incest. Both pollute the village *bongas* and the families involved.

[46]See also, Furer-Haimendorf, Christoph von, 'The After Life in Indian Tribal Belief', *Journal of the Royal Anthropological Society*, London, 83(1), Jan-June 1953, pp. 37-49; Mary Douglas (1966:201-2).

As we have seen in Chapter III, the Santals believe that, on the death of an individual, his social personality is not annihilated but rather transformed.[47] As some of the expressions used to denote the death of a person indicate, according to Santal belief, the soul, after leaving the body, becomes a *bonga* joining the abode of its deceased ancestors. We thus have expressions like, 'nitok doe hapramena', meaning, 'he has become a *bonga*'. This belief in the soul of a person becoming a *bonga* and joining the abode of his ancestors, predominates, as we shall see, in all the rituals and ceremonies connected with death. The Santals believe that one becomes a *hapram bonga* only after all the funerary rites have been performed in his honour. If a person dies an unnatural death, or in the case of a woman dying in pregnancy or childbirth, they do not achieve full spiritual status and their ghosts are believed to continue hovering around the world as *bhuts* or *curins*.

Some of the current ideas about future life have a moral content. Thus, the Santals believe that their future life is determined by the good or bad deeds a person has committed in his earthly life. Ideas regarding punishment and reward show that the sufferer will be comforted, the good man rewarded, while the wicked man will be punished by *Jom Raja* who, along with *Hudar Raja*, is the regent of the nether world. If a person, during his life-time in *noapuri* has treated others unjustly, in *hanapuri* he is made to carry rotting meat on his head, wrestle with huge worms or sit immersed in excrement. Special tortures are also meted out to those who transgress the tribal code of morality and to those who, as we have seen, fail to show the traditional tribal marks, *sika* and *khoda*, on their bodies. On the other hand, he who leads an honest and kind life in *noapuri* will be rewarded in *hanapuri*.[48]

When a Santal dies, his house and village become polluted. The village is bereft of its protective *bongas* and the household is deprived of the care of its *orak bongas*. No marriages,

[47]Refer to Du Toit, B.M., 'Some Aspects of the Soul-Concept among the Bantu-Speaking Nguni Tribes of South Africa', *Anthropological Quarterly*, Washington, 33(3), July 1960, pp. 134-42; Firth, Raymond, *The Fate of the Soul: An Interpretation of Some Primitive Concepts*, Cambridge: Cambridge University Press, 1955.

[48]Mukherjea (1962:228-30) and Bodding (1942:187-8).

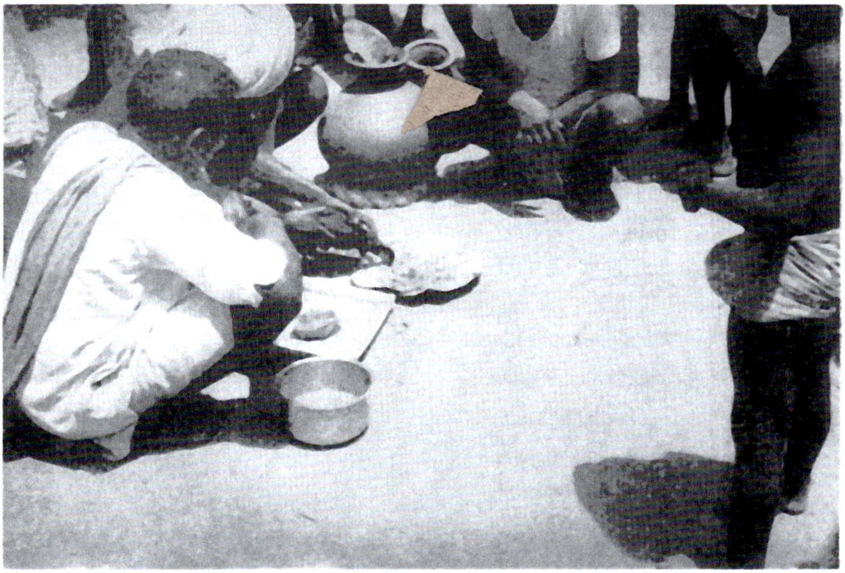

Bhandan: The villagers offerig sacrifices to their *hapramko bongas* (ancestral spirits).

Rejoicing that the ritual pollution brought about by the death of a person has been removed.

The *Janam Chatiar* ceremony: Women dancing in the courtyard after the *Nim Dak Mandi* ceremony.

The village priest offering sacrifies of pigeons to *Manjhi Haram* at the *Manjhithan*.

festivals or any public worship can be performed within the village until the funerary rites have been performed. The pollution is due to the belief that death is a victory of the malignant agencies. It is an insult to the benevolent *bongas* whose major concern is the Santals' well-being. Through death, the *jaher bongas* of a village and the household *bongas* are polluted. Besides, as long as the funerary rites are not performed, the soul of the departed person still remains a menace to all the living members of his household. As a result, when a Santal dies, the family and village co-operate in performing the funerary rites.

On a death occurring in a village, a loud chorus of lamentations and wailing is set up by the female relatives of the deceased.[49] The *godet* is told and he, in turn, informs all the villagers, starting with the headman. All the deceased's relatives, living within a reasonable distance, are also apprised of the occurrence. The body is then prepared for burial.[50] It is anointed with oil and turmeric, dressed in new clothes and laid on a *parkom* (stringed bed) which is brought out into the courtyard. In the case of a woman whose husband is still alive, vermilion is put on her forehead by a female relative. A piece

[49]According to Durkheim (1967:434ff), in the case of mourning, the social pressure is to bear witness, by significant actions, to the people's sorrow and perplexity. The people concerned have to show that they are not indifferent to what has happened. The family members must react to the loss of one of their members by renewing their collective sentiments. The sharing of similar emotions produces a sense of comfort compensating for the original loss.

See also Malinowski (1954.49); Bodding (1942:175); Radcliffe-Brown (1964:285ff) and Archer (1974:327-8).

[50]Though many authors like Bodding (1942:176-8); Culshaw (1949:150); Datta-Majumder (1956:90); and Archer (1974:330-2) speak of cremation as the Santal way of disposing of a dead body, no cremation has taken place in Pangro since 1946. From information gathered from Santals in other parts of the district, burial seems to be the main way of disposing of a corpse in Santal Parganas. The reason often given is the difficulty in obtaining sufficient firewood.

According to these authors, burial was considered an exception and was resorted to in the case of children who die before puberty, men and women who die from certain contagious diseases such as leprosy, smallpox and tuberculosis, persons who die an unnatural death or without their *Caco Chatiar* ceremony, and by women who die in pregnancy or childbirth.

of cloth containing some money, a brass plate (*thari*), drinking vessel (*bati*), and other gifts donated by the family and near kinsmen as a token of mourning, are placed on the cot which is carried by four of the deceased male relatives or friends. Women do not go to the burial place.

On reaching the outskirts of the village, a grave (*gadlak*) facing north to south, is dug deep in the ground by some of the villagers.[51] All the ornaments are removed from the body and so are the gifts placed on the cot. These are taken by those present and sold, buying *handi* and *paura* in return. A cloth is laid in the grave and the body is carried around the grave three times. The chief mourner then puts some burning embers into the deceased's mouth. The body is lowered in the grave, its head facing the south. Branches are put into the slots prepared. These serve as a kind of canopy over which other branches are laid. The cot is broken and the wood is placed on top of the branches. The chief mourner, followed by the other relatives and villagers throws earth into the grave until it is filled. A mound of soil is raised on the grave around which some stones are also placed so as to keep away any stray animals. An earthenware water pot (*kandha*) and a winnowing fan containing some paddy are left beside the grave, which is purified by the sprinkling of cowdung mixed with water.[52] The mourners then go for their purificatory bath, after which they anoint themselves with oil and turmeric. The chief mourner has his head shaved completely.[53]

As a rule, the eldest son is the chief mourner in the case of the deceased being a man. If the deceased has no male children, then the right of placing the burning embers into the corpse's mouth, descends in this order on the following persons: father, brother, senior kinsman on the male side. In the case of a woman, it is the husband who performs this ritual. If she is a

[51]The Santals do not have a specific burial ground. Bodies are usually buried in the deceased's lands at some distance from the village. Graves are not places of cult and are not long remembered.

[52]The *hatak* filled with paddy signifies that the body is provided with food and, therefore, it does not have to return to its house in search of food.

[53]As in the case of *Janam Chatiar*, the shaving of the chief mourner's head expresses the transition of the deceased from one state to another.

widow, her eldest son does this. When asked the meaning of this ritual of putting burning embers into the corpse's mouth, the spontaneous answer received was that this was a remnant of the times when dead bodies used to be cremated. On further probing, I was told that the one who applies the embers is looked upon as the deceased's successor in the management of his household affairs. It is he who meets the expenses of the funerary ceremonies.

The next phase in the funerary ceremonies is known as *Tel Nahan* or 'oil washing'. It is also known as *Umul Ader* or 'bringing in the shadow'. The soul or spirit of a man is identified with his shadow which in turn is credited with a number of powers. This purification ceremony, performed on the fifth day after death, is said to be of great importance. Until it is performed, the dead person will remain in the clutches of the hostile agency which brought about his death and is thus a menace to his household and village. Through this ceremony, the villagers are safeguarded against such dangers while the deceased's soul is freed from its shackles. It now dwells inside the family's *bhitar*. The village *bongas* cease to be unclean, the village is purified and feasts and public worship can once more be performed. Though the deceased's immediate family members still remain, as they say, 'in the shadow', his other kinsmen are free to perform weddings and offer sacrifices.

The *Tel Nahan* ceremony starts when the village men gather at the dead man's house. After all have been shaved, some male relatives of the deceased accompanied by other villagers go to the grave. Here, the chief mourner collects a handful of earth which he burns and puts into a new earthenware pot. On returning to the end of the village *kulhi*, where they are met by the womenfolk, the pot is smashed to pieces and the burnt earth is sprinkled with water and turmeric.[54] Then everyone

[54]The burnt handful of earth is said to be reminiscent of the *jan baha* which literally means 'flowers of bone' but which, in the context of cremation, meant a piece of the frontal portion of the skull and two bits from the collar bone. These bones used to be rescued from the funeral pyre and, after sometime, a special ceremony was observed in which these bones were immersed into the Damodar river (*Nai Gada*) or into any stream or pond.

goes for his purificatory bath, the chief mourner carrying the burnt earth on a leaf plate. After taking a bath and rubbing themselves with oil given by the deceased's family, the chief mourner, surrounded by his male relatives and villagers, makes offerings of oil cakes and *sal* twigs to *Maran Buru, Pilcu Haram* and *Pilcu Budhi*, and to the departed soul. He implores *Maran Buru* to lodge the deceased's soul in the 'shadow of the house' till he reaches his final rest. He also invokes the departed spirit to accept his new temporary abode.

Everyone then returns to the deceased's house for the *Umul Ader* ceremony. Here, two persons are said to become possessed, one by *Maran Buru* and the other by the spirit of the deceased. They are given water and rice-beer to drink. One of the deceased's relatives then asks the spirit of the dead person the cause of his death—whether he left of his own free-will or whether it was through some disease or through someone's hostility. Once the villagers are satisfied with the answers given, the two individuals impersonating the spirits resume their normal roles. The sacrificial animal is offered to the spirit of the deceased by the chief mourner. Each of the houses in the village, or in certain cases those who can afford to, provides a fowl for the purification of the village and to celebrate the departed spirit's release from the underworld. All these animals are slain with a blow on the back of the head. They are not beheaded as in other sacrifices. When the food is ready, the people present are served. They are also given rice-beer. The flesh from the animal's head is reserved for the chief mourner and his family. After everyone has had his fill, they return to their homes happy that their village has been purified.

Though with the *Tel Nahan* ceremony, the departed spirit is said to have been released from the underworld, he has not yet reached his final abode. He is still, as it were, in transit. It is only with the *Bhandan* ceremony that he finally joins the realm of his ancestors. With this ceremony, the deceased's relatives bid the departed their last farewell and send him happy and honoured to his abode. All mourning comes to an end and the deceased's immediate family once more is free to sacrifice to their *bongas*, attend festivals, and celebrate marriages.

As such, there is no specified time when this ceremony should be performed. It all depends on the economic situation of the deceased's relatives. Thus, in the case of Singrai Marndi, his relatives performed the *Bhandan* ceremony a year after his death, while Lokhon Tudu's *Bhandan* was performed six months after. On the fixed date, all the villagers and deceased's relatives assemble in the deceased's house. Here the chief mourner's head is once more completely shaved, while the other villagers have their beards shaved. On returning from their purificatory bath, all are given *taben* and *khajari* to eat and rice-beer to drink. Three persons are possessed by the spirits of the dead person, the founder of the village and *Maran Buru* respectively. The dead man is made to re-identify himself. Then the three spirits are asked whether they were satisfied with all the ceremonies already performed in honour of the departed spirit. On giving their assent, the three men emerge from their roles and are given rice-beer.

A goat is brought into the courtyard. After preparing the *khond*, the chief mourner offers the goat to the spirit of the dead person invoking him to protect his living relatives and keep away any harm or misfortune. The animal is then slain by the *jog manjhi* who strikes it with the butt-end of an axe. The side on which the animal falls is retained by the deceased's family, while the other side is given to the villagers. Rice-beer libations are also made in the dead man's honour. Fowls are offered to each ancestor spirit of the family, mentioning each one by name. Rice-beer libations are also made in their honour. After each libation, all those present drink.

Meanwhile, several relatives and fellow villagers bring goats and fowls to be offered in the name of the departed spirit. While offering these animals, the giver mentions his name saying, 'Take note, this animal is being offered to you by so and so'. When all the sacrifices are over, the flesh is dressed and cooked with rice. Besides the uncooked portion set aside for the dead man's family and relatives, two other portions are made. One is eaten by all those present, the villagers and the household members, the other portion is divided among the villagers who take their share back to their homes. Before the food is served, the chief mourner offers some of the food to the departed spirit invoking it to accept the food and to purify the household completely. The whole night is spent in feasting, dancing and singing.

In this way, all the funerary ceremonies come to an end. The dead man's family is free to resume normal relations with the world of men and spirits. Judging by what has been said here, we can rightly apply Radcliffe-Brown's findings on burial customs among the Andaman Islanders to the Santal funerary rites. In both cases, the burial customs can be visualised and explained 'as a collective reaction against the attack on the collective feeling of solidarity constituted by the death of a member of the social group' (1964:286). We can also say that the main object of the Santals' funerary rites is twofold: (*i*) to rid the living survivors of the death pollution and of the evil attentions of the departed spirit which is believed to haunt them until it is united with the ancestor spirits; and (*ii*) to release the departed spirit from the underworld and help it find final rest in its abode.[55]

As we have seen in Chapter III, the Santals are constantly conscious of their relation and dependence on their spirits. This intimate relationship is concretely manifested in the various rituals performed. In Chapter IV, we have seen how this relationship is expressed in the Santal seasonal rites and festivals, most of which are associated with their agricultural cycle. In this chapter, we have described and analysed the various rites and ceremonies through which Santal society seeks to bring the world of the spirits into relation with the individual in the critical junctures of his life.

The main impact of Van Gennep's theory was on the study of the mechanism of rituals with special emphasis on the rites of passage. He rightly pointed out that the passage from one stage to another in an individual's life-cycle does not by itself explain the complex ceremonies which accompanied it. Each ritual has specific protective, propitiatory, purificatory and

[55]According to Malinowski (1965), funeral rites provide a useful catharsis of the emotions of those most closely affected. They are also an expression of the new adjustment of statuses and roles in a group after the death of a member.

As already mentioned in Chapter III, ancestor worship ritually brings the spirit of the deceased back into the community reaffirming the connections between the dead and the survivors.

productive purposes. However, he has failed to clearly demonstrate the association of these rites with the social structure of the society in which they are performed. A later generation of social anthropologists like Durkheim, Radcliffe-Brown, Evans-Pritchard, Forde, Turner, Junod and others, were more concerned in analysing the social function of these rites rather than elaborating on their mechanism. Thus, Radcliffe-Brown (1964) in his analyses of the rites of passage performed by the Andaman Islanders shows how these rites deal with the 'social personality' of the individual.

Likewise, in the analytical description of the nature and function of the rites of passage prevalent in Santal society in Pangro, attention has been paid to the symbolic social values of the rituals and ceremonies performed. It has been shown how in their congregational aspect, these rites and ceremonies help to re-enact the community's relationship of dependence and fellowship with their spirits. In so doing, they reinforce the community's own solidarity and reaffirm its own values.

As we have seen, the critical junctures in the life-cycle of an individual are replete with danger. The individual is himself in danger. He also passes this danger on to his family, village and tribe at large. Besides the individual, his family and village are also defiled. The village *bongas* are polluted. No festivals, marriages or public sacrifices, can be held unless the purificatory rituals are performed. In view of this, we can say that the main object of all the rites and ceremonies attending birth, initiation, marriage and death, is twofold:—(*i*) to remove the pollution attendant on the individual's household and village, and to protect them against any calamities at the hands of the evil spirits and powers; (*ii*) to purify the individual himself, keep him away from any hostile agencies, and to ensure for him the security and care given by the benevolent spirits. Thus, the *Janam Chatiar* reveals an anxiety to integrate the new-born child into its father's clan, subclan and *bongas*. *Caco Chatiar* reveals an anxiety to integrate the initiated person into a new relationship with his *bongas*. Various marriage rituals manifest the anxiety for the future welfare of the married couple, guarding its luck, and warding off evil spirits and impersonal powers. The funerary rites help the departed spirit to liberate itself from the underworld and to finally join the abode of its ancestors.

We have also seen how these ceremonies serve as occasions for emphasising the relations of mutual harmony and dependence between the individual and his society and how, in so doing, village solidarity is strengthened. The whole Santal village community acts like one man. Their presence is required to give sanction to the proceedings. The person who conducts each ritual is merely the active representative of the community. The feasting, social reunion and rejoicing that mark their successful termination, make it clear that each rite of passage is a matter which concerns not only the individual who enters into it, but the whole community. The various gifts bestowed upon him, are a clear expression of the general goodwill towards him.

In our study of the various rituals and ceremonies in an individual's life-cycle, one clearly notices the Santals' strong preoccupation and belief in magic and ominous signs. This is most evident in the various precautions taken by the pregnant mother; the magico-religious rites like cicatrization for boys and tattooing for girls; the extreme care paid to good or bad omens during the several visits to either of the groom's or the bride's party; the use of ominous pots and water, etc. In the next chapter we shall, therefore, study the nature and function of magic in Santal religious beliefs and practices.

Chapter VI

Magic and Witchcraft: Nature and Function

As we have seen in Chapter III, the Santals, like many other tribals, have evolved a system of beliefs and practices to face the unknown supernatural world which, according to them, is peopled with a large number of supernatural spirits and powers. In the foregoing two chapters, we examined the religious beliefs and practices through which the Santals have established a close relationship with their spirits or *bongas*. This study of Santal religion would be incomplete if we do not consider the question of magic, which, as much as religion, pervades the daily life of the Santals.

Much has been said and written about the role of magic in primitive societies. There are innumerable ethnographic descriptions of how magical rites are performed. The term magic has been used so widely and in such a variety of senses that Hutton Webster (1948) rightly says that the range of magic is almost as wide as the life of man.[1] For many years, there has been a controversy among scholars as to whiether magic is to be classified with religion or not. As Evans-Pritchard points out, 'Anthropologists still distinguish between or pointedly do not distinguish between, as the case may be, magic and religion among primitive peoples in terms of categories

[1]Webster, H., *Magic· A Sociological Study*, Stanford: Stanford University Press, 1948.

derived from an analysis of ideas of our own culture' (1954:7). The last part of this statement might seem too harsh especially when one considers the field studies of people like Malinowski among the Trobriand Islanders. What, however, remains true is that a distinction between magic and religion has been made by several generations of social analysts using different criteria.

Frazer took the position that magic and religion are separate and different phenomena. He defined religion as 'a propitiation or conciliation of superhuman powers which are believed to control nature and man', and regarded magic as 'the erroneous application of the notion of causality' (Radcliffe-Brown, 1959:137). During the magic period, man, according to Frazer, was not yet reasonable, but merely superstitious. Reason in turn gave rise to religion, and later to science.[2] Radcliffe-Brown (1959:137) points out that the application of this distinction to the Polynesians, met with certain difficulties. According to Tylor, magic is a pseudo-science based on an inaccurate association of ideas, divination being a 'sincere but fallacious system of philosophy'.[3]

Similar to Tylor's view is Malinowski's conception of magic; according to him, the Trobriand Islander's magic begins where his positive science ends.[4] He refers to this distinction as a 'clear cut division' in the Islander's mind. The Trobriand Islander believed that the empirical conditions subject to control 'are coped with by knowledge and work', while the supra-empirical conditions are controlled 'by magic' (1954:28-9). Malinowski does speak of various similarities between magic and religion. Thus, for example, both 'arise and function in situations of emotional stress', both 'open up escapes from such

[2]A similar opinion is held by R.R. Marett, 'Magic', in J. Hastings (ed.), *Encyclopaedia of Religion and Ethics*, Edinburgh: Clark, 1915, Vol. 8, pp. 245-52. According to him, religion includes all salutary ways of dealing with supernatural powers while magic includes all bad ways of dealing with them.

[3]Tylor, E.B., *Primitive Culture*, Vol. 1, New York: G.B. Putnam's Sons, 1920, 6th edition, pp. 117-41.

[4]Malinowski noted that in spite of the considerable empirical knowledge and skill which the Trobriand Islanders possessed with regard to fishing and gardening, their means of subsistence, they considered magic as indispensable to the success of gardening.

situations', both are 'surrounded by taboos and observances', both are 'strictly based on mythological tradition'.[5]

He, however, sees important differences between the two, the most definite being that 'while in the magical act, the underlying idea and aim is always clear, straightforward and definite, in the religious ceremony there is no purpose directed toward a subsequent event'. On the one hand, a magical rite 'is carried out as a means to an end, it has a definite practical purpose which is known to all who practice it'.[6] On the other hand, a religious rite 'is not a means to an end but an end in itself'. A religious rite 'expresses the feelings' of all concerned (1954:37-38). In other words, while magic is instrumental, religion is expressive. Another aspect of Malinowski's theory is that he does not attribute magic to any 'mystic' frame of mind but rather to psychological frustration. In most primitive societies, it is magic that gives man confidence in the face of difficulties and uncertainties. It supplements man's practical abilities and thereby enhances his confidence. Thus, he points out that:

> Magic, from many points of view, is the most important and the most mysterious aspect of primitive man's pragmatic attitude towards reality .... It enables man to carry out with confidence his most vital tasks and to maintain his poise and his mental integrity under circumstances which without the help of magic would demoralize him by despair and anxiety, by fear and hatred .... (1954:138-40).

In applying Malinowski's criterion, one encounters various difficulties. First of all, it is not clear as to what Malinowski meant by 'definite practical purpose'. Second, his view that a

[5]Malinowski (1954:87-8).

[6]Among other distinctions which Malinowski makes between magic and religion we find:(i) The techniques used in magic are simpler than those used in religion; (ii) The belief in magic is extremely simple while in religion there is a whole supernatural world of faith; (iii) The mythology of religion is more complex and more creative than that of magic; (iv) In religion everyone takes an active part while magic is in the hands of specialists; (v) While in religion the contrast between good and evil is very little, in magic it is very strong (1954:88-9).

religious rite 'is not a means to an end' is too extreme a view. Surely the Santals, like other tribals, do think of their religious rites as means to ends. Through their religious rituals, they do believe that they would accomplish something. As Radcliffe-Brown points out, 'In all ages men have hoped that by the proper performance of religious actions or observances they would obtain some specific benefit' (1959:153). Similarly, Lowie, seconded later by Radin, shows that even in the religious situation, one may find the Winnibago practitioner 'compelling' the spirits. Furthermore, the magician has clearly more than a craftsman's attitudes towards his apparatus and beliefs.[7] The positive function of magic as emphasised by Malinowski, that it enhances confidence, does not exhaust its relationship with social structures and processes. Magic also contains a set of human activities by means of which men act out aggressions, and seek to inflict injury upon others. In this respect, magic becomes a disintegrative phenomenon.

For Emile Durkheim, there is a 'marked repugnance of religion for magic and in return, the hostility of the second towards the first' (1967:58-62). He defined magic as something antithetical to collective solidarity and, therefore, hostile to society. According to him, the essential distinction between magic and religion lies in the fact that religious rites are connected with a religious society or church, while 'there is no church of magic'. Religion is inseparable from the idea of a church while the associations of magicians, where they are to be found, are in no way indispensable to the working of magic. In the second part of his definition of religion, Durkheim emphasises the fact that religion is a collective phenomenon. The religious beliefs and practices are always common to a definite group, whose members feel themselves united by the simple fact that they have a common faith. Magic has no community even if it is widely diffused in a society. 'It does not result in binding together those who adhere to it, or in uniting them into a group leading a common life' (1967:60). Magic has a clientele, just as a medical doctor has a clientele. A priest has

[7]Refer to Lowie, Robert, H., *Primitive Religion*, New York: Boni and Liveright, 1924, p. 142; Junod, Henri, A., *The Life of a South African Tribe*, New York: New Hyde Park, 1962, p. 486; Goode (1964:49).

a congregation. As a result, while in magic the client goes as an individual to a magician, in religion, he goes as a member of a group to the priest. Though this distinction is of a considerable theoretical importance, Durkheim's statement that, 'Magic takes a sort of professional pleasure in profaning holy things' (1967:58), does not adequately explain Santal magic. As Radcliffe-Brown points out, 'It is difficult to apply (this distinction) in the study of the rites of simple societies' (1959:137).

Some scholars, like Frazer and Radin, have considered magic to be the primary stage of religious ideas of the primitive people. Frazer's argument proceeds by a kind of Hegelian dialectic. According to him magic, classified as primitive science, being defeated by its own inadequacy, was supplemented by religion. From the thesis of magic emerged the antithesis of religion and the synthesis, modern effective science, replaced both magic and religion. This theory is, however, untenable. To consider magic as a preliminary stage leading to religion, or even as a source of religion, is not only opposed to the data of cultural history but is an ideological dogma that misapprehends the dialectics of cultural history and tells reality what it has to look like.[8] As Dubre remarks, 'Religion and magic are embedded in the texture and dynamics of culture and symbolization, both as expression and as limitation of dialectical existence' (1975:49).

There are some scholars who claim that magic and religion never occur separately and Lowie, for instance, includes magic in religion. A similar position is taken by Goode according to whom, 'Magic and religion are not dichotomies, but represent a continuum and are distinguished only ideal-typically' (1964:55). For Herskovits, 'Magic is regarded as an integral part of the Dahomean religious system'. In Firth's Tikopia, the magical and religious practitioner are the same.[9] However, these positions, like the others already mentioned, cannot be applied universally. In view of the lack of agreement on the definitions

[8]Evans-Pritchard remarks, 'No one can put to the test of observation a theory that magic preceded religion' (1956:314).

[9]Firth, Raymond, *We The Tikopia*, New York: George Allen & Unwin Ltd., 1936; *Primitive Polynesian Economy*, London: Routledge, 1939; Lowie, R.H., op. cit.; Herskovits, M.T., *Dahomey*, New York: Panther House, Vol. 2, 1938, p. 362.

of magic and religion and the nature of the distinction between them, the actual relationship between the two remains an open question for further discussion. The significance of these theoretical issues for Santal magic will be better understood in the analysis of the nature and function of magic as practised by the Santals.

OJHAISM

In our analysis of the Santals' religious universe, we have seen that, apart from the various benevolent and malevolent *bongas*, the Santals believe in a class of mischievous impersonal spirits and evil powers which are not objects of worship but which have to be scared away through exorcism or magic. To this class belong innumerable mysterious impersonal powers which are believed to reside in or are connected with various natural or artificial objects. In his day-to-day life, the Santal also has to cope with a number of inexplicable supra-normal phenomena. To deal with all these mysterious impersonal forces and powers, the Santals have recourse to various magical practices which are marked by an attitude of defiance, control and domination.

Whereas religion among the Santals, as among other primitive tribes, is essentially the business of the community—the village, the subclan or the household—magic is reserved only for the specialist. This distinction is also evident in the fact that the ministers of Santal religion are different from those of Santal magic. The Santals also distinguish between beneficent and maleficent magic. Magic intended to produce evil is known as black magic in contrast to the socially and psychologically beneficent white magic. The minister of white magic is known as *ojha* or diviner and medicine-man, whereas the one of black magic is known as *dan* or witch and sorcerer.[10] The *ojha* seeks to expose and counteract the anti-social activities of the sorcerer and witch and the evil influence of the impersonal forces or powers. His magic is regarded as useful so long as he does not make use of it to harm his fellow-men.

[10]It appears that in other parts of North India, the *ojha* is a dealer in black magic. See Crooke (1925:423).

A Santal *ojha* is believed to possess special powers through which he is able to perform certain things that are outside the knowledge and power of the ordinary people. As we have seen in Chapter III, the Santals believe that an *ojha* has special retained *bongas* as a result of which, whilst the ordinary Santal stands in fear of the malevolent spirits and impersonal powers, the *ojha* does not show any fear. On the contrary, the *ojha* does not exhibit any reverence when he addresses the malevolent *bongas* but threatens and conjures them. He tries to use one *bonga* against another appealing to the power and knowledge of his tutelary *bongas*.[11]

Apart from this power to communicate directly with the spirits, the *ojha* is also a physician having a superior knowledge of the magical properties of common substances and objects. He also professes to know how to find out and deal with the causes of misfortune or illness. This he does by taking recourse to divination, maintaining that his body is possessed by a spirit who speaks through him, indicating the nature of the disease, its natural or supra-normal cause and helping him to find out the will and desire of the malevolent spirit. According to tradition, the Santals believe that their ancestors learnt the art of *ojhaism* from a personage called *Kamru Guru*. There is no cause whatever to doubt the correctness of their statement. One thing is certain, namely, that *Kamru Guru* is venerated above all the other tutelary *bongas* of the *ojhas*. He is also invoked in the majority of *mantars* (magic spells). The ancestors passed on their knowledge to their own disciples who, after undergoing a period of training, receive a formal initiation or *sid*.

Among the Santals, only men can become *ojhas*. A female who professes intimate familiarity with the *bongas* is looked upon as a witch and persecuted. Every *ojha* has to build and sustain his own reputation. This he can only do by demonstrating his power to others. In so doing he not only receives the respect of others but also makes a considerable personal profit. He may also develop a wide practice for he is not confined to

[11]Dubre reports that the *angakog* among the Central Eskimos and the *tonralik* in Alaska, have a personal relationship with their spirits (1975:203-4).

his own village but may go wherever he is summoned. In Pangro, there are five *ojhas* of whom Bharat Soren has the widest practice. He is even called upon by Santals from the neighbouring villages. On the other hand, the people of Pangro, like other Santals, are not bound to use the services of the *ojhas* residing in their own village. In fact Pitho Murmu, during the illness of his wife Solma Besra, called upon an *ojha* from Adro who enjoys a very good reputation in the area.

The Christian households in Pangro, like in other places, are forbidden to have recourse to any *ojha* in case of sickness or any other misfortune. They are taught that the *ojha's* work is the work of the devil. An interesting case, involving the cure of a Santal Christian, occurred during my stay in Pangro. A Christian woman was one day bitten by a snake while she was working in her fields. When she was brought to her house her body was already swollen. The medicine given by Gangaram Marandi who, as we have seen, is a homoeopathic doctor, did not help. On hearing the news, Bharat Soren without being called upon, went to her house. After reciting a number of *mantars*, he gave her some herbal medicine.[12] The following morning, the woman was seen working in the fields as if nothing had happened. This incident enhanced Bharat's reputation. He went around saying that, through his charms and medicine, he could cure even where the Christian gods could not. An *ojha*, however, is not always so successful.

Like the *naeke*, an *ojha* is expected to observe a stricter way of life than the ordinary people. He is to fast and abstain from sexual intercourse prior to any divination or exorcism. This is due to the Santals' belief that, as a result of his work, an *ojha* makes many spiritual enemies whose displeasure he incurs. He is said to stand between the greed of the evil spirits, impersonal forces and witches, on the one hand, and mankind, on the other. Not to offend his tutelary *bongas* who are constantly watching him, he must pay special care not to have sexual relations with any woman apart from his wife. Unlike the *naeke*, the *ojha's* position is not hereditary. He does not receive any public

[12]The Santal *ojhas* have quite a number of *mantars* which they specially use in connection with snake-bites. Bodding (1925:116-122) records sixty-six such *mantars*.

remuneration for his work but is paid for by the particular households who consult him and this only if the person is cured or the misfortune is removed.

The Hindu influence on the Santal *ojha* institution cannot be denied. Thus, for example, the very name *ojha* is not a Santal word but a Hindi word meaning, 'a diviner, soothsayer, sorcerer, exorcist, magician'. Many of the *mantars* used by the *ojhas* are not in Santali but in a corrupt form of Hindi or Bengali. The very word *mantar* is derived from the Sanskrit *mantra*. Besides, as we have seen, most of the *saket bongas* invoked by the Santal *ojhas* have names of Hindi origin. Such similarities between the Santal *ojhas* and the Hindu *ojhas*, however, must not be taken to mean that both are, at the present time, or for that matter have ever been, the same. Whatever the origin of *ojhaism* may have been, this institution has been adapted by the Santals to their own social and cultural system.[13]

After this general description of the *ojha*, we shall now come to his *modus operandi*. Like other tribes, the Santals look upon most diseases as something unnatural, ascribing them to the agency of evil spirits and forces, witches and the evil eye.[14] This, however, does not mean that the Santals let a matter rest with taking only so-to-say 'religious' precautions. They do acknowledge the natural causes of certain illnesses. They cannot avoid seeing effect and immediate cause. As a rule, they can also point out to the material nature of a common disease. They make use of symptomatical remedies such as fomentation and massage and administer medicines made from a large number of plants, herbs and other natural objects. Bodding records a list of 305 Santal prescriptions for various human

[13]See Datta-Majumder (1956:114-5) and Biswas, P.C., *Santals of the Santal Parganas*, Delhi: Bharatiya Adimjati Sevak Sangh, 1956, p. 109.

[14]The main ambition of a Santal is to live happily with his family. To do so, it is considered necessary to be in good health. Hence there is something abnormal in being ill.

Majumdar drawing upon the ideas and practices of north and north-eastern tribes, came to the conclusion that Indian tribes attribute disease to hateful humans and wicked spirits, *Matrix of Indian Culture*, Lucknow: Universal Publishers, 1947:109ff. See also Malinowski (1954:31).

diseases and fifteen veterinary medicines.[15] They also have their own physicians called *raranics* (one who administers medicine).[16] There is, however, scarcely a grown-up Santal who is not cognisant of some of these medicines called *rehet ran* which literally means 'root medicine'.

The most common of the natural causes of diseases is the spraining or dislocation of any *sir*, which term is used in a broad sense to mean muscles, nerves, arteries and veins. The best remedy for such complaints is *iskir* or massage. Some diseases like rabies, epilepsy, scabies, ringworms, etc., are said to be caused by different kinds of worms (*tejo*). Among other natural causes, are bad diet, eating unclean things, bathing in dirty water, etc. But when anything different from the common diseases occurs, the Santals are at a loss, and take recourse to magic, being greatly influenced by the belief that the ultimate cause of disease may be found in evil spirits and forces, witches or sorcerers. Such conceptions determine a sick person's treatment.

When a person falls ill, his relatives first try to apply the medicines they know of. If these do not work, a *raranic* is summoned. He identifies the disease and prescribes the herbs to be applied. When, however, the illness persists, the patient and his relatives suspect that some supra-normal agency is at work and they call in an *ojha*. It is interesting to note here that in case of sickness, very few of the Santals of Pangro call upon Gangaram Marandi, the homoeopathic doctor. They believe that if they go to him, then the *bongas* will get jealous and will see to it that the illness will not be cured. Moreover, modern medicines are regarded as futile. As a result of their belief that the ultimate cause of a prolonged disease lies in the supernatural, it is only the *ojha* who can reach that realm.[17]

[15]Bodding, Paul Olaf, 'Santal Medicine', *Memoirs of the Asiatic Society of Bengal*, Calcutta, 10(2), 1927, pp. 135-426.

[16]The difference between a *raranic* and an *ojha* lies in the fact that while the *raranic* gives only medicine, the latter has or rather professes to have power to drive away the supernatural mischievous agents. The *raranic*, though he might have a good knowledge of herbs and roots, is ignorant of incantations and sacrifices.

[17]Evans-Pritchard (1956) remarks that the Nuer regard medicines as something strange and foreign. They think easily in terms of spirits but not in terms of medicine.

When the *ojha* is called in, he first enquires for how long the patient has been ill and what type of treatment he has received. He then feels the pulse of the patient and looks at his tongue. The Santals believe that the *ojha* can diagnose the cause of the disease in this way. He recites various *mantars* (magic spells) and sings some *jharnis* (magical incantations) over the patient. As a result of their inherent magical powers, these *mantars* and *jharnis* are said to have the power to drive away all evils. Through them the *ojha* coaxes and threatens the malevolent agent. If the patient does not recover, the *ojha* takes recourse to divination so as to ascertain the ultimate cause and origin of the disease.

Divination has been and is resorted to by various people throughout the world, taking many forms and appealing to innumerable supernatural agents.[18] It is known by various names. Winick records forty-seven different forms of divination.[19] As the Latin root of the term divination (*deus* meaning a god) indicates, the source of divination is the supernatural. Although divination mainly aims at gaining knowledge of the future, many tribes in Central India use divination to discover the causes of unknown events and afflictions.[20]

Among the Santals, divination is not performed only in the case of disease but also in other types of misfortune. In the case of Sagram Hasdak, it was resorted to in order to find out the cause of his and his daughter's illness and the death of his cattle. On reaching the house of Sagram Hasdak, Bharat Soren, one of the *ojhas* of Pangro, sat down in the courtyard and asked for a *lota* of water, some mustard oil and a few *sal* leaves. He then selected two *sal* leaves and, after looking at each one of them intently, he folded and creased them so as to

[18]See Moore, O.K., 'Divination: A New Perspective', *American Anthropologist*, Wisconsin, 59(1), Feb. 1957, pp. 69-74; Turner, Victor, W., *Ndembu Divination: Its Symbolism and Techniques*, Manchester: Manchester University Press, 1961; Park, G.K., 'Divination and Its Social Context', *Journal of the Royal Anthropological Institute*, London, 93(2), 1963, pp. 195-209; Bascom, William, *Ifa Divination: Communication between Gods and Men in West Africa*, Bloomingtion: Indiana University Press 1969.

[19]Winick, C., *Dictionary of Anthropology*, New York: Philosophical Library, 1956

[20]See Majumdar, D.N., *Fortunes of Primitive Tribes*, Lucknow: Universal Publishers, 1944, p. 30; Crooke (1925:308-16); and S.C. Roy (1937:393-5).

make marks across the surface. Putting the leaves aside, he dipped his right index finger in the oil and sprinkled a few drops on the ground invoking his tutelary *bongas* to guide him in determining the correct cause of the sickness. Thereupon, he took one of the leaves and put oil marks on it, at the same time indicating which oil mark was to stand for natural causes, which one for *bongas*, and which one for witches. He then rubbed each oil mark separately uttering various *mantars* appealing at the same time to his tutelary *bongas* to come to his aid and to exercise their power. Placing the two leaves on top of each other he rubbed them together, muttering *mantars* in the process. Holding both the leaves towards the sky he removed the covering leaf, and proceeded to investigate the result, pronouncing the cause of the disease in accordance with the way in which the oil spots were found in the different parts of the leaf. The underlying idea behind such a divination is the belief in sympathetic magic whereby an intentional imitation of a desired result produces that result through spiritual sympathy.

Having performed the divination, the *ojha* informs the patient's relatives of what is to be done. The treatment which follows depends on what the divination reveals as the maleficent agent. Thus, as mentioned in the case of Sagram, his *kisar bonga* was exorcised through spirit-possession. In Kapre's case, the *Tak Taki* ceremony proved to be of no avail. If divination shows that the illness is due to natural causes, medicines will be administered. In the case of an evil spirit being found, the *ojha* performs the *Bul Mayam* ceremony, the object of which is to appease the interfering spirit so that he will not create any further mischief. Blood is regarded as a beneficent power possessing the greatest potency which can counteract the evil influences of harmful agents. This is done in the same manner performed by the *kudam naeke* in propitiating the *bahre* and *sima bongas*, with the exception that, besides the invocations addressed to the particular *bonga*, the *ojha* utters various *mantars*.

If the patient does not recover, the *ojha* has recourse to another form of exorcism. In the case of Mongla Tudu, her sickness prevailed in spite of all the precautions taken by Samu Soren, another *ojha* from Pangro. Seeing this, Samu did not want to lose face and he resorted to the practice described here.

On reaching Mongla's house, he sat near the *parkom* (stringed bed) on which she was lying. Taking a twig he drew a circle on the floor. He then brought out the two *sal* leaves with which he had earlier performed the *Sunum Bonga* divination and looking at the one on which the oil marks were made, he drew the same pattern inside the circle. Thereupon, he spat on the marks putting his left heel down on the circle and finally rubbing out the marks he drew. This form of exorcism known as *Ak Raput*, which literally means 'to break the figure', was repeated several times with the aim of undoing the deception created by a possible witch. Samu, then asked for a leaf plate, some charcoal and some burnt clay from the fireplace. After grinding the latter into powder, he made a circle on the leaf plate in the centre of which he drew some figures. After looking at the leaf plate for some time, he upturned it. This process was repeated twice. Thereupon, he again drew a figure on the plate, in the centre of which he put some *adwa caole* and *sindur* marks. Then Mongla was made to sit down on a *gandop* (wooden stool) in front of the leaf plate facing Samu. A fowl was brought and after putting *sindur* marks on its head, Samu told Mongla to touch the fowl. After which, he let the fowl feed on the *adwa caole*.

Then Samu performed a type of exorcism called *Bulau*. He took the fowl and moved it three times round Mongla's head and body. The fowl was again made to feed on the rice and the ceremony was repeated again. The *ojha* then took some cowdung which he smeared on the ground thus obliterating the first circle made. Thereupon, he collected some earth which he mixed with some cowdung, and put the ashes in a leaf cup. After wrapping everything in a leaf plate along with the fowl, he walked straight out of the house without ever looking back. In doing so, the Santals believe that the evil spirit is transferred to the fowl. After a few moments, Mongla's male relatives followed Samu to the outskirts of the village where the fowl was sacrificed in the name of one of the *sima* or *bahre bongas*. When this was over, everyone returned to the house and Samu made a *sindur* mark in the courtyard followed by *saket*, a vow to sacrifice a castrated goat to his tutelary *bongas* in the case of Mongla's recovery. The Santals believe that if a cure is effected and the patient does not fulfil this vow, an early relapse or even a more fatal complication will result.

In Mongla's case, however, there was no recovery, her illness lingered on and her relatives, doubting Samu's efficacy, decided to call upon Bharat Soren.[21] In this case, Bharat did not perform the *Sunum Bonga* ceremony but took recourse to another method of divination called *Dali Thenga*. For this, Bharat required the services of two of his disciples. Everyone assembled in the courtyard as Bharat's aides brought two big bamboo sticks which they spread lengthwise on the ground. Bharat uttered some *mantars* invoking his *saket bongas* to help him in the divination and marked both the sticks with *sindur*. Then his aides, taking the two sticks at each end, began shaking them, sometimes bringing them closer to one another, sometimes far apart. Now and then, Bharat uttered the name of a *bonga*. The sticks 'reacted' at each name. He kept on mentioning the names of various *bongas* till finally the sticks came very close to one another and did not move apart.[22] This was a sign that the *bonga* named was causing all the mischief. Bharat, therefore, entreated Mongla's relatives to propitiate this *bonga* with a fowl and to promise a goat's sacrifice to the same *bonga* on Mongla's recovery. But still the illness prevailed. So Bharat resorted to performing a mock funeral hoping that, by doing so, he would deceive the *bonga*, making him think that Mongla had died and consequently, he would stop harassing her.

Bharat made a tiny figure out of a banana stalk to represent Mongla, and with small twigs and thread he made a tiny bedstead. These he brought to Mongla's house. Adjacent to one of the legs of the bed on which Mongla was lying, Bharat, using a stick, drew a circle on the ground making a number of magic marks in the circle as previously described. He then exorcised Mongla by blowing over her, commencing at the head and finishing at the feet. Thereupon, he placed the model bedstead, containing the figure, in the centre of the magic

[21]In some cases, the patient's relatives do begin to doubt the *ojha's* medicinal knowledge, his ability to accurately recognise the nature of the illness and, what is more important, his ability to appease the malignant agent.

[22]For a similar custom see S.N. Roy, 'Some Popular Superstitions of Orissa', *Man in India*, Ranchi, 5(3), Sept. 1925, pp. 210-34.

circle, putting some *adwa caole* and *sindur* marks around it. After sprinkling water on the fowl he had brought with him, he marked its head, wings and legs with *sindur*. The fowl was then made to feed on the *adwa caole* in the name of *Jom Raja* and *Hudar Raja* who, as we have seen, are considered to be the guardians of the netherworld. Taking the fowl in his hands, he touched it on every part of Mongla's body. Then the fowl was made to feed on the *adwa caole* again, making it face in the four directions. In each direction, one of the fowl's legs or wings was broken. The magic marks were destroyed and Bharat, followed by Mongla's husband and eldest son, went to the village outskirts. There, Bharat, using twigs, built a tiny funeral pyre upon which he placed the bed and the figure. Then stripping himself completely, he set fire to the pyre. As he did so, he pretended to wail for Mongla's departed spirit. When everything was reduced to ashes he dug a hole and buried the ashes. The whole ritual was concluded by the sacrificing of the fowl in honour of the malignant *bonga*, invoking him to depart. This is a case of *mimetic magic* which seeks to drive away the evil powers through mimicry. In spite of all this Bharat did not prove himself successful.

Such then are the several methods of divination and exorcism used by an *ojha* to find out the cause of a sickness and to try and cure the patient, counteracting the mischief brought about by evil spirits and impersonal powers. In tackling an illness, an *ojha* shows great optimism. Except in obviously hopeless cases, he always exhorts the patient and his relatives not to be afraid or harbour any anxiety, since he professes to have the power to cure the disease. Whenever an *ojha* is unable to bring about a cure, he offers a number of explanations to the people concerned, so as to save his reputation. He never admits that the lack of success is due to his own inability or the insufficiency of his remedies, but he remarks that the destructive spirit or power has gained the upper hand.

To the observer, many of the methods employed by the *ojha* seem meaningless. It is difficult to say whether the *ojha* actually believes in the possibility of any revelation brought about through the various methods of divination. In any case it is to the *ojha's* interest to build on the Santals' belief that prolonged sickness is the result of a supra-normal power and, therefore, his services are required to appease these powers. The Santals want to make sure against all possibilities. Very few would dare challenge an *ojha's* vision, believing that such a distrust might involve disrespect of the supernatural, resulting in greater calamities. Whatever be the outcome, they feel at peace with themselves believing that, on their part, they have done all that was expected from them. Thus, while the manifest function of divination is often ineffective, its latent function is effective. At the psychological level, it cures anxiety and helplessness infusing hope and confidence while at the social level it manifests the Santals' belief and dependence on their *bongas*.

Once a cure is ascertained, the relatives of the patient inform the *ojha* that they are ready to fulfil their vow and perform the *saket* sacrifice. A day is fixed and the *manjhi, paranik* and various relatives are invited. After taking his purificatory bath, the *ojha* prepares the *khond* in the courtyard and sacrifices the *saket* animals, invoking the *bonga* to whom the vow had been made. The heads of the animals sacrificed are kept aside for the *ojha*. The livers and lungs are cooked in rice and eaten by the *ojha, manjhi, paranik* and the household head. The rest is divided into three portions, one for the *ojha*, one for the household head and the other is given to all those present. After everyone has eaten and drunk rice-beer, the *ojha* is given his fee (*dadni*) which, in Pangro, amounts to five rupees and a *dhoti*.

As mentioned earlier, the *ojha's* work is not hereditary. The Santals recognise a regular science of *ojhaism*. It is customary for young men of a village to go through an elementary course of training in this science since it is considered proper for a Santal man to have some knowledge of *ojhaism*. In Pangro, this course lasts for one month, starting in *Bhador* (August-September) and ending in *Asin* (September-October), the time of the *Dasae festival*.[23]

During this course, the disciples assemble every evening for about two hours in the *ojha's* courtyard. Here they are taught various *mantars, bandhons* (charms) and *jharnis* to be used on

[23]Because of the connection with this festival, the *ojha* in charge of this course, is called *dasae guru*. According to Culshaw (1949:94), in Sarenga, the course in *ojhaism* used to last from the month of May till October.

different occasions. They have to learn the words and the manner of application, while in the case of *jharnis*, they also learn the melody. Certain elementary medicines to be used when the *mantars*, *bandhons* and *jharnis* prove ineffective, are also taught. The course also comprehends various songs, dances, play-acting, and methods of spirit-possession (*rum*), most of which are to be used during the *Dasae Daran* as we shall see later. I should like to emphasise here that this is only a preliminary course in *ojhaism*. It does not make the participant fit to practice as an *ojha*, but only gives him a first insight into this science. To be initiated as an *ojha*, one has to undergo a rigorous and specialised training as an apprentice to an *ojha*.

This short course of instruction comes to an end two or three days before the *Dasae Parab* which is the common name among the Santals for *Durga Puja*. The disciples are now ready to commence the *Dasae Daran* which literally means the '*Dasae* wandering about' or 'begging expeditions'. Anyone who has undergone instruction and who still remembers the songs, dances and methods of spirit-possession can participate. The participants who are known as *dasae kora* dress in skirts and small waistcoats and attach peacock feathers to their heads.[24]

On the morning of the *Dasae Daran*, all those taking part accompany the *dasae guru* to a place on the outskirts of the village. Here the *dasae guru* sacrifices three fowls and two pigeons to *Kamru Guru* and the other *saket bongas*, imploring them to keep watch over the *dasae kora* so that no harm may befall anyone of them during the *Dasae Daran*. The fowls are then singed, cooked with rice and eaten by all those present. Thereupon, the *dasae kora* enter the village dancing and singing along the *kulhi*. This ritual is called *Belboron*.

On reaching the *manjhi's* house, they enter the courtyard single file, singing and swaying as they go along. Meanwhile the *dasae guru* sprinkles some water mixed with flour on the entrance door, after which he is given a stool to sit on. The *dasae kora* then begin their impersonifications or play-acting. Most of the things they personify are animals. This continues until a woman of the house gives them some maize-cobs. In the

[24]This is the only time when Santal men are allowed to wear women's attire.

same manner, they visit each house in Pangro and also the Santal houses in the neighbouring villages returning in the evening to the *dasae guru* house where they leave their spoils. This 'wandering and begging' continues for two or three days.

On the last day of *Durga Puja*, all the participants accompany the *dasae guru* to Sahibganj, dancing and singing all the way. They visit each *Durga* shrine, in front of which they dance, sing and play-act. Late at night, all the *dasae kora* from various villages assemble in a big field on the outskirts of Sahibganj where each village tries to outdo the other in its singing, dancing and play-acting.

A week or so later, the animals which were bought after having sold the maize are killed and the flesh divided equally among all the participants. When asked about the reason behind *Dasae Daran*, the answer received was that it was an expression of appreciation, on the part of the villagers, of those who had undergone the course of instruction in the elementary forms of *ojhaism*. This is considered to be beneficent not only to tbe persons so instructed but also to the village community as a whole in their fight against the evil spirits and powers.

WITCHCRAFT

As we have seen, in the *Sunum Bonga* method of divination, one of the oil marks placed by the *ojha* on the *sal* leaf stands for a witch as a possible cause of a sickness or misfortune. Usually, at an early stage of a sickness, a witch is not accused of being the mischievous agent, although the possibility is not ruled out. The reason for the *ojha's* caution is due to the fact that declaring the presence of a witch is considered to be a very serious matter and no one would think of tackling such a matter on his own. However, if in spite of all the medicines and exertions of the *ojha* described earlier, a patient does not recover, the latent suspicion of witchcraft comes to the surface and the *ojha* feels compelled to announce the presence of a witch as the cause of the illness. Here it is interesting to note that, according to Santal belief, there is a natural enmity between an *ojha* and the witches who attempt to hinder him in his work. Witches are said to have the power to prevent their presence and activities from being shown up in the *Sunum Bonga* method of divination and, instead, throw the blame on others, thus completely misleading the *ojha*. Once witchcraft is suspected, the case does not remain restricted merely to the patient's household but becomes a public affair. The help of the village community is sought since a witch is considered to be a very dangerous public menace, an enemy to humanity.

Among the Santals, as among other aboriginal tribes, there is a strong belief in the potent evil powers of a witch.[25] In fact, the most dreaded of magical effects are those resulting from witchcraft. Witches are believed to be productive of the greatest misfortunes. The Santals have always been obsessed by the menace of witchcraft. Early in 1867 Man noted, 'no reasoning with them, nor ridicule can dissuade them of their belief in witches and the necessity of their being at once murdered' (1867:29). Witches are said to be the thorns of the Santal social fabric. They undermine society and bring about injury and death. As Kolean Haram remarks, 'The greatest trouble for us Santals is witches. Because of them we are enemies of each other. If there were no witches we would have lived happily' (Bodding, 1942:160). Even today, very few are those Santals who do not believe in witchcraft. Thus, for example, in his study of Santal workers living in *bustees* (village-like settlements) outside the industrial city of Jamshedpur, Martin Orans points out that, after fifty years of urbanisation, witchcraft remains a parallel solution to Santal problems.[26] The belief in witchcraft being so strong, it is not strange that a suspicion is always present that witches may be at work when a sick person does not recover.

While amongst the Mundas, Oraons, Bhils and other tribes, a witch can be either a man or a woman, among the Santals

[25]See Creagh Coen, T.B., 'Witchcraft in the Dangs', *Man in India*, Ranchi, 15(3), Sept. 1945, pp. 187-8; Crooke (1925:419-39); S.C. Roy (1937:409-10); Bodding, P.O., *Witchcraft among the Santals*, Oslo: A.W. Broggers Boktrykheri, 1940, pp. 257-326; Hivale, Shamrao, 'Pradhan Ideas about Witchcraft', *Man in India*, Ranchi, 15(3), Sept. 1945, pp. 146-8; Marwick, Marvin G., (ed.), *Witchcraft and Sorcery*, Harmondsworth: Penguin Books, 1970.

[26]Orans, Martin, 'A Tribal People in an Industrial Setting', *Journal of American Folklore*, Philadelphia, 71(281), July-Sept, 1958, pp. 422-6.

only women are believed to practice witchcraft. Women are, from time to time, regarded as being imbued with strange mysterious powers. There is behind this belief a myth according to which women learned the art of witchcraft from *Maran Buru* whom they deceived by going to him in their husbands' place. According to this legend, *Maran Buru* as a recompense for his mistake taught the menfolk the art of countering witchcraft.

The science of witchcraft gives women power to transform themselves and to cause harm. Though some diseases are generally considered curable by human skill or in a natural way, if a witch casts her evil eye on the patient, then the illness may prove fatal. The Santals believe that very often witches can influence evil *bongas* by their feminine charms and make them do their bidding. Vice-versa, evil spirits are sometimes said to use witches as mediums for their nefarious actions. Though they work in close collaboration, witches are different from *bongas*. Besides being experts in black magic, witches are believed to know sorcery, making use of material objects in influencing the evil spirits. This corresponds to Evans-Pritchard's (1965) distinction, based on his study of the Azande, between witchcraft as an influence and sorcery as a magic art using material objects.

Like *ojhaism*, the power of witchcraft is not inborn but is acquired through training in secret. The magic power of witchcraft can be acquired by a woman of any age. A belief, however, prevails that it is the witches themselves who take the initiative. They are believed to entice and sometimes even to force girls to become their disciples so that 'the seed may live on when they themselves die'. The training is said to be imparted during very dark nights in a forest or an open plain, and consists in the teaching of *mantars*, charms and songs. Once a girl has mastered these things, she is introduced to the *bongas* whose names she must learn. She is then married to a *bonga* from whom she learns the art of 'killing'. At the end of her training, she is commanded by her witch tutor to practise what she had learnt upon one of her own relatives. If she refuses, she is said to become mad and die.

Witches are said to cause harm either through contact or through the long-range influence of sympathy. There are six methods by which a witch causes disease or any other calamity to an individual, a household, or a whole village. The first is to 'eat' up a victim by supposedly taking out his liver and eating it after cooking it with rice.[27] The liver is considered to be the seat of the vital principle. This method, however, cannot be resorted to without her *bonga's* permission and unless one member of the victim's family is a witch. Another method is for a witch to take the form of a black cat and, entering her victim's house at night while he is sleeping, to lick saliva from his mouth. After some time the victim falls ill and very often the illness proves fatal. A similar method is reported by S.C. Roy (1972:191) in his study among the Oraons.

Sometimes, a witch draws a picture of her victim and does the killing *in effigie*. This is what Frazer called imitative and contagious magic. In the next three methods, the witch does not do the nefarious work herself but commissions evil spirits to do it for her. Thus, as in the case of Kapre Kisku, a witch was believed to have localised a *thapna bonga* in a stone and buried it in Kapre's house or cowshed. The Santals believe that if anyone steps on such a stone, he is struck by disease and sometimes even death. *Thapna bongas* can also be buried in a whole village. A similar method is the strewing of disease germs over which spells have been pronounced in various nooks and corners of a village. Contact with such germs is believed to cause serious illness sometimes proving fatal unless counteracted. According to a traditional myth, these germs are annually collected by the witches from a big water tank situated in Kundli village near Barhait. The last and most common method is when an evil spirit is the cause of all calamity.

Once witchcraft is suspected as being the cause of a villager's disease or any other mischief, the village officials are immediately informed, and the case becomes the village community's affair. The first precaution is taken by the *manjhi* who, walking along the *kulhi*, in a loud voice warns the witch to desist from her work and set the patient free. The oil divination, as a result of which witchcraft has come out, has to be confirmed by three other *ojhas* from neighbouring villages. If, after

27. Among the Oraons it is believed that witches extract the hearts out of their victims.

performing divination by *Sunum Bonga*, these three *ojhas* do not reach the same verdict, then the matter is dropped. If, however, agreement is reached that witchcraft is at work, steps are taken to locate the witch. This is done through another form of divination.

The menfolk of the village accompany their *manjhi* to the banks of the water tank. Here a number of freshly cut *sal* twigs are placed in the mud. As each twig is planted, *sindur* marks are put on it. These twigs represent the various households in the village. Some *adwa caole* is scattered among the twigs and the *jaher bongas* are invoked to make the twig representing the guilty household dry up. The twig that withers first is taken as a clear sign pointing to the direction in which the villagers must look for the answers to their suspicions. This form of divination, however, only helps to locate the house where the witch resides. No individual names are mentioned. It is only the *jan guru* who has the powers to reveal the exact identity of the culprit. He is the orthodox witch-finder for the Santals who believe that he 'knows' through revelation.

Once a woman is declared by the *jan guru* to be a witch, vigorous action is taken by the villagers to punish her and to rid their village of her presence. Formerly, the action taken depended on whether the witch's victim was still alive or not. If the victim was still alive, the culprit used to be given a severe beating by all the villagers and punished with a heavy fine. If the victim died, preventive action often led to dastardly murders. Though witches are nowadays normally no longer murdered, evidence relating to witchcraft and murder has been documented. According to the statistics published for the Santal Parganas for the period 1931-40, out of the seventy-eight cases of homicide by Santals brought before the courts, it was definitely established that sixteen were due to accusations of witchcraft.[28] Gupta reports that the incidence of murders connected with witchcraft is heavy in the tea-growing areas of the Duars

[28]Naqavi, S.M., 'Santal Murders', *Man in India*, Ranchi, 23(3), Sept. 1943, pp. 236-52. See also J. Shore, 'On Some Extraordinary Facts, Customs and Practices of the Hindus', *Asiatic Researches*, Calcutta, 4, 1795, pp. 331-50; E.G. Man, (1867:29) and S.P. Prasad, 'Witchcraft among the Santals of Mayurbhanj', *Adibasi*, Orissa, 8(4), Jan. 1966-67, pp. 6-22.

inhabited mainly by Santals, Mundas, Oraons, Kols and Kharias.[29] The brutal persecution of a suspected or declared witch is a result of the desire to punish all anti-social mischief-makers.

As a result of such murders, the Government has discouraged the profession of the *jan guru*. Still, however, there are some who continue, in secrecy, practising as *jan gurus*. Thus, I was informed that there is one *jan guru* in a village called Jerle in Mandro Bungalow. The people of Pangro do not remember any case of murder connected with witchcraft ever taking place in their village, though some still speak of such a murder taking place, about thirty years ago, in Ambadiha about fifteen miles away. This, however, does not mean that there were no witchcraft cases in Pangro. We have already mentioned how in the case of Kapre Kisku's protracted illness, a *thapna bonga* was revealed by the *Sunum Bonga* divination. In spite of all the efforts of Bharat Soren, including even the *Tak Taki* method of exorcism, Kapre, instead of recovering, grew worse and was on the point of dying. The villagers suspected Juna Hembrom, Kapre's daughter-in-law, of witchcraft. They did not go to the extreme of consulting the *jan guru*, but they acted on the supposition that since Juna and Mongla could not get along well together due to the fact that Juna had no male offspring, she was having her revenge. She was severely beaten and ran away from the village.

Owing to the belief that witches possess the power of seducing the *bongas* and since it is not easy to ascertain who is a witch and who is not, the names of the *orak* and *abge bongas*, as already mentioned in Chapter III, are never disclosed to women. The belief in the dangerous potentiality of women to seduce evil spirits and wreck vengeance on their enemies is reflected in the fact that participation in all sacrifices are taboo for women. They are barred from eating the flesh of animals sacrificed to the *abge bongas* or to *Maran Buru*. A married woman is also barred from entering her father's *bhitar*. The Santals' abhorrence of witchcraft is also reflected in the fact that divorce is easily granted in the case of a woman suspected of being a witch. Here the *Sakam Orec* ceremony (Chapter V) is not

[29]Gupta, R.K., 'Witchcraft Murders in the Duars', *Man in India*, Ranchi, 40(4), Oct.-Dec. 1960, pp. 307-19.

performed and the woman's relatives have to return the bride-price they received.

THE EVIL EYE

There are various other procedures through which magical effects are said to be obtained. In the opinion of the Santals, like many other tribals, the evil eye and bad omens may also cause disease and misfortune. The belief in the danger resulting from the evil eye prevails widely in Northern and Central India.[30] Though, as we have seen, the Santal like the Munda, attributes certain misfortunes to the direct action or malice of some evil spirit or impersonal power, he also recognises the application of the evil eye as a source of trouble and mischief. The Santals believe in women possessing a malevolent eye or *hoe hisit*, as it is called, that can bring ruin on a person, destroy his household members, domestic animals, crops and houses. All witches are believed to invariably possess an evil eye. Some men also are said to possess 'evil shadows'. Similarly, certain animals and snakes are believed to have this mischievous power. Thus the *Bitkil dhond bin*—a huge water snake with black and white stripes on its skin—is credited with an evil eye capable of causing disease and death through its glance.

Children are more liable to be the victims of the evil eye than adults, and women more than men. Thus, children and women need special protection, particularly at moments of crises such as childbirth or marriage. We noted in Chapter V that the Santals believe that at no moment in life is a person more vulnerable to the evil eye than while still in the mother's womb and at birth. In certain circumstances, persons are considered to have the evil eye only temporarily and this in relation to a specific individual. People possessing an evil eye are particularly averse to the sight of the happiness or abundance of others to such an extent that the Santals believe that in many cases the evil eye of women is applied because of a great envy which eats them up. As a result of this belief, the Santals are very careful not to boast of a good crop. In fact, when asked

[30]Crooke (1925:276-307).

how their crop was they always understate it by saying that a lot of the crop was destroyed due to some reason or other. In those houses where they have a number of *bandis*, a manifestation of wealth, they try to hide them lest somebody should get jealous and cast his evil eye on them. One Santal when asked why he does not work more in his fields answered, 'If I exert myself too much I am liable to become a victim of jealousy and hence susceptible to some evil eye'.

The effect of an evil eye can bring about the destruction of any object. Thus, when it is directed on a healthy child, he is believed to fall sick, have bowel complaints or fever and cry constantly and unnecessarily. If directed on a pregnant woman it may cause a miscarriage, difficult labour or a physical deformity in the child. When directed on a man while eating or rather, on his food, the victim loses his appetite or suffers from indigestion. A cow or a *bitkil* (female buffalo) on which the evil eye has been cast, ceases to yield milk or yields very little. If the evil eye is cast on maize, then, though to the observer it looks healthy, it is rotten inside the cob. Similarly, the affected rice-crop does not mature fully.

The Santals believe that it is easier to prevent the evil eye from falling on a person than to cure a victim so smitten. In the latter case, the aid of an *ojha* is sought to neutralise, through the recitation of *mantars* and the chanting of *jharnis*, the mischief done and to remove the spell. Among the various devices used by the Santals to ward off the evil eye, we have already mentioned in Chapter V, the *Met Halan* ritual performed by the midwife on the very day the child is born. Cowrie shells or other amulets are worn on the waist of a child attached to the *dora* (loin string). Soot is also applied around the child's eyes whenever taken out of the house. During the marriage proceedings, various rituals like the *Cumaura* and *Parchau* as we have seen, are performed which, though not exclusively to ward off the evil eye, are intimately connected with it. To avert the evil eye, women put on iron amulets and rings. These are also used as a protection against evil powers. The *mantars* and *jharnis* which the youth learn during their elementary course in *ojhaism* also help to counteract the evil eye. It is because of the belief in the evil eye that during the *Disom Sendra* the hunters do not mention the names of their villages but refer to them by using other terms. The supposed intimate relation between a name and its owner is believed to offer a very potent means to the witch or sorcerer to cause mischief.

OMENS AND AUGURIES

Even in the most ordinary affairs of life, the Santals assign supernatural reasons to certain events in the natural phenomena. They believe that these natural phenomena may have a prophetic significance. Though it is difficult to establish why a coming event, good or bad, should be foreshadowed in a particular manner, the fact remains that the Santals, like many other people all over the world, have held fast to the belief in omens and auspicious moments.[31] The omen is considered as a reliable indication of overwhelming good or evil which is in the offing. We having already seen in Chapter V, the importance given to the reading of ominous signs during the marriage procedures, especially when the groom's and bride's party visit each other. The preoccupation with ominous pots and water is a manifestation of the same belief.

According to their tradition, omen reading plays a great part in selecting the site for a new village. According to Campbell (1915:213-28) usually a few men accompanied their headman to inspect the site in a forest which had been reported to be a likely place. If, on entering the forest, they saw any of three kinds of quails flying, then they used to say, 'Some day in the future, a village established here will be deserted'. If, however, they saw these birds hatching eggs, or if they met a tiger or saw its footmarks, then they used to say, 'Some day in the future, a village founded here will thrive and become prosperous'. Omens are also taken in selecting the site of a house. Thus, when Ganesh Murmu separated from his father and wanted to set up a separate house, he kept a fowl at the site where he was to build his house. After five days, on the fowl remaining alive, Ganesh sacrificed it to *Maran Buru* and started building. Had

[31]See Crooke (1925:310-6); Beidelman, T.O., 'Kaguru Omens: An East African People's Concepts of the Unusual, Unnatural and Supernormal', *Anthropological Quarterly*, Washington, 36(2), April 1963, pp. 43-59.

the fowl died, the site would not have been considered auspicious.

It is not possible to mention here all the ominous'signs observed by the Santals. We shall, however, mention a few. If hens are seen touching or pecking each other with their beaks, guests are expected. If hens are seen spreading out their wings in the sun, rain is expected. The sight of a vulture alighting on the roof of a Santal house, indicates a coming death in that house. Similarly the hoarse cry of a jackal near a village foretells death in that village. If the milk of a pregnant woman escapes, it is apprehended that her child will be either still-born or die shortly after birth, for such milk is regarded as the tears of the child in the womb. If an earthenware water-pot suddenly breaks by itself, it is a sign of unforeseen calamity. If game is killed at the outset of a hunt, it presages good fortune during the rest of the hunt. The year in which the evening star (*hiduk ipil*) is more evident than the morning star (*bhurkak ipil*) indicates a famine. It is inauspicious to eat cooked rice on the *kharai* (threshing floor). If a goat enters the *kharai*, it is considered unlucky. Pigeons are supposed to be auspicious signs. A sty, *toke*, is said to be a sign of a liar. The interstices between a stringed bed (*parkom*), must always be odd in number otherwise the bed is considered unlucky. Similarly, the stringing of a *parkom* should be finished in one day lest the bed should 'eat up' the person who uses it. A fresh *bandi* is never opened to give rice on loan or in charity, lest the good luck of the house should go with it. Similarly, when a Santal sells any domesticated animal like a goat, sheep, cow, pig or buffalo, he must first pull out a few hairs from the animal's hind part, otherwise the luck of his family will depart with the animal.

The principle of sympathetic magic underlying omen reading appears to lie at the root of dream interpretations. Santal women are great believers in dream interpretation, regulating their behaviour according to what their dreams foretell.[32] The Santals also believe in auspicious and inauspicious days. Mondays and Thursdays are considered unlucky days.

[32]For a further study about dreams in primitive religions refer to S.C. Dube, 'Dreams in Two Primitive Tribes', *Man in India*, Ranchi, 29(1), Jan-Mar. 1949, pp. 18-28; Presler (1971:116-23).

No money transactions are carried out and no *bandis* are opened on these days lest the house be impoverished.

As mentioned earlier, it is very difficult to say what makes a good or bad omen. In most cases, the Santals themselves do not know, though a few did mention certain myths to account for their beliefs. One thing is certain, that the grip which this belief exercises on the Santal mind is so strong that, notwithstanding the modern rapid scientific progress, it still continues to shape the daily lives of the Santals.

TABOOS

Protection against the malevolent spirits and especially against the impersonal powers is sought by the Santals through a system of taboos or negative magic. The various taboos prevalent among the Santals are considered to be the best way of keeping oneself out of harm's way avoiding a direct or indirect contact with the malevolent powers.

The English word 'taboo' is derived from the Polynesian word 'tabu' which, in the Polynesian languages, simply means 'to forbid', 'forbidden' and which can be applied to any sort of prohibition. Realising that in this manner the word taboo has a much wider meaning than that used by anthropologists, Radcliffe-Brown preferred to regard a taboo as a ritual prohibition which he defined as 'a rule of behaviour which is associated with a belief that an infraction will result in an undesirable change in the ritual status of the person who fails to keep to the rule' (1959:134-5). Though different societies conceive of this 'change in the ritual status' differently, they have a common idea that an infraction results in misfortune.[33] It is interesting to observe how in the Santal mind, the concepts of sorcery, breach of taboo and *bonga* intrusion have become closely interwoven with one another. Though, as we have seen, *bonga* intrusion is generally aided by the human agency of the sorceress, the witch's power would be rendered ineffective unless the victim had not previously committed some breach of taboo.

[33]See Goode, (1964:113-4); Crooke (1925:381-413); Majumdar, D.N., *Races and Culture of India*, Bombay: Asia Publishing House, 1961.

The taboos which the Santals consider to be important and which are frequently observed by them are here classified according to the method adopted by Stith Thompson in his book *Motif Index of Folk Literature*.[34]

Taboos Connected with Supernatural Beings

In general, we can say that the goodwill of the *bongas* is positively achieved through sacrificial offerings, negatively through the observance of taboo rules.[35] Many of the taboos operative in the Santals' daily life can be directly traced to the urge to safeguard the 'interests' of the *bongas*. The fact that women are kept away from participation in the *jaherthan* that they cannot be present when sacrifices are offered, nor eat of the flesh of any animal there offered, has already been mentioned. So also the taboo on women not to eat the flesh of animals sacrificed to the *abge bongas* and to *Maran Buru*. Nobody can cut any of the sacred trees in the *jaherthan* or collect fallen branches. Women are barred from climbing these trees. The *kulhi* or village street is equally sacred. Accordingly, no one can drive a plough along the street, it must be carried on the shoulders. Similarly, to drag a clod crusher or leveller through the *kulhi* is tabooed. Other taboos are related only indirectly to the belief in spirits.

Sex Taboos

MARRIAGE

As already mentioned it is tabooed to marry outside the tribe or inside one's clan. Having sexual relations with persons from the above categories is also tabooed, so are adultery, homosexuality and bestiality. Such breaches are believed to incur the wrath of the spirits and to bring immediate punishment.

[34]Elwin (1955:513-29).

[35]Frazer, James, *The New Golden Bough*, New York: Mentor Books, 1964.

CHILDBIRTH

In Chapter V we have described two categories of taboos imposed on the parents of a child while still in the womb. One category is meant to protect the mother and child from the evil spirits and evil eye, while the second category is meant to protect the child from any physical or mental deformity.

RITUALS

To protect the religious functionaries prior to their ritual operations, certain taboos are enjoined on the *dihri, naeke* and *kudam naeke*. As already mentioned, these three are barred from having sexual relations on the night preceding their ritual performance. The same can be said of the *ojha* prior to any divination. The sexual act is said to be a mysterious power and is consequently tabooed before and during such auspicious occasions as rituals, divination and hunting expeditions.

WORK

Santal women must avoid a number of actions which men are permitted or even expected to do. Thus, women are not only barred from ploughing but it is also inauspicious for a Santal woman to even touch the plough.[36] Women are also tabooed from roofing a house, striking with an axe, shooting an arrow, stringing a *parkom*, playing on a flute, wearing male clothes. All these acts are, in varying degrees, suggestive of the male role. Such breaches would be regarded by the *bongas* as symbolic perversions.

FOOD TABOOS

EATING CERTAIN THINGS

The Santals in general have a taboo on the eating of the flesh of horses, cats and dogs. Several *khuts* have different

[36] Paramanik, Pramananda, 'Santal Superstition regarding Ploughing'' *Vanyajati*, Delhi, 4(4), Oct. 1956, pp. 154.

taboos regarding the kinds of food which must not be eaten. Thus, for example, the Gua Hembroms cannot eat eels. It is tabooed to eat uncooked rice for it is considered to be 'the food of the *bongas*' and if anyone eats it he will impoverish the house. Cooked food touched by a non-Santal especially by a *Deku* or a Muslim is taboo. The belief behind such a taboo is the fear of evil spirits and powers connected with alien people.

EATING BEFORE CERTAIN TIMES

As mentioned earlier, no Santal can eat of the first fruits of the *matkom* or the winter rice-crop before the *Baha* and the *Janthar* festivals are performed. Such breaches will incur the wrath of the *bongas*. It is taboo for a *dihri* and a *naeke* to break the rule of fasting before performing a sacrificial ritual. Likewise the *ojha* is also tabooed from eating before divination.

EATING AT CERTAIN PLACES

It is tabooed to eat in the *kharai* or threshing ground. Among other food taboos, we find that men and women cannot eat together. A person who is eating cannot serve food to himself but must tell someone else to serve him in case he wants more.

KINSHIP TABOOS

Besides the food and sex taboos, the Santals have also some tabooed relations between whom not only marriage or sexual relations must be avoided, but even their close contact is tabooed. Thus, the relation between a Santal and his younger brother's wife (*bokon bahu*) and between a woman and the husband of her younger sister (*ajhnarea*) is marked by many taboos, all of which are intended to prevent physical contact between the two. They cannot be alone either in a room or in a courtyard. They must never sit near each other or on the same bed, nor can they touch each other. During the *Baha* festival, they cannot throw water on each other. The relations between a woman and her younger brother's wife (*ajhnarea*) and a man and his wife's younger brother's wife (*bahonharea*) are governed by the same taboo. The taboo against touching the person is also extended to clothes, beds and food belonging to each other. Similarly, the mentioned relatives by marriage, together with parents-in-law (*balaea*) and husband and wife are tabooed from mentioning each other's name. When a reference to such names has to be made, they can be referred to by teknonymy, that is, in terms of the relation to their children.[37] When they have no children, they call each other using some general expression. This practice is observed not only when they are speaking to, or, about each other, but whenever they may have to mention their particular names. Breaches of this taboo are said to be punished in the next world.[38]

Miscellaneous Taboos

TABOOS AGAINST DOING CERTAIN THINGS AT CERTAIN TIMES

Like the Andamanese (Radcliffe-Brown, 1964:139), the Santals are tabooed from whistling at night lest the noise should attract the *bonga kuri*. Though women are not permitted to take part in the hunt, there are certain taboos which they must observe to protect their husbands from any dangers while they are away. These prohibitions are similar to those enjoined on widows. No woman may wear flowers in her hair nor bangles on her hands, both being signs of her married status.

SUBCLAN TABOOS

Besides food taboos, various subclans observe other taboos. Thus, as already mentioned, some of the Murmu *khuts* are tabooed from building houses with four-cornered roofs.

From what has been seen, it is evident that magico-religious beliefs also exist in the form of taboos which in turn reinforce

[37]For a similar custom among the Andaman Islanders, see Radcliffe-Brown (1959-146).

[38]Bodding, Paul Olaf, 'On Taboos and Customs Connected therewith among the Santals', *Journal of the Asiatic Society of Bengal*, Calcutta, 67(1), Pt. 3, 1898, pp. 1-24.

these beliefs. In most of the socio-religious taboos mentioned, a transgression incurs the displeasure of the *bongas*. Hence, an expiation has to be undergone. On the other hand, observance of these taboos ensures a certain protection. Certain taboos, especially those regarding sex are dealt with by the village council.

Another phenomenon found among the Santals and among various tribes throughout the world is what the Santals call *rum* or spirit-possession. Lewis called this phenomenon ecstatic religion.[39] According to Santal traditions, in choosing a *jaherthan* for their village, some Santals become possessed and the spirits are said to speak through them, demarcating the exact place where they want the sacred grove to be. Similarly, through spirit-possession, the stones at the foot of the *jaher* trees are said to be put at the command of the spirits themselves. Spirit-possession also occurs, as we have seen, during the *Umul Ader* and *Bhandan* funerary ceremonies and also in exorcising a *kisar bonga* and a *naihar bonga* from a house. Part of the *Baha* festival is called *Bonga Lagao*, during which three men are said to become possessed by *Jaher Era*, *Moreko-Turuiko* and *Maran Buru*. The Santals believe that through spirit-possession the *bongas* manifest their wishes to men.

RELATION BETWEEN MAGIC AND RELIGION

To the non-Santal, the various magical beliefs and practices described in this chapter might appear absurd, illusory and even erroneous. However, in order to understand the nature of such beliefs and practices, a sociologist must look at these 'social facts' not from his point of view but from that of the Santals. In other words, one should consider the nature and social function of these beliefs and practices as understood by those who take part in them. As already mentioned, the Santal has his own way of relating himself to nature and natural forces. He is aware of natural causes and conditions and of his own physical efforts to control them. Age-long experience

[39]Lewis, I.M., *Ecstatic Religion: An Anthropological Study of Spirit Possession and Shamanism*, Hermondsworth: Penguin Books, 1971.

of natural events, of animal and plant laws, has taught him how nature works. Out of observation and common knowledge he knows the time of rain, the possibility of good crops and he can also forecast future courses of nature. From one natural event, he can predict other natural events. To this extent, he is not fully dependent upon unseen forces. He is, however, also aware that, despite all his experimental knowledge and concentrated efforts, success may not always follow. Results are affected by agencies outside his sphere of control. When any evil befalls his household or his village community, he believes that some malevolent spirit or impersonal power is at work.

The Santals' ideas regarding the causes of disease or calamity can be classified into three categories: supernatural, human and physical. The action of *bongas* and black magicians like witches and sorcerers, come under the first two categories respectively. The Santals also acknowledge natural causes of certain illnesses. That these three categories are not mutually exclusive can be seen from the fact that in most cases, witches work through their *bongas* to cause disease or calamity. Similarly, a *bonga* or an impersonal power, may be the cause. This explains why an *ojha* usually combines both the medical and magical methods in treating a patient or a misfortune. This belief that most of the diseases and misfortunes are due to malevolent *bongas*, impersonal powers, witches or sorcerers, does not render the Santals mere passivists. They have developed remedial measures to cope with such unnatural problems. Among the most potent remedies we find magic, omens, and taboos. These are an essential part of the Santals' belief. They help them to react to the unknown and unknowable.

We can, therefore, say that, underlying the beliefs and practices in magic, omens, dreams, spirit-possession, and taboos, there is the same truth, namely, the conviction that one's personal welfare, as well as that of society, depends on establishing a balance between man, nature and the spirit world. By taking recourse to such activities, the Santals manifest their deep faith that such a balance can be achieved. As the idea behind their religious beliefs is alliance with the benevolent spirits and through them control of the malevolent *bongas*, the idea behind their magical beliefs and practices appears to be the need of avoiding, controlling and counteracting the harmful influences and energies of their physical and super-physical environment. This is the nature and function of such beliefs and practices. In other words, though the manifest function of magic even to the Santals may be a failure in the sense that it does not produce the effects that are expected or hoped for, the latent functions of magic are valuable. At the cognitive level, they provide explanations for physical and moral events which are otherwise inexplicable. At the affective level, they cure anxiety and helplessness, ritualising the Santals' optimism. At the social level, they help to increase the community's dependence and solidarity with their benevolent spirits.

Having analysed the nature and function of magic as practised by the Santals, we are now in a better position to show what the actual relationship is between magic and religion in the mind of the Santal. We shall also briefly examine as to what extent we can apply to the Santals some of the theories mentioned in the beginning of this chapter. We shall start by saying that magic is not absent from the Santal's dealing with the spirits. It can be used for social as well as anti-social ends as *ojhaism* and witchcraft show. The witch or sorceress accomplishes her nefarious activities through the aid of her 'husband' *bonga* from whom she actually learns the art of 'killing'. Witches and evil spirits work in close collaboration. The *ojha* or minister of white magic, on the other hand, invokes the aid of his tutelary spiririts or *saket bongas,* to foil the mischievous activities of the malignant spirits or of those spirits used by witches and sorcerers.

The Santal makes more than a mere 'ideal-typical distinction' between magic and religion. Thus, Goode's theory does not seem tenable in the case of the Santals. This is evident from the following differences. The ministers of Santal magic are different from those of Santal religion. This contradicts Firth's hypothesis, according to which the magical and the religious practitioners are the same. Similarly, while no training for worship or initiation is necessary for one to become a *naeke,* an *ojha* has to undergo a long course of training, after which he is formally initiated. Moreover, while the *naeke's* office is hereditary, that of the *ojha* is not. Broadly speaking, in religion proper the *naeke's* relation to the spirits is one of reverential fear, dependence, submission and propitiation. An alliance is sought with the benevolent spirits invoking their protection through sacrificial offerings, libations and invocations. In magic, the attitude of the *ojha* is one of defiance, control and domination through divinations, exorcisms and the use of *mantars* and *jharnis*. Another difference is that while the *naeke* relates more with personal spirits, the *ojha* deals more with impersonal spirits and powers. Thus, not only are the objects of magic and religion different but the attitudes of the *ojha* and the *naeke* also differ.

In spite of these differences, the Santals' perception of religion and magic are not mutually exclusive. The *ojha's* mission is like that of the *naeke* insofar as both aim to attain curative results that endure to the benefit of the Santals. Magic, consequently, overlaps the sphere of religion, which, however, covers experiences where the arts of magic do not reach, while magic also works independently in some situations. For the most part, however, the various approaches are simultaneously pursued. Magic and religion are often found together as parts of the same ritual and custom. This is evident in such marriage rituals as the *Dak Bapla*, *Cumaura* and *Parchau*; in the rites of cicatrization for boys and tattooing for girls; in the constant use of ominous pots and water in various rituals; in the use of lucky charms; in the various taboos, etc.

In consonance with Malinowski's theory, both Santal magic and religion are surrounded by taboos and observances based on mythological traditions. In situations of emotional stress, both contribute to the Santals' morale by infusing hope and confidence. However, in applying to Santal magic and religion, Malinowski's basic distinction between magic as instrumental and religion as expressive, one meets with certain difficulties. Santal religion can never be characterised as being purely expressive. Though, as seen in Chapters IV and V, the expressive aspect of Santal religion is very evident in their rituals, festivals and ceremonies, one cannot leave aside the instrumental aspect, namely, to invoke the protection of the benevolent *bongas* on the one hand, and to ward off the evil *bongas* on the other. Thus, in Chapter IV, we have analysed the various religious rites and ceremonies by which the Santals seek to ensure prosperity to their village community.

In our analysis of the Santals' rites of passage (Chapter V,) we have seen how these rites and ceremonies are mainly concerned with securing the active help of the benevolent spirits and the passive forbearance of the malevolent ones so as to ensure the safety and well-being of the individual. Likewise, to say that Santal magic is merely instrumental is not totally correct. Magic helps to reinforce certain values in the Santals. It contributes to human morale by infusing in the Santals feelings of hope and confidence in their efforts to cope with the unknown and the unknowable. This positive function of magic has been emphasised by Malinowski himself in his study of the Trobriand Islanders. Moreover, magic strengthens the Santals' conviction that a balance between man, nature and the spirit world is possible of achievement.

Another element which Malinowski failed to stress in his study of magic, is the negative aspect of magic. His emphasis does not exhaust the relationship of magic to social structures and processes. Magic among the Santals, as among other tribals, also comprises a set of human activities in which persons like witches and sorcerers, using sacred forces (what Durkheim called 'impure sacred forces') and agencies, achieve anti-social results and ends which are detrimental to the welfare of the individual. Paradoxically, however, these dysfunctional or anomic characteristics of black magic can be seen to have a positive functional significance for social control. Whiting, in her study of the Paiute Indians, has shown how sorcery, by inculcating a fear of magical retaliation for evil in the members of the tribe, restrains actions which would otherwise violate the rights of others.[40] Similarly, O'Dea attests to the significance of this social control function, remarking that, 'witchcraft and sorcery, by representing all that is forbidden in dramatic form... help to set out in bold relief what is held to be moral and good' (1969:107-8). This is exactly what is happening among the Santals. Moreover, the *ojha's* efforts to counteract and undo the evil caused by witches and sorcerers 'reinforces and re-confirms all that is the opposite of the evil practices'. (Ibid).

Durkheim's basic distinction, that in magic the client goes as an individual to a magician, while in religion he goes as a

[40]Whiting, Beaticre B., *Paiute Sorcery*, New York: Viking Fund Publications in Anthropology, No. 15, 1950.

member of a 'church' to the priest, does not adequately explain the distinction between Santal magic and religion. Though, magic ritualism, among the Santals, is the speciality of the *ojha*, once witchcraft is suspected, the case is not restricted merely to the afflicted person or to his household. It becomes a public affair, and the village community as a whole tackles the matter. This is evident from the various actions taken in verifying the result of the divination, in locating the witch and in punishing or getting rid of her. The *manjhi*, as the representative of the village community, warns the witch to desist from her nefarious work. Representatives of the village are sent to three other *ojhas* to confirm the *Sunum Bonga* divination. The whole village assembles to perform the divination through which they locate the witch's residence. Together, they go to the *jan guru* and, as a group, they punish the culprit. In this manner the afflicted person does not approach the magician as an individual but as a member of the village community. In fact, we can say that it is the village community as a whole which approaches the magician on behalf of the afflicted person. Moreover, the marked repugnance which, according to Durkheim, exists between magic and religion, especially the fact that 'magic takes a sort of professional pleasure in profaning holy things' and that 'in its rites (magic) performs the contrary of the religious ceremony' (1967:58), is not evident in the case of Santal magic and religion.

In conclusion, we can say that both magic and religion help the Santals to confront the unknown supernatural world and restore confidence to the mind of the community and the individual in situations which involve frustration and deprivation. In spite of this intimate relation which the Santals make between magic and religion, it is clear, from what we have said here, that the Santals do make a distinction between religious and magical elements. This, however, should not be understood to mean that magic and religion are considered to have a mutually exclusive character. Both the magical and the religious sphere are constantly overlapping each other in the Santals' life. This is evident from the various magico-religious rituals and customs prevalent among the Santals. It would, therefore, seem that wherever magic plays a role in man's life, it cannot be completely devoid of religion. Nor can we ever expect to find a religion that has eliminated magic completely. In either case, no study of religion can or should refrain from considering the aspect of magic.

Chapter VII

Conclusion: The Process of Change and Adaptation in Santal Religion

In this study an attempt has been made to portray Santal religion not as a set of abstract beliefs, or in isolation, but as an essential part of the Santal social structure. We have seen how the relationship between the Santal religious universe and the social structure is so intimate that one cannot be fully understood without the other. In the course of our study, we examined the Santal religious universe (Chapter III), that is, the supernatural spirits and powers which are believed to people the invisible world. We noted how the Santals actually regard themselves as being completely surrounded by these spirits or *bongas* and by impersonal powers which constantly manifest themselves, shaping the course of nature and of human events. Our analysis showed how the Santals are not mere worshippers of malevolent spirits as various scholars and missionaries have posited.

As a result of the power attributed to these spirits, the Santals firmly believe that it is necessary to harbour friendly relations with them. The intimate inter-relationship between the Santals and their spirits is concretely manifested in their seasonal rites and festivals which mark every important stage in their annual agricultural cycle (Chapter IV). In our analysis we have shown how, in bringing about success in an agricultural enterprise, religious and magical beliefs and rituals are as indispensable as the economic activity itself. The Santals' dependence on their spirits is also manifested in each stage of an individual's life-cycle. In Chapter V, our analysis was concerned with the various rituals and ceremonies which accompany the birth, initiation, marriage and death of every Santal. We have shown that the main object of all these rites and ceremonies is twofold: (*i*) to remove the pollution attendant on the individual's household and village community and to protect them against any calamities at the hands of the evil spirits; and (*ii*) to purify the individual himself, keeping him away from any hostile spirits and to ensure for him the security and protection given by the benevolent spirits.

Different from religion but closely related to it is Santal magic (Chapter VI). Here, an attempt was made to examine the nature and function of magic and witchcraft. In the course of our analysis, we focused on the *ojha* or medicine-man, witchcraft, evil eye, omens and auguries, and taboos. We noted how the spheres of Santal magic and religion overlap one another and how both are simultaneously pursued in the Santals' attempt at confronting the unknown supernatural world.

To sum up, we can say that the life of every Santal is cast within the framework of his religious and magical beliefs. These regulate his relationships with the visible and the invisible world around him. Underlying all religious and magical rituals and ceremonies is the conviction that the welfare of the society and of the individual depends on establishing a balance between man, nature and the supernatural universe. Though some of these practices may appear very strange to the non-Santal, to the Santal they are the means through which prosperity, safety and confidence for himself and his community can be secured. As the Santals' social organisation at the village, *Bungalow* and tribal levels aims at alliance and solidarity between its members, so also the Santals' religious beliefs, rites and festivals aim at bringing about an alliance with the benevolent spirits invoking their protection and through them controlling the malevolent *bongas*. Similarly the idea behind *ojhaism* is an avoidance and control of the harmful powers and influences which as in the case of witchcraft and sorcery are considered anti-social and thus a menace to solidarity. In what follows it is proposed to discuss two points: (*i*) to what extent can Santal religion, as we have described it, be classified as *Animism* or *Bongaism*, and (*ii*) to what extent has this system of beliefs and practices reacted to the impact of other religious systems like Hinduism and Christianity.

ANIMISM

The tribal religions in India have long been characterised as animistic. Thus, in the Census of 1901, the tribals were enumerated as animistic while in the 1911 Census they were classified as tribal animists. *Animism* from the Latin *anima*, meaning 'soul' is the doctrine whereby inanimate objects as well as living things are endowed with indwelling souls. Tylor popularised the term in his work, *Primitive Culture*. He showed how this belief originated in a mistaken but consistent interpretation of dreams, visions, hallucinations and similar phenomena.

It is true that the Santals believe in a host of spirits who are said to populate the world. It is also true that mountains, rocks, rivers, trees, etc., are believed to be inhabited by various powers. However, to describe Santal religion as animistic appears to us to be inaccurate, if not actually a misnomer. To show the inexactness of this term, it is important to first show the weakness of Tylor's theory. Being a rationalist, he explained religion as a mere intellectual effort to understand and control natural phenomena and biological events. In other words, he made early man too contemplative and rational. Second his approach was too individualistic. He tried to explain religion as mere individual action rather than as a social phenomenon. Finally, when confronted with the belief in a supreme deity prevalent among various primitive tribes, he tried to shun the difficulty by tracing the existence of such beliefs to the preaching of Christian missionaries. Various field studies reveal a great many aspects of early religion which cannot be placed in Tylor's scheme of *animism*.

Let us now come to Santal religion as we have described it in this study. We have shown how Santal religion is essentially social. The various beliefs and practices help to strengthen the Santals' social unity and contribute to the existence and maintenance of the social order. Santal religion permeates every aspect of the Santals' life. It colours their economy, tribal laws and customs. As we noted earlier, there is no individual approach to the spirits. Fellowship with them is maintained through sacrificial offerings made on behalf of a particular social unit which is sometimes the whole village and sometimes as small as the household and through ceremonial eating and drinking. Moreover, Santal worship centres round its sacred places—the *jaherthan*, *manjhithan* and *bhitar* which are communal in character.

It is inaccurate to think that the Santal attributes all the phenomena of nature and all the goods and ills of life to the *bongas* or to the mysterious impersonal powers. We have shown how, as a result of the observation of the processes of nature and through elementary reasoning based on such observation, the Santals have accumulated a certain amount of practical knowledge. They are aware that this experimental knowledge coupled with physical effort ordinarily produces definite desired results. They also acknowledge the natural causes of disease, making use of symptomatical remedies such as fomentation and massage. Their knowledge of medicines, made up from a large number of plants, herbs and other natural objects, manifests the Santals' knowledge of nature and of the things around them.

Our study of the Santals' beliefs and practices has shown that Santals do believe in a supreme deity whom they call *Thakur Jiu*. Though there is no specific worship in his honour, he is far from being a mere abstract conception. He is reverentially invoked in all important rituals, in solemn oath-takings and in the readmitting of an ostracised person into Santal society. Contrary to Tylor's view, the Santals' belief in this supreme deity cannot be attributed to the preaching of Christian missionaries.[1] According to their tradition, the earlier belief of the Santals centred round *Thakur*. Besides, the

[1]Andrew Lang indicated the existence among some Australian natives of the belief in what he called a 'high god', *The Making of Religion*, London: Longmans, Green & Co., 1898. Pater Schmidt (1931) adduced a lot of evidence to prove that this belief in a supreme deity was universal among all the peoples of the simplest cultures. He also showed that this belief could not be discarded as an irrelevant fragment of mythology, still less as an echo of missionary teaching.

Santals did not come in contact with Christian missionaries before the middle of the nineteenth century.

That the Santal religion differs from *animism* can also be seen in their ancestors' worship which occupies an important place in their religious beliefs. It keeps the memory of the dead alive and welds the community of the living into one with those who have lived in the past. All the spirits of the deceased members are regarded as forming one family with their living descendants and kinsmen whose welfare is now their special concern. The Santals look upon their dead ancestors with filial love and intimacy. Veneration of their ancestors is very deep. Special shrines, appropriate rites and appointed times for rituals commonly characterise their ancestor worship. Apart from periodical worshipping, the ancestral cult is also closely connected with the Santal festivals. Thus, in all festivals, public or private, rice-beer libations are made on their behalf. They are also given a very special place in the house, the *bhitar*. At the end of life, people look forward to being reunited with their loved ones. The performance of ancestor worship clearly suggests that the departed ancestors play a definite and decisive role in the Santals' life in general and in their religious beliefs and practices in particular.

Animism, as an explanatory theory of religious behaviour, does not take into account the emotional aspects of religion. For the Santals, however, the religious rituals and ceremonies evoke an emotion that goes beyond a mere response to practical needs. They bind the community together in their beliefs and give them a sense of the sacred. Collective ritual and rejoicing have served to intensify the emotional appeal of religion. Their major festivals and forms of worship can only be partially understood unless they are seen within the context of religious emotion or enthusiasm. It is interesting to note that S.C. Roy used the term 'spiritism' in designating the religion of the Kharias (1937: 332) and of the Oraons (1972:1). Elwin (1955) supports the concept of 'spiritism' in his study on the Savara tribe of Orissa. The latest Government Census Reports have also given up the use of the term *animism* to designate tribal religions.[2]

[2]For a further study of animistic beliefs among India's tribal

BONGAISM

Majumdar discards the idea that *animism* is the only form of religion among the tribals of India and offers an alternative view. In his analysis of the religious beliefs and practices of the Hos (1937), he opines that their religion is based on the theory of *Bongaism*, a term he himself coined. He maintains that the basic belief of the Hos lies in an impersonal and supernatural power, a force, called *bonga*. It pervades all space and is believed to take any shape or form. This power renders life to all animals and plants. He shows how the Hos have derived the idea of *bongas* from the original idea of a vague and mysterious power which 'evidences itself and is identified with things or objects of his environment'.[3] He identifies this power with the concept of *mana* as it is found in Melanesia. He does not restrict his view of *Bongaism* merely to the Hos but, by reference, implies that it is also validly applicable to describe the religious beliefs and practices of the Mundas and the Santals.

This extension of the view of *Bongaism* from the Hos to the Santals is inadequate to explain Santal religion. It fails to describe the Santals' perception of and relationship with their *bongas*. It is true, as we have seen, that the Santals do believe in a number of impersonal powers which are believed to cause havoc in nature and in the Santals' lives. There is, however, no evidence to show that either now, or in the past, the Santals have held beliefs which would justify one in maintaining that the word *bonga* can mean an impersonal and all-pervading power. Though it is true that Santal religion is one of power or of many powers, one is not justified in assuming that all these powers are either indeterminate or devoid of form and function.

The Santals have long attained the stage when man not only objectifies but also personifies the supernatural powers whom he propitiates. They not only differentiate between their

societies, see Crooke (1925:25ff); Presler (1971:51-5); and Vidyarthi (1977:239:41).

[3]D.N. Majumdar, *The Affairs of a Tribe A Study in Tribal Dynamics*, Lucknow: Universal Publishers Ltd., 1950, p. 278.

various spirits but have also a conception of individual spirits as distinguished from group spirits. They not only personify their *bongas*, allotting them fixed abodes, but also ascribe the more important among them with a more or less definite form and individuality.[4] Thus, as we have seen in our analysis of the *Baha* festival (Chapter IV), *Jaher Era*, *Maran Buru* and *Moreko-Turuiko*, are visualised in the shape of human beings. Similarly, spirit-possession also occurs in exorcising a *kisar bonga* and a *naihar bonga* from a house (Chapter III) and during the *Umul Ader* and *Bhandan* funerary ceremonies (Chapter V). According to tradition, in choosing a *jaherthan* for their village, some Santals become possessed and the spirits are said to speak through them to demarcate the exact place where they want their sacred grove. Similarly, through spirit-possession, the stones at the foot of the *jaher* trees are said to be put at the spirits' command.

Let us now come to the innumerable impersonal powers which are believed to cause havoc in nature and in the lives of the Santals. As seen in Chapters III and VI, the belief in these impersonal powers is one which the Santals share with the peasantry of North India (Crooke, 1925:183-226). They are not called *bongas*, but the Santals use the same terms which their neighbours use and speak of *bhuts*, *curins*, *rakas*, *ekagudias*, etc. This has led Culshaw to conclude that

> while there is much in the *bonga* cult that is distinctive of the Santals, they seem to have absorbed the general beliefs of the region regarding spirits that are not worshipped but feared (1949:92).

They are not directly connected with Santal religion. To evade and control them, the Santals take recourse to various magical rites and practices. While in their dealings with their *bongas*, the Santals call upon the services of the *naeke* and the *kudam naeke*, in dealing with these impersonal powers, they seek the services of the *ojha* and *jan guru*. The latter's attitude is mainly one of defiance, control and domination over these impersonal powers.

[4]For a similar argument regarding Oraon and Munda religion, see S.C. Roy (1972:81-2).

Finally, in the Santal language, I have not come across any term which is equivalent to the term *mana* of the Polynesians. Though the Santali grammar distinguishes between animate and inanimate, 'the distinction is not between living and dead matter, or between spirit and matter but between what, according to Santal ideas, has a soul and what has not'.[5] The Santal conception of animate and inanimate does not always coincide with what we may consider naturally one or the other. The Santals regard as animate those beings which are capable of independent action and movement. Certain words may, according to meaning, be constructed with either form. Thus, the word *buru*, when it refers to spirits, is animate and when referring to mountain it is considered as inanimate. The word *bonga*, however, is always constructed with an animate form. Basing himself on this argument, Culshaw concludes that:

> If there were any evidence of the word *bonga* being regarded as impersonal , and, therefore, (for a Santal) as inanimate, we would expect to find it reflected in the way in which the word is constructed in speech.[6]

In other words, it would seem that one must look elsewhere than in the Santals' belief in *bongas* for traces of a concept analogous to *mana* or to *Bongaism* as implied by Majumdar.

One thing is certain, that Santal religion like any other religion, cannot be defined by its subject-matter in a narrow sense as spirit worship or as ancestor worship or as the cult of nature. As Malinowski pointed out, 'The 'ism' of religion.... must be given up for religion does not cling to any one object or class of objects' (1954:36).

IMPACT OF HINDUISM AND CHRISTIANITY

I shall now examine in what manner and to what extent Santal religion, as described in this study, has reacted to its contact

[5]Bodding, Paul Olaf, *Materials for a Santali Grammar*, Pt. 2, Benagaria: Santal Mission Press, 1929, p. 29.

[6]Culshaw, W.J., 'Some Notes on Bongaism', *Journal of the Asiatic Society of Bengal* (*Letters*), Calcutta: 5, 1939, pp. 427-8.

with the impinging forces of Hinduism and Christianity. An important point to remember from the very beginning is that religion, like culture, has everywhere been undergoing a certain degree of change through a process of acculturation.[7] Acculturation includes those processes of change which result from contact conditions. One can distinguish two major types of acculturation: (*i*) incorporation; and (*ii*) directed change.[8] A process which facilitates the retention of original customs as well as the acceptance of new elements is called syncretism.[9]

The various forms of response to directed change can be classified under three main processes—assimilation, fusion and reaction. The process of fusion, or, as it is sometimes called, accommodation or reinterpretation, does not result in a complete assimilation which, in actuality, rarely takes place, since some features of the older culture always tend to survive. The process of reinterpretation consists in reinterpreting the meaning of the pre-existing element in such a way as to suit the form of the new element that has to be accepted. The reaction process frequently takes the form of nativistic movements.[10]

[7]The term was first given currency by certain American anthropologists who were interested in the study of the changing cultures of North American Indians. Redfield, R., R. Linton and M.J. Herskovitz, 'A Memorandum for the Study of Acculturation', *American Anthropologist*, Wisconsin, 38(1), Feb. 1936, pp. 149-52. See also M.J. Herskovits, et al, *Acculturation: The Study of Culture Contact*, New York: American Anthropological Association, 1938; R. Beals, 'Acculturation', in A.L. Kroeber, (ed.), *Anthropology Today: An Encyclopaedic Inventory*, Chicago: University of Chicago Press, 1953.

[8]Incorporation takes place when people of different cultures maintain an inter-change without pressure being applied by the dominant group over the other. The borrowerm, without losing its own identity, integrates in its own way elements from another culture.

Directed change takes place when one culture applies pressure over another with the result that the dominant group seeks to change the way of life of the dominated group.

[9]See M.J. Herskovits, 'Problem, Method and Theory in Afro-American Studies', *Afroamerica*, 1, 1945, p. 19.

[10]For a study of such movements among tribals see Raghaviah, V., *Tribal Revolts*, Nellore: Andhra Rashtra Adimjati Sevak Sangh, 1971; Jay, Edward, J., 'Revitalisation Movements in Tribal India', in L.P. Vidyarthi, (ed.), *Aspects of Religion in Indian Societies*, Meerut: Kedar Nath Ram Nath, 1961, pp. 282-315; Gough, Kathleen, 'Indian Peasant Uprisings', *Economic and Political Weekly*, Bombay, 9(32-34), August

Before settling down in Santal Parganas, the Santals, according to their traditions, have always been wandering from one place to another. It is only natural, therefore, that their religion, like their language and culture, has been influenced by the peoples with whom they came into contact. Santal religion has come under the impact of Islam, Hinduism, and Christianity. Its present day forms suggest that Hinduism has had the greatest influence, followed by Christianity.

ISLAM

Islam has had practically no effect at all. This is rather surprising especially when one takes into account that, for more than five centuries, from the thirteenth century onwards, the Santals were in contact with the Mohammedans. The area round Rajmahal and some other portions of Santal Parganas were of strategic and economic importance to the Mughal rulers.[11] In fact in 1592, Rajmahal was established as the capital of Bengal by Man Singh, Akbar's Viceroy in Bengal and remained so till 1660.

There is, however, a remarkable abhorrence, among the Santals, of the Mohammedans whom they call *Turuk*, a term which carries a connotation of contempt. According to their tradition, the sojourn of the Santal ancestors in 'the corrupt and defiled land' of the Muslims was attended with such grave harassment that contact with Muslims must be avoided. Some Muslim traders from Bara and Chota Madansahi, do visit Pangro regularly either to sell cattle or to buy paddy or straw. The Santals of Pangro, like many other Santals elsewhere, however, do not accept food from these Muslims. This is due to the belief that if they were to do so, their benevolent spirits would be defiled and would take away all their protection.

1974, pp. 1391-412; Singh, Kumar Suresh, *Dust Storm and Hanging Mist. Study of Birsa Munda and His Movement*, Calcutta: Firma K.L. Mukhopadhyaya, 1966; Fuchs, Stephen, *Rebellious Prophets*, Calcutta: Asia Publishing House, 1965.

[11]Roy Chaudhury, P.C. (1965:49-56).

HINDUISM

The tribals of India have been influenced by the traditions of their neighbouring communities, the dominant community often being the Hindu community. From very early times, there have been several points of contact between the Hindus of the area and the tribal communities living within it. This is evident from the fact that tribals have borrowed heavily from the ideas and institutions of the Hindus.[12] This influence, however, does not justify the statistical manpiulation of religion in the Indian Census material, according to which tribal India is practically Hindu by religion. According to the 1961 Census data, only 4.19 per cent of the tribals declared themselves as followers of a tribal religion while 89.39 per cent have been declared as Hindu by religion.[13]

Commenting on the Census data, Orans noted that, 'The Indian Government's figures on Hindu religious identification are largely an artifice of Census methods, and.... often of coercion as well' (1965:89). A similar view is expressed by Culshaw who remarks that the fact that in the 1931 Census, 50 per cent of the Santals were returned as Hindus indicated, 'the heightened political consciousness of the enumerators more than any real division within the tribe' (1949:15). In other words, although one does find a lot of similarity between various tribal beliefs and the Hindu religious beliefs and practices, the picture of total absorption of tribal religions by Hinduism, as implied by the Censuses is rather misleading. This is not to say, however, that certain tribes, like for example the Bhumij, the Parahiyas and the Tharus have not been largely absorbed in the Hindu social order.[14] What is meant is that as it is an extreme viewpoint to

[12]Bose. N.K., 'The Hindu Method of Tribal Absorption', *Science and Culture*, Calcutta, 7(4), October 1941, pp. 188-94; Kalia, S.L., 'Sanskritisation and Tribalisation', in T.B., Naik, (ed.), *Changing, Tribe*, Chindwara: Tribal Research Institute, 1961.

[13]Vidyarthi (1977:237). I refer to the 1961 Census data because of the fact that no mention is made of tribal religions in the 1971 Census Paper 2 of 1972 which deals with the religion of India's population.

[14]See S. Sinha, 'Changes in the Cycle of Festivals in a Bhumij Village', *Journal of Social Research*, Bihar, 1(1), Sept. 1958, pp. 24-49 and 'Tribal Cultures of Peninsular India as a Dimension of Little Tradition in the Study of Indian Civilisation'. *Journal of American*

deny any impact of Hinduism on tribal religion, so also the views that tribal religion is a backward form of Hindu religion[15] or that the distinction between tribal religion and Hinduism is meaningless,[16] is another extreme and as such not tenable. In this context, N.K. Bose remarks that:

> One might indeed say that tribes can be regarded as being fully absorbed in the Hindu fold if Brahmin priests perform Brahminical ceremonies for them during the three critical events of birth, marriage and death. If the latter are still celebrated by tribal rituals, then the communities are still true to their own faith in spite of the fact that, in the outer fringes of their culture, they participate in some of the ceremonies of their Hindu neighbours.[17]

Moreover, one must not brush aside the fact that the tribal population has contributed to the building of Hinduism. Majumdar, in his study among the Hos of Singhbhum, has referred to the concept of trans-culturation which reflects the reciprocal impact of a tribal culture on the Hindu castes living in tribal areas.[18] Kalia (1959) has described the process of 'tribalization' among the Khasas of Uttar Pradesh and Madhya Pradesh, concluding that the high caste Hindus have accepted the beliefs and ritual practices of the tribal people among whom they are staying.[19]

Another point to be kept in mind is that one must not

Folklore, Philadelphia, 71(281), July-Sept. 1958, pp. 504-18; Sahay, K.N., 'A Study in the Process of Transformation from Tribes to Caste: Parahiyas of Lolki. A Case Study', *Journal of Social Research*, Ranchi, 10(1), Mar. 1967, pp. 64-89; Srivastava, S.K., *The Tharus—A Study in Culture Dynamics*, Agra: Agra University Press, 1958.

[15]Ghurye, G.S., *The Scheduled Tribes*, (3rd edition), Bombay: Popular Prakashan, 1963, p. 20.

[16]Elwin, Verrier, 'The Loss of the Nerves: A Comparative Study of the Contact of People in the Aboriginal Areas of Bastar State, Central Province of India', 1952.

[17]Bose, N.K., *Tribal Life in India*, New Delhi: National Book Trust, India, 1971, p. 66.

[18]Majumdar, D.N., *The Affairs of a Tribe: A Study in Tribal Dynamism*, op.cit.

[19]Kalia, S.L., op.cit.

confuse the movement of even large numbers of Santals to Hinduism with the more complex question of the absorption of Santal religion into Hinduism.[20] Datta-Majumder (1956: 124) shows how, though various Santals have been converted to Hinduism, their change of affiliation has not meant a complete break with earlier religious conventions. They have retained many of their tribal beliefs and customs.[21] Similarly, though there have been formal mass conversions of tribals to Hinduism, these were rarely a complete break. Most tribes have retained a large portion of their traditional beliefs and practices.[22]

Earlier, writers referred to the process of Hinduisation and prophesied that the primitive religions would fade out of Indian life. More recently, however, scholars have criticised the theory of Hinduisation or Sanskritisation[23] because it goes far beyond the facts discovered in fieldwork. The theory is correct in insisting that various tribal religions have undergone considerable Hindu acculturation.[24] It, however, goes too far in assuming the elimination of tribal religions.[25] Both the terms

[20]Roy, S.N., 'The Conversion of Santal to Hinduism', *Journal of the Bihar and Orissa Research Society*, Patna, 2(1), March 1916, pp. 87-8.

[21]Similarly, S.C. Roy (1970:269) points out that there are large numbers of Hinduised Mundas who, though they no longer join in their old national forms of worship have not yet dispensed with the office of the village *pahan* who still offers the customary sacrifices to the village spirits.

[22]In the eighteenth century, the Manipuris, Koches and Kacharis were declared by the Brahmins true Hindus of Kshatriya status and provided with fictitious genealogies. See Fuchs, Stephen, *The Aboriginal Tribes of India*, Delhi: The Macmillan Co. of India, 1973, p. 70. Similar transformations have occurred in Gujarat and other parts of India.

[23]The theory as expounded by M.N. Srinivas does not confine itself to Hindu castes but shows how it also occurs among tribal and semi-tribal communities such as the Bhils of Western India, the Gonds and Oraons of Central India. *Social Change in Modern India*, Bombay: Allied Publishers, 1966, p. 6.

[24]See Bailey (1959); Shah, P.G., *Tribal Life in Gujarat*, Bombay: Bharatiya Vidya Bhavan, 1964; Nath, Y.V.S., *Bhils of Ratanmal*, Baroda: Maharaja Sayajirao University of Baroda, 1960.

[25]Refer to McKim Marriott, 'Little Communities in an Indigenous Civilisation', in McKim Marriott (ed.), *Village India*, Bombay: Asia

Hinduisation and Sanskritisation seem to imply an identity crisis, connoting that those who have adopted a number of Hindu deities or begun to imitate Hindu rituals have forsaken their traditional religion.

The influence of Hinduism on Santal religion cannot be discounted. For at least a thousand years before the advent of Islam in the thirteenth century, the Santals may be said to have been in contact with the Hindus (Datta-Majumder, 1956: 53). As a result, various aspects of Santal life—material, social, economic, linguistic and religious—have been affected by Hindu culture. In this section, on the basis of the data on Pangro which has already been discussed in the previous chapters, an attempt will be made to analyse the exact nature of the influence which Hinduism has had on the religious beliefs and practices of the Santals. The influence of Hinduism on other aspects of Santal life has been discussed by other scholars such as Amir Ali, Banerjee and Kochar.[26]

In the four foregoing chapters, we have seen how the very name *Thakur*, which the Santals use to denote their supreme deity, is of Hindu origin. Hindu deities like *Siva*, *Lakshmi*, *Parvati*, *Ram*, *Kali*, *Durga* and *Krishna* have been adopted and given a place in the Santal pantheon of *bongas*. Similarly, the Santals have also certain festivals, like the *Chata*, *Pata* and *Jatra* which are believed to be of Hindu origin. As Kolean remarks, 'From the *Dekus* we have, from time to time, taken over many festivals, but among these there is only one festival that the whole village celebrates, viz., the *Karam*' (Bodding, 1942: 158).[27] Though, as we have seen in Chapter VI, the majority of the Santals of Pangro do not worship *Durga* or *Dibi* as it is called by the Santals, *Dasae Parab*, the Santali name for

Publishing House, 1961, pp. 175-227; Cohn, Bernard S., 'The Changing Status of a Depressed Caste', in McKim Marriott, (ed.), ibid., pp. 54-79.

[26]Amir, Ali, *Then and Now—A Study of Socio-Economic Structure and Change in Some Villages near Vishva-Bharati University, Bengal*, Calcutta: Asia Publishing House, 1960; Banerjee, Hemendra Nath and Biman Kumar, Das Gupta, 'The Santal of Madhupur, Purulia District', *Bulletin of the Department of Anthropology*, Calcutta, 8(2), 1959, pp. 55-62; Kochar, V.K., 'Profile of a Tribal Village', *Vanyajati*, Delhi, 12, 2, April 1964, pp 80-95.

[27]See Datta-Majumder (1956:49).

Durga Puja, is a big feast for the Santals. Following the Hindu custom, new clothes are bought for the household members and also for the servants. This feast also marks the end of the course in *ojhaism*. All the Santals of Pangro and of the neighbouring villages flock to Sahibganj to see the various shrines and to take part in the festivities.

The institution of the *ojha* shows a great deal of Hindu influence. Most of the *saket bongas* invoked by the Santal *ojhas* have names of Hindu origin. The term *ojha* is not a Santal word but a Hindi word. Similarly, many of the *mantars* (magic spells) used by the *ojhas* are not in Santali but in a corrupt form of Hindi or Bengali. The very word *mantar* is derived from the Sanskrit *mantra*. The work of a Santal *ojha* resembles, to a certain extent, that of his Hindu counterpart. The Hindu influence on *ojhaism* is so great that Bodding (1925b: IV) and other writers, have been led to believe that the Santals have borrowed the whole institution of *ojhaism* from the Hindus.

We noted in Chapter V that some of the marriage and funerary ceremonies described are closely analogous to certain Hindu practices. Similarly, when a couple cannot secure the birth of a child, as a last resort they approach the *bongas* said to be latent in certain Hindu shrines. Moreover, one of the largest fairs which the Santals of Pangro and of the neighbouring villages attend, is the one held at Moti Jharna on *Shiva Ratri* symbolising the marriage of *Mahadev* with *Parvati*. No Santal marriage, except, among Santal Christians, is performed in Pangro and in the neighbouring villages before this fair.

The Santal belief in *orak bongas* has its counterpart in the Hindu belief in *Grha-Lakshmi*. The Santal *jaherthan* may be compared with the Hindu *Panca-vati*. Though there is a difference regarding the species of the trees, the sacred nature of both places and the same number of trees, point to this. *Maran Buru* has his counterpart in the Hindu deity *Mahadev* or *Siva*. As mentioned in Chapter III, Culshaw (1949:92) is of the opinion that the Santals borrowed the belief in *curins, bhuts, rakas* and *ekagudias* and impersonal powers from their neighbours. Ritualistic importance attached to such articles as cowdung, vermilion, turmeric and cowrie shells, is also shared by both groups. Similarly, blood sacrifice is an important element in both Santal worship and Hindu *Sakti* cult.[28]

Some scholars have tried to explain these similarities by assuming that the Santals have borrowed them from the Hindus. Except in certain obvious cases, however, this hypothesis is not tenable. While not denying the Hindu elements to be found in *ojhaism* as prevalent among the Santals, various authors have shown that Bodding's idea of the Santals' borrowing this practice from the Hindus is invalid. Thus, according to Datta-Majumder, a closer scrutiny of the circumstances reveals the operation of a different process. He points out that:

> the culture complex of magic (in the form of *ojha*-science) was lent and re-borrowed, came back where it started, but in the process of diffusion and re-diffusion it gathered new experiences and underwent novel changes (1956:114-5).

Orans sees a process of emulation operating in the borrowing of Hindu words in the *mantars* which the *ojha* uses, pointing out that 'it is rather a case of connecting status and efficacy which is expressed in the Santal reference to Hindus as '*big* and *knowing* people'' (1965:126).[29]

Risley's view that *Sindradan* (the applying of vermilion on the bride's forehead) has been borrowed by the Santals from the Hindus, is also of doubtful validity.[30] Basing himself on the importance of the red colour in Santal ritual practices and also on the fact that, as in the case of *itut bapla*, a Santal boy can marry a Santal girl by merely rubbing *sindur* on her forehead, Datta-Majumder (1956:127-8) sees *Sindradan* as a process of diffusion and re-diffusion. Orans (1965:96) records the saying of a certain Mr. F. according to whom it is the Hindus who borrowed the use of vermilion from the Santals. Judging that such an important ingredient of culture is not usually borrowed, it is preferable to consider it as a case of cultural similarity.

[28]For further similarities between Santal and Hindu beliefs and customs see Mitra, Archana, 'Notes and News', *Folklore*, Calcutta. 13(5), May 1972, pp. 193-4.

[29]See Culshaw (1949:23).

[30]Risley, H.H., *The Tribes and Castes of Bengal*, Vol. 1, Calcutta: The Bengal Secretariat Press, 1891, p. 230.

Various authors have seen the throwing of water by the Santals on one another during the *Baha*, as an example of cultural borrowing of *Holi*.

The other close similarities mentioned can only be explained by the principle of reciprocal borrowing which seems to have operated throughout the long period of contact between the Santals and the Hindus. Conclusions, however, must be drawn with extreme caution. There has been so much mutual borrowing that it is almost impossible to point out with certainty who borrowed from whom.

The motivation to borrow Hindu deities can be ascribed to the hardships suffered by the Santals at the hands of their Hindu landlords and money-lenders whom they called *Dekus*, a term which signifies the indifferent or hostile outsider who is to be shunned.[31] This might seem a contradiction. A question arises as to how it is that the Santals tried to improve their rank by emulating a number of ritual practices prevalent among the Hindu oppressors whom they wanted to expel. We shall now try and explain this phenomenon. As we pointed out in Chapter II, the material conditions of the Santals were so desperate that they rebelled against their oppressors in 1855. The claim of Sidhu and Kanhu that it was God's wish that the Santals revolt against the oppressors gave the leaders the authority they required to be accepted by the Santals and to start the rebellion. The gods could not fail them.

The defeat of the Santal rebellion, however, shook their belief in the efficacy of their *bongas*. As a result of relative deprivation and constant exploitation, the Santals were anxious to try any means to improve their economic condition. They now had principally three directions to which they could turn—Islam, Hinduism and Christianity. For reasons already mentioned earlier, the choice of Islam was out of the question. This left only two alternatives—Hinduism and Christianity. Considering the milieu in which they were, it is understandable that the Santals adopted the socio-religious practices of the Hindus. It was believed that by doing so they would improve their

[31]Mahapatra, Sitakanta, 'The Insider Diku: Boundary Rules and Marginal Man in Santal Society', *Man in India*, Ranchi Vol. 56, No. 1, Jan.-March 1976, p. 38.

economic status. As Orans pointed out, 'The goal of rank improvement is suggested by a number of ritual practices emulative of Hindu customs which accompanied the rebellion' (1965: 33). Though the Hindu elements were more prevalent, the Christian influence, as we shall see in the next section, must not be underestimated.

The realisation that the path to better economic conditions through military force was closed, marked the beginning of a new consciousness which manifested itself in various movements, the first of which was called the Kharwar movement which led to increased Hindu acculturation.[32] It is not known exactly when the movement actually started. It, however, achieved prominence in 1871 when Bhagirath Manjhi of Godda sub-division, who added the title of *babaji* to his name, announced that he would restore the Golden Age if the Santals returned to the worship of one god and cleansed themselves of their sins. As the 'king' of the 'New Santal Raj'[33] he endeavoured to liberate the Santal country from the oppressors. By exhorting the people to worship the Hindu deity *Ram*, whom he identified with the Santal *Cando*, he assured them that their lands would be recovered. Their present oppression, he explained, was a divine punishment for abandoning the worship of the one god and turning to the veneration of minor and evil

[32]According to Skrefsrud, the word *Kharwar* 'is the ancient name of the Santals and in their minds is inseparably associated with the Golden Era of their history, namely the time when they lived in Campa in absolute independence and had no rent or tribute to pay but only to bring a small annual offering to their leaders in virtue of their office'. A.P. Jha, 'Nature of the Santal Unrest of 1871-75 and the Origin of the Sapha Hor Movement', *Indian Historical Records Commission Proceedings*, 35, No. 2, Feb. 1960, pp. 103-13.

The various Bhagat Movements which have emerged among the Oraons, Bhils and several tribes of Chotanagpur constitute in many ways the most sanskritised groups among the tribal communities. See S.C. Roy (1972:227-97); Doshi, *Bhils: Between Societal Self-Awareness and Cultural Synthesis*, New Delhi: Sterling Publishers (P) Ltd., 1971, pp. 166-75. The closing years of the nineteenth century saw the rise of an eclectic religion amongst the Mundas. Known as Birsa Dharam after its founder Birsa Munda this religion is a mixture of Hinduism and Christianity. S.C. Roy (1970: 188-95); Singh, Kumar Suresh op.cit.

[33]Kathleen, Gough, op.cit., p. 1396.

spirits.[34] When the number of his followers began dwindling, since they were unable to recover their land, Bhagirath changed the style of his preaching, particularly after the severe famine of 1874. He told the people that the rebellion had failed because they had committed the sin of having sexual relations with non-Santal women. Only if they purified themselves would god, or, *Ram Cando*, restore their lands. He instructed the people not to let fowls or pigs pollute the Burma rice (imported by the Government because of the famine), and to bathe daily before cooking their food.

The new norms of behaviour which Bhagirath sought to impose on the Santals certainly reflected Hindu notions of ritual purity and pollution. The people, however, began to lose faith in Bhagirath when they found that they had to repay the Government for the Burma rice which they had thought was a gift. Later, when he attempted to politicise the movement by instigating the Santals to refuse payment of taxes on the land they cultivated, Bhagirath was arrested and imprisoned.

After Bhagirath, the movement was kept alive by several *babajis* who claimed to have received a mandate from *Ram Cando* to work for the economic upliftment of the Santals. In general, they were more preoccupied with religious ideas than with political action. In 1880 Dubia Gosain, who came from the vicinity of Deoghar, introduced the worship of the *babaji* in the manner of reverence paid to the *sanyasis* by the Hindus. He smeared his body with ashes and kept long hair and also started taking *ganja*. Using the Census operations of 1881, he instigated the Santals to clamour for a tribal administration. The Santals objected to the numbering of their houses and the recording of their names. The British Government took immediate action, arresting Gosain and placing the entire area under the control of the police and the army.

After this, although mention is made of an outbreak during the 1897 famine, the Kharwar movement went underground and in the next few decades it split into three distinct sects—the

[34]His teaching was in keeping with the Santal traditions that their ancestors had no *bongas* but only worshipped *Thakur*, the supreme deity.

Sapha Hor, *Samra* and *Babajiu*.[35] Even after their division, the three sects retained the same practices, sharing in common the worship of *Ram Cando*. Later, however, these sects became more sharply differentiated with the *Sapha Hor* emerging as the more sanskritised and exclusive. The members of the *Sapha Hor* observed strict commensal norms which forbade eating in the houses of those who did not belong to the sect. These 'outsiders' were not invited to participate in ceremonies and life-cycle events of the *Sapha Hor* members. They abandoned what they considered to be degrading practices such as the keeping and eating of fowls and pigs and the drinking of *handi* or other intoxicants. They could eat their morning meal only after taking a purificatory bath. They also recognised *Mahadev* as their one god.

In 1930, a new reform movement started by Bangam Manjhi attracted a lot of followers. His teachings supported the practices of the *Sapha Hor*, particularly the daily purificatory bath and abstaining from meat and liquor. To these, Bangam added the exclusive use of khadi clothing and exhorted the Santals not to dance anywhere except in their village. In May 1930, 210 Santals were invested with the sacred thread or *janeo* (Fuchs, 1965:57). The *janeo-dhari* Santals (those who wear the sacred thread) regarded themselves as socially superior to those who did not wear the thread. They were reluctant to intermarry or to have social intercourse with the non-*janeo-dhari* Santals. A wide cleavage separated the two groups.

As a result of the Kharwar movement, especially the working of its three sects, the Santals were generally moving towards Hinduisation with increasing ambivalence. The emulation of Hindu socio-religious practices was regarded as a means of improving their economic status. But in the 1930's, political events external to Santal society, helped to check this drift

[35]The name *Sapha* is derived from the word *sapha* which means 'to clean' and refers to the cleansing out of what were considered to be objectionable practices. *Samra* was the village in Godda sub-division where the founder of this sect lived. *Babajiu* was the name of the sect which represented the original group. See Bodding, P.O., 'The Kharwar Movement among the Santals', *Man in India*, Ranchi, 1(3), Sept. 1921, pp. 222-32; 'A Santal Sect', *The Modern Review*, Calcutta, 31, March 1922, p. 358.

which seemed to be threatening their tribal solidarity. The path which the Santals were following was altered profoundly. This change was marked by a shift in emphasis from the socio-religious to the political aspect with a native socio-cultural resurgence.

With the spread of the National Freedom Movement, a new political consciousness emerged that was marked by a sense of an exclusive Adivasi identity. In 1938, Jai Pal Singh, an Oxford-educated Christian Munda, started in Ranchi an Adivasi political movement which, twelve years later, came to be known as the Jharkhand Party.[36] It aimed at establishing a tribally dominated State, asserting its tribal identity and autonomy of the region. It declared that the Jharkhand was the homeland of the Adivasis and that there was little hope of their regeneration unless the non-Adivasi exploiters quit the area.[37] Though it did not originate among the Santals, the ideology of the Jharkhand movement coincided with the aspirations of the Santals. As a result, many Santals became members. Having emulated their Hindu neighbours to a great extent, yet desirous of maintaining their identity, the Jharkhand movement, though essentially a political movement, gave the Santals an opportunity to create a 'great tradition' of their own. As Orans reported:

> The movement is spoken of in the following terms 'we should not leave our religion; we should continue to use rice-beer; we should have our worship at the sacred grove;

[36]The word Jharkhand literally means 'a tract of forest'. Chotanagpur, Santal Parganas and other adjacent districts belonging to the States of Bengal, Orissa and Madhya Pradesh are considered to be parts of the Jharkhand by the protagonists of the party.

[37]In January 1955, a memorandum was submitted to the State's Reorganisation Commission for the formation of a separate State of Jharkhand to be made up of six districts of Bihar and nine districts of Bengal, Orissa and Madhya Pradesh. The homogeneity, the geographical contiguity, the economic feasibility, the ethnic identity and the administrative separativeness were emphasised. This demand, however, was rejected. For a more detailed study of the Jharkhand Movement see Sharma K.I., 'Jharkhand Movement in Bihar', *Economic and Political Weekly*, Bombay, 11(1-2), Jan. 10, 1976, pp. 37-43.

also we should not stop eating beef. We will call our religion *Sarna Dhorom*' (1965:106).[38]

It can now be seen that continuous first-hand contact between the Santals and the Hindus did create a condition favourable for acculturation and generally led to reciprocal borrowings. By itself, however, this contact was not a sufficient cause for any radical readjustment. It was mainly with the Kharwar movement that the acculturation of the Santals to Hinduism was accelerated. The material conditions of the Santals facilitated the success of this movement. In fact, the movement has been periodically stirred into new life especially after recurring disasters of famine and epidemic which were believed to be signs of God's displeasure.

The socio-religious aspect of the movement consisted in the adoption of certain Sanskritic beliefs and practices such as the introduction of various Hindu deities in the Santal pantheon, the addition of the *Pata* and *Chata* to the Santal festival cycle, the avoidance of the meat of fowls and pigs, the giving-up of liquor, and the daily purificatory bath. The movement, however, has lost its hold and many have relinquished it, going back to ordinary Santal worship. Since the 1920s, efforts have been made by more than one Hindu organisation, mainly by the *Vaishnavas* to bring the Santals into the Hindu fold by giving them *Suddhi* or ceremonial purification.[39] The Arya Samaj has actively campaigned to convert the Santals, persuading them to declare themselves as Hindus. But so far the impact has not been very strong.[40]

The adoption of a number of Hindu deities, festivals, customs and concepts, however, has not changed the basic character of Santal religion. The belief in the *bongas* is still strong. Similarly the most important annual festivals described in Chapter IV and the rites of passage (Chapter V) are still

[38]*Sarna* is the Munda word for 'Sacred Grove' while *Dhorom* is the Oriya word meaning 'religion'.

[39]See Mukherjea (1962:380-1).

[40]The same thing is recorded by S.C. Roy in his study of the Oraons (1972: 293). He attributes the failure of the Arya Samaj mainly to its somewhat abstract conception of God which does not satisfy the Oraons' emotional needs.

observed in many Santal villages. Though some Santals have been converted to Hinduism, this has not meant a complete break with their earlier religious conventions. They still retain a number of their tribal beliefs and practices. In spite of newer accretions and borrowings, the Santals have preserved the essential core of their religious traditions. As Mukhopadhyay pointed out, 'the religion of the Austrics is still a distinctive culture and . . . can be seen in its pristine glory even today' (1965:14-5).

In short, we can say that, though all aspects of Santal life have been affected by contact with the neighbouring Hindus, the degree of change is least in the Santal religious sphere. This, by and large, has also been the case among those Santals who migrated to industrial areas such as Chittaranjan (Mohsin) and Jamshedpur (Orans) or to the tea gardens of West Bengal (Das and Banerjee) and Assam (Giri).[41]

CHRISTIANITY

The study of cultural change among the Santals as among other tribals in Chotanagpur and north-east India, would be incomplete without taking into account the influence of Christian missionaries.[42] While the impact of Hinduism, as we have seen in the preceding section, has been felt for several centuries, Christianity is a relatively modern force in the area. The Santals first began to attract the attention of Protestant

[41]Mohsin, Mohammed, Chittaranjan, *A Study in Urban Sociology*, Bombay: Popular Prakashan, 1964; Orans, (1965); Das, Amal Kumar and H.N. Banerjee, *Impact of Tea Industry on the life of the Tribals of West Bengal*, Calcutta: Tribal Welfare Department, Govt. of West Bengal, 1964; Das, Amal Kumar and S.K. Banerjee, *Impact of Industrialisation on the Life of the Tribals of West Bengal*, Calcutta: Tribal Welfare Department, Govt. of West Bengal, 1962, See also Mukherjee, Bhabananda, 'Santals in Relation to Hindu Castes', *Man in India*, Ranchi, 40(4), Oct.-Dec. 1960, pp. 300-06; Presler (1971: 236-37).

[42]The first impact of Christian missionaries in tribal areas was felt by the Khasis of Assam in 1813, the Oraons of Chotanagpur in 1850 and the Bhils of Madhya Pradesh in 1880. For an account of Christian missions among the Oraons, see S.C. Roy (1972: 243-6); among the Mundas, see S.C. Roy (1970: 132-4, 138-9, 144-52, 177-84, 201-3); among the Bhils, see Doshi, op.cit., pp. 175-7.

missionaries in the first half of the nineteenth century. The American Free Will Baptist Mission was the first mission to take up regular mission work among the Santals. When Eli Noyes, on 29 December 1838, 'came to a small village in the heart of a dense jungle' somewhere on the borders of Bengal and Orissa, a new factor was introduced in Santal history. In a few years, mission stations were opened in the western portions of Midnapore district and in Orissa.[43] The Church Missionary Society of England was the next mission to take up work among the Santals. The Rev. E. Droese, a German missionary, started work among the Mal Paharias at Bhagalpur in the beginning of the 1850s. He also opened up a few schools among the Santals of that area.

The main Christian missionary activity among the Santals of Santal Parganas started after the Santal rebellion had directed public attention to their affairs. It was the time when exploitation and oppression were most poignantly felt. In 1862, the Rev. E.L. Puxley and the Rev. W.T. Storrs of the Church Missionary Society, began to work in the northern part of the new district. On 26 September 1867, Mr. Boerresen, a Dane and Lars Olsen Skrefsrud, a Norwegian, took up residence at Benagaria in Dumka sub-division. Their mission was known as The Indian Home Mission to the Santals.[44] The United Free Church of Scotland began work in the south-western part of the district in 1870. In 1884, the American Methodist Episcopal Mission started work in the Pakaur sub-division. Other Protestant societies that have made notable contributions to missionary work in the district are the Plymouth Brethren at

[43]See Hodne, Olav, 'Early Missionary Work among the Santals', *Santal Theological Seminary: Fiftieth Anniversary, 1916-1966*, Benagaria: Santal Mission Press, 1966, pp. 4-11; Culshaw, W.J., 'Early Records Concerning the Santals', *Man in India*, Ranchi, 25(3), Sept. 1945, pp. 191-3.

[44]In 1910, this name was changed into The Santal Mission of the Northern Churches. As time passed, the work done by the Lutherans among the Santals in Santal Parganas spread to the Santals in the States of Assam, Orissa, and West Bengal. This was the reason why a new name, The Northern Evangelical Lutheran Church, was given. See Gausdal, Johannes, 'The Santal Evangelical Lutheran Church', in C.H. Swavely, (ed.), *The Lutheran Enterprise in India*, Madras: The Federation of Evangelical Lutheran Churches in India, 1952, pp. 106-22.

Jamtara, Karmatar and Mihijan; the American Seventh Day Adventists at Karmatar; the Wesleyan Mission and the Bengal Baptist Dipti Mission at Sahibganj and Rajmahal.

One of the first Catholic missionaries to work among the Santals was Fr. L. Knockaert, a Belgian Jesuit who worked in the district of Purnea from 1900 till 1925. On 16 April 1923, Fr. J.B. Anselmo of the Foreign Mission of Milan started work in Santal Parganas proper. He, however, could not remain long there. Seven years had to pass before Fr. B. Cauchi, a Maltese Jesuit, set up camp in Hirampur village about ten miles away from Pakur on the 5 January 1930. Since then, the Catholic Church has established itself in the district founding thirteen mission stations.[45]

One cannot study the impact of Christianity on Santal religious beliefs and practices without taking into consideration the influence of Christian missionaries on other spheres of Santal life. This is due to the fact that all the work of the missionaries was evangelical in nature. They aimed at a final conversion of the people to what they considered to be the only path to salvation. We shall, therefore, briefly portray some of the more important aspects of Christian missionary work among the Santals.

The Christian missionaries were the first to study and promote Santal language and culture. As we noted in Chapter II, they introduced a script to the Santal language, adopting the Roman script and adding various diacritical marks.[46] Their grammars and dictionaries are still considered the best source for the study of the Santal language.[47] Christian missionaries, especially Skrefsrud and Bodding, have left us invaluable data on the various aspects of Santal culture and way of life.

[45]For a historical study of the work done by the Catholic missionaries in Santal Parganas see Troisi, J., '50 Anni fra i Santals', *Popoli e Missioni*, Milan, Nov. 1974, pp. 4-7.

[46]The Santals did not have a script of their own and at first the Bengali script was used followed by the Devanagari script in some parts of Bihar. The Oriya script was also used in certain parts of Orissa.

[47]As early as 1845, Rev. Jeremiah Phillips published in Santali, *An Introduction to the Santal language*. In 1873 Skrefsrud published A *Grammar of the Santhal Language*. Bodding's *Materials for a Santali Grammar* published in two parts over 1923-29, is still considered the best source for an advanced study of the Santal language.

The Christian missionaries have also been the pioneers in the spread of education among the Santals. Education has been part of their missionary activity from the very beginning, to such an extent that missionary work and education have proceeded side by side. Rev. Jeremiah Phillips founded the first Santal primary school in 1845. The schools which the Rev. E. Droese had started in 1850 at Bhagalpur soon achieved great importance. Mr. G. Yule, the then British Commissioner at Bhagalpur, noticed that the Santals who had attended these mission schools did not take part in the rebellion. As a result, when the rebellion was over, he proposed to the Government that schools be established all over the new district of Santal Parganas in co-operation with the Church Missionary Society. In 1862, the Government sanctioned a grant-in-aid equal to half of the expenses of the Santal schools already established or those to be established under the supervision of this Protestant society.[48]

By the end of the nineteenth century, a number of schools and boarding houses managed by the Protestant and Catholic missions were opened in different parts of the district for the education of Santal boys and girls.[49] There are also four teachers' training schools in the district. Most of the Santal leaders have been educated in these mission schools.

The missionaries' work in the district was not only confined to education. The record of Christian missionaries has also been very creditable with regard to medical care and social welfare. The missionaries run a number of hospitals and dispensaries which are used not only by Christians but also by non-Christians as well as by Hindus and Mohammedans in the vicinity.[50]

[48]Gausdal, op. cit., pp. 106-22.

[49]Among the best schools run by the Santal Mission of the Northern Churches we find those at Bandarjuri, Basetkundi, Kaerabani, Koraya and Moharo. The Church Missionary Society has schools at Taljhari, Patra, Bhagaya and Dhorompur. The American Methodist Episcopal Mission runs schools at Chandrapura and Pakur. The Catholic missionaries run two Cambridge schools, at Sahibganj and Madhupur, three high schools, at Dudhani, Guhiajori and Tinpahar, and a number of middle and primary schools. For an account of the spread of missionary education in Santal Parganas see K.K. Basu (1954:178-83).

[50]The Santal Mission of Northern Churches runs a hospital at Mohulpahari which also serves as a training centre for nurses and

As we stated earlier, contact with Christianity took place at a time when the Santals were economically destitute, faced with starvation and overcome by the helplessness of their situation. Wherever the oppression of the landlords and money-lenders was mostly felt, the Santals turned to the Christian missionaries who helped the down-trodden Santals to secure justice for themselves. The missionaries have been foremost in bringing facts of oppression to the notice of the authorities.[51] In many instances, they also fought in the law courts for the vindication of the Santals' rights against their oppressors.[52] Moreover, pecuniary assistance in the form of loans at reasonable rates of interest, was given to the Santals to help them recover their lands and also to buy seeds and agricultural implements.[53]

These educational and philanthropic activities of the missionaries have undoubtedly been of immense benefit to the Santal Christians and have also indirectly benefited the non-Christians as well. They made a deep impression on the Santals and, in many cases, acted as an impetus to conversion. A number of Santals became Christians as a result of their contact with Christian teaching in mission schools. Moreover, non-Christian parents began realising that the children of their Christian converts were improving their economic condition and prospects through education imparted in mission schools. The study and promotion of the Santal language and literature together with the printing press which Skrefsrud started in Benagaria in 1879

midwives, and a big leper colony situated between Katikhund and Gopikandor. The Church Missionary Society runs a big hospital at Hiranpur and a dispensary at Dhorompur. The American Methodist Episcopal Mission has a hospital at Chandrapura about twenty-four miles from Pakur, and a dispensary at Pakur itself. The Catholic missionaries have five dispensaries and one leprosy clinic in the district.

[51]McAlpin, M.C., *A Report on the Condition of the Santals in the Districts of Birbhum, Bankura, Midnapore and North Balasore*, Calcutta: Bengal Secretariat Press, 1909.

[52]Knockaert, L., *Two Months among the Santals (6th Feb.-27th Mar. 1915)*, Calcutta: Catholic Orphan Press, 1951; *Further Progress among the Santals (21st Feb.-15th April 1916)*, Calcutta: Catholic Orphan Press, 1917.

[53]Giri, S.Y., 'Santhals of Assam', in V. Raghaviah, (ed.), *Tribes of India*, Vol. 1, New Delhi: Bharatiya Adimjati Sevak Sangh, 1969, pp. 231-33; Culshaw, (1949:64-5).

helped to circulate religious and educational books among the Santals in their own language.

Most of the early Christian converts, however, were converted in order to gain freedom from oppression. As Knockaert reported in his journal, 'Show the Santal an interest in his land and you have found a way to his heart'.[54] By defending the poor Santals against the extortion of the landlords and money-lenders, many Santals were induced to join the Christian fold. They thought that in order to deserve the powerful patronage of the influential missionaries, they had first to do what the missionaries asked from them in matters of religion. The influence which the European missionaries carried with the Government during the British days gave a further impetus to conversion.

Having shown how the Christian missionaries have exercised a certain influence on various spheres of the Santals' cultural life, we are now in a better position to analyse the influence which Christianity had on Santal religion in particular. Despite the unceasing work of the missionaries and of the various inducements which they offered, only a small proportion of the Santals in the district of Santal Parganas has entered the Christian Church.[55] Similarly, the influence of Christianity on the Santal religion has been extremely limited. When one analyses the factors as to why Christianity has not made more headway, one has to take into account the various traditional backgrounds of the missionary societies, especially of the pioneer missionaries.

Puritanism is one of the reasons why Christianity has not made a greater impact. The conservative and puritanical stands regarding drink and sex to be found in some of the Christian traditions represented by the missionaries, especially the Lutherans and the CMS, led to the propagation of total abstinence from rice-beer drinking and from participation in certain social dances. These Protestant missionaries considered the drinking of rice-beer as degrading and the dances as obscene. They also exhorted their converts not to play the *tamak* and the

[54]Knockaert, op. cit., 1914, p. 20.

[55]Only about four to five per cent of the total Santal community in Santal Parganas are Christians.

tumdak, the Santal traditional drums, lest they be tempted to participate in the tribal dancing. Their insistence on the obscene character of these dances has infused in the Santal Christian a sense of immorality. In view of these puritanical sanctions, Santals frequently object that if they were to become Protestants they would have to give up their *raska* which is an essential part of their right way to live.

The word *raska* is often on the lips of the Santals and it is dear to their hearts.[56] They turn from their difficulties and sorrows to find solace in one or other of the many ways in which they can experience *raska*—dancing, singing, drinking and eating. Pleasure means more to the Santals as a living experience than its English equivalent can suggest. As the Santals think of it, 'pleasure' is pre-eminently a social phenomenon. In view of all this, the lives of the Santal Christians who are excluded from participating in these traditional manifestations of tribal rejoicing, appear colourless.

The most deep-rooted objection, however, is the fact that the Christian method of evangelisation often tended to draw the Santals out of their own milieu, consequently posing a serious problem to tribal solidarity and making the converts feel insecure. The Santals saw in Christianity, especially as preached by the rigid Protestant sects, something that threatened to become a disintegrating influence in their society. The majority of the participants to the All-India Santal Social Assembly (13-16th April 1978) agreed that large-scale conversion to other religions directly resulted in a loss of identity. The individual Santal knows of no security apart from his village and tribe. His life is moulded within the framework of tribal laws and customs which regulate all his relationships with the visible and the invisible world. The aim of all these customs and regulations is to secure prosperity and safety both to the individual and to his tribe as a whole.

We shall now analyse the differential approach of Protestantism especially of the Lutheran and CMS missionaries and of Catholicism to the Santal religious and cultural institutions.

[56]Traditionally, when a Santal meets another from a distant place, one of the first questions asked would be 'How is pleasure in your region'?

Both Catholicism and Protestantism, like other semitic religions, are highly normative and intolerant of divided allegiance. Both of them, by claiming uniqueness in terms of religious identity, demanded from their Santal converts a drastic change in their religious adherence. Accepting the Christian theology involved a rejection of the belief and worship of *bongas*. Any sort of religious compromise was ruled out. The efforts of the Christian missionaries were by and large aimed at destroying, as far as possible, the faith of the Santals in their *bongas*. As we pointed out in Chapter III, they identified *Maran Buru* with Satan, the cause of all evil. All *bongas* were, in turn, thought of as demons.

In order to protect the faith of their converts and to safeguard their Christian identity, the missionaries tended to be highly normative, in the sense that they set norms to control the behaviour of their members both within and outside the religious sphere. The converts were cut off from any activity that savoured of *bonga* worship. They were forbidden to partake of any ritual sacrifice and ceremony in honour of the village *bongas*, the *abge*, *orak* and ancestral *bongas*. They were also tabooed from calling upon the services of an *ojha* in the case of sickness or any other calamity and from contributing in cash or in kind to the offerings associated with village festivals. This highly normative approach as a boundary maintenance mechanism in the cultural and social sphere, was not used uniformly by the Protestant and Catholic missionaries. The Protestants, especially the Lutheran and CMS missionaries, tended to be more rigid, sanctioning other forms of behaviour which had very little to do with religion. This Protestant approach was determined largely by their puritanical religious tradition, which, as mentioned earlier, made them disapprove of rice-beer drinking and dancing. The Catholic missionaries tended to be more accommodating and liberal regarding those customs which were not in direct conflict with the Christian faith. Thus, for example, their converts were not completely discouraged from rice-beer drinking and dancing unless carried to excess.

Moreover, the Protestant missionaries thought that in order to convert the Santals, they had to isolate them from their own milieu. The Santal way of life, values and norms had to be changed and the values, attitudes, behavioural patterns and way of life of the 'colonisers' had to be adopted. It is indeed a paradox that the very people who were the first to study and promote Santal culture, exhibited such ethnocentric tendencies. They tended to identify Christianity with their own particular culture and often evaluated various Santal laws and customs against this background which they tried to impose on the Santals. Change was, therefore, unidirectional and adaptation, if any, was indeed minimal. They tended to take away the Santals from the moral and social sanctions under which they had lived and grown. This attitude is very well expressed in Bodding's remark that the Protestant missionaries tried to make Christian Santals rather than Santal Christians. In other words, what they considered to be of primary importance was the fact that a person was first a Christian and then a Santal. Trying to evangelise the Santals by such a 'substituting' approach, tended to disrupt the tribe's unity and cohesion. It alienated the Santal convert from his own tribe. He was immediately aware of certain tensions and cleavages which issued progressively in a breaking away from his old way of life, beliefs and practices.

In Chapter IV we pointed out that the Santal village festivals are a potent source as well as a reflection of the community solidarity. The whole village takes part. Dancing and rice-beer drinking occupy a very important role on all these festive occasions. They add to the social character of these community celebrations. Rice-beer is so important that nothing of a public character can be ratified without the drinking of *handi*. The ceremonial drinking of rice-beer ratifies the alliance entered into by the Santals with their *bongas*. The provision of rice-beer is also important in showing hospitality to visitors. As a consequence, the ban on rice-beer drinking and on participation in tribal dancing has excluded the Santal Christians from the communal rejoicing, which takes place during the village festivals. As a result:

> it is impossible to live in a village at the time of the great Spring and Harvest festivals without becoming acutely aware of the gulf which divided the Christians from their neighbours, and without realising that the Christians are themselves deeply conscious of the gulf (Culshaw, 1949:176).

Another main factor in producing tension lies in the sphere of marriage laws. Although the village Santal Christian abhors the thought of inter-marriage, a few individuals have ignored the rule of tribal endogamy and have contracted marriages against which there are no Christian sanctions. Similarly, while cross-cousin marriage is not tolerated among the non-Christians, among the Santal Christians it is not prohibited. On the other hand, while there is no bar for a Santal non-Christian to marry more than one wife, this practice is strictly prohibited among the Santal Christians. Similarly, divorce can be obtained by the Santal non-Christian, but is completely tabooed for a Christian. It naturally follows that no Christian can enter into *sanga* marriage or marriage between divorcees. *Kirin jawae bapla* or marriage by the purchase of a husband for an unmarried mother is likewise tabooed for a Santal Christian. Christians are also discouraged from marrying non-Christians unless the latter are willing to be baptised.

A cleavage between the converts and their community also arises as a result of the substantial changes in the rites and ceremonies which surround a Santal's life-cycle. While for the Santal non-Christian the most important birth ritual and ceremony is the *Janam Chatiar*, for the Santal Christian it is Baptism. In the former, the child is given the protection of the tribal *bongas* and those of his father's, in the latter he renounces all association with the *bongas*. The pastor officiates during the baptism ceremony which usually occurs sometime during the child's first year and which takes place in a church and not in the child's house. In some places, most of the villagers gather for the ceremony, while in other villages only Christians take part.

The preliminaries for a Christian marriage are much akin to a Santal non-Christian marriage. The role of the *raebaric*, the exchange of presents and the payment of bride-price are usually observed in Christian families just as in non-Christian ones. The parents of Christian girls tend to demand a higher bride-price than the non-Christians. The marriage ceremony, however, is shorn of the tribal rites invoking the spirits. Thus, the *Dak Bapla*, the *Ul Sakam Tol* ceremonies and the sacrificial offerings at the *manjhithan* are not observed. The ceremony has to be conducted in accordance with the provisions of the Indian

Christian Marriage Act. It is normally held in a church and is officiated at by a pastor. While among the non-Christians, the most important part of the marriage ceremony is the *Sindradan*, or smearing of the bride's forehead with vermilion, among the Christians, the exchange of rings by bride and groom marks them as husband and wife. The applying of *sindur* is tabooed. The bride and groom are not dressed in saffron clothes, nor is the bride carried in a *daura*. Similarly, while among the non-Christians the whole village is a witness to the marital contract, among the Christians four relatives, two from the groom's party and two from the bride's party act as witnesses. In the funerary ceremonies, there is little trace of non-Christian customs and modes of thought. Non-Christians normally keep away from the house of the dead person and will have nothing to do with the disposal of the dead body. The pastor officiates in this ceremony. The grave is dug lengthwise from east to west and the head of the corpse is placed towards the west. The subsequent *Tel Nahan* and *Bhandan* ritual ceremonies are altogether absent.

Becoming a Christian is not in itself an offence for which there is any established penalty. However, as a result of the rigid Protestant norms of behaviour not only in the religious sphere but also in the social and cultural spheres of Santal life, the converts are, by and large, being alienated from their village communities. Moreover, converts also become estranged from their own kinsfolk. They are prohibited by their own religion from taking part in the ritual offerings and ceremonies which are associated with the worship of the *abge*, *orak* and ancestral *bongas*. These ritual practices and ceremonies as noted in Chapter III, act as a strong unifying force among the household and family members. In view of this, the influence of kinsfolk often serves to hinder a person from becoming a Christian.

A change in religion has similarly brought about changes in food habits, attitudes to education, health and sanitation, etc. We have already seen how Santal Christians were encouraged to take to tea instead of rice-beer. Santal Christian women are adopting the use of sarees, blouses and petticoats, while men are taking to wearing pants and shirts. The level of aspiration of the Santal Christians is higher than that of the non-Christians. They send their children to mission boarding schools after which, those who are economically better off, go to college either in Sahibganj, Dumka or Ranchi. The educated Santal Christians are following a wide range of occupations, most of which are unknown to the older generation of Santals. Santal Christians are also politically more active than the non-Christian Santals. In short, it can be said that the Santal Christian tends to cease being a typical representative of his community.

Cutting themselves off from many aspects of their old community life, the converts find themselves members of a new community, the Christian community.[57] This community is more than a mere aggregate of individuals and households. It possesses a social life of its own. Its corporate life manifests itself in a new symbolism and is fostered by a new ritual. In the traditional framework, a Santal village functions as an 'isolate' entity insofar as it has its own sacred places—the *jaherthan* and the *manjhithan*, and religious functionaries—the *naeke* and *kudam naeke*. The new community, however, cuts across the village boundaries centering on the church and the pastor.

The Santals of Pangro have a small brick-walled chapel which serves as the socio-religious centre of the Christian community. Every Sunday afternoon, the Christians of Pangro gather together for their religious services during which they pray and sing together. The prayers are conducted by Bhattu Murmu who acts as a village catechist. Once a month, however, Daniel Hasdak, a Santal pastor belonging to the Church Missionary Society, conducts the services which are also attended by Protestants from the neighbouring villages of Nirepara and Adro. Baptisms and marriages are also conducted in this chapel. Such services also serve as an occasion for social intercourse. The main festivals of the Christian community are Christmas, New Year and Easter. As described in Chapter IV, Christmas is celebrated as the Santal *Sohrae*. The traditional *Janthar* festival is celebrated by the Christians on New Year's day.

Catholic missionaries have been trying to incarnate the Christian message into the Santal milieu by blending the Santal

[57]Culshaw (1949:175-94).

tribal customs with the Christian liturgical rites. An attempt is also being made to integrate a number of traditional Santal festivals connected with agricultural activities like the *Baha*, *Erok*, and *Hariar* into the Christian annual festival cycle. In this manner, the Santal Catholics are not only allowed but encouraged to express the Christian reality through their own life and culture. This adaptation process, though still in its infancy, has met with considerable success. This can be seen from the fact that there are more Santal Catholics in the district than Protestants. Besides, in the last few years, there has been a steady flow of Santal Protestants into the Catholic Church.

On the one hand, Christianity has brought about an intra-village fusion insofar as the convert is to a certain extent alienated from the village community into which he was born. On the other hand, it has promoted inter-village cohesion of Christian groups. This cohesion among Santal Christian groups is also extended to Christians from other tribes. This sense of belonging, however, is stronger among Catholics than among Protestants because of the latter's sectarian nature of their religious allegiance.

From the data presented in this chapter it appears that the more normative a religion is the less seems to have been its impact on Santal religious beliefs and practices. Thus, a highly normative religion like Christianity which sets norms to control the behaviour of its members not only in the religious but also in the social and cultural spheres, appeared to the Santals to threaten their social and cultural autonomy and, to a certain extent, their tribal solidarity. As a result, it is very difficult for an individual Santal to become a Christian. Though not ostracised from his community, he is in many ways alienated from it. In view of this, as Culshaw remarks:

> The most usual response to the appeal of the preacher is expressed in the words: 'Yes your religion is good and some day we shall all become Christians: but—we shall wait until all of us can do it together' (1949:169).

Hinduism, on the other hand, as a more tolerant and less normative religion, allowed the Santals to borrow new religious ideas and practices in such a way that the autonomous charac ter of their religious, social and cultural institutions was not undermined. Unlike the adoption of Christian beliefs and practices, Hindu beliefs and rituals could be grafted on to the Santal religion without necessitating its assimilation or total absorption into Hinduism. Another point to be kept in mind is that 'popular Hinduism' is widely diffused and affects the Santals in numerous ways without their being conscious of it.

This relationship between the normative character of a religious tradition and its impact on Santal religion needs, however, to be further specified so as to explain its complex nature. Thus, we notice a differential influence of the religious trends within Hinduism on Santal religion. It would appear that while 'popular Hinduism' which is less normative, has had a considerable impact on Santal religion, 'sectarian Hinduism' which is highly normative, has exercised only a passing and relatively peripheral influence on Santal religion. As we saw in Chapters III and IV, the Santals have borrowed a number of deities, festivals, customs and concepts from 'popular Hinduism' which, by and large, have become an integral part of Santal religion without, however, changing its basic character. On the other hand, the religious symbols and practices, such as the giving up of the use of beef and rice beer, taking to vegetarian-ism and *ganja* instead, adopting the habit of daily purificatory baths and the use of the sacred thread, which were borrowed from 'sectarian Hinduism', were used only to manage specific crisis situations. Many Santals who had become members of such Hindu sects as the *Sapha Hor*, *Samra* and *Babajiu*, after some time relinquished them and went back to their traditional beliefs and practices. Similarly, in Christianity itself, certain Protestant sects, for example, the Lutherans and the Church Missionary Society, which were highly normative not only within but also outside the religious sphere, tended to be less influential in their impact on Santal religion. Catholicism, on the other hand, being less normative and more liberal and tolerant of Santal social and cultural autonomy, had a greater appeal for the Santals.

We have seen how Santal religion, has been able to interact with two major religions, Hinduism and Christianity, without losing its distinctive identity and its appeal for the majority of the Santals. The belief in the *bongas* is still strong. Similarly, the more important annual festivals (Chapter IV) and the rites of passage (Chapter V) are still observed in many Santal villages. These religious beliefs and practices bind the community together to the tribal spirits and to their ancestors and, thereby, their tribal solidarity is strengthened. This study, therefore, suggests the need to re-examine the commonly accepted anthropological assumption that the survival of tribal religions is rather doubtful when they are in continuous contact with and subjected to the impact of dominant religious traditions.

Appendix I

DISTRICTWISE DISTRIBUTION OF THE SANTALS IN THE STATE OF BIHAR, 1971

		Total Population	*All Scheduled Tribes*	*Santals*
BIHAR		56,353,369	4,932,767	1,801,304
Patna Division		11,953,452	42,540	619
Patna	Dist.	3,556,945	2,276	197
Gaya	,,	4,457,473	1,538	406
Shahabad	,,	3,939,034	38,726	16
Tirhut Division		17,896,941	25,394	229
Saran	Dist.	4,279,253	1,433	19
Champaran	,,	3,543,103	22,860	79
Muzaffarpur	,,	4,840,681	766	32
Darbhanga	,,	5,233,904	335	99
Bhagalpur Division		15,462,751	1,449,225	1,204,138
Monghyr	Dist.	3,892,609	54,916	44,425
Bhagalpur	,,	2,091,103	75,056	49,714
Saharsa	,,	2,350,268	9,159	5,941
Purnea	,,	3,941,963	155,813	100,239
Santal Parg.	,,	3,186,908	1,154,281	1,003,819

		Total Population	*All Scheduled Tribes*	*Santals*
Chotanagpur Division		11,040,225	3,415,608	596,318
Palamau	Dist.	1,504,350	287,150	47
Hazaribagh	,,	3,020,214	331,798	203,165
Ranchi	,,	2,611,445	1,516,698	1,407
Dhanbad	,,	1,466,417	155,645	126,163
Singhbhum	,,	2,437,799	1,124 317	165,536

Source: *Census of India 1971*, Series 4, Bihar, Part V, ST-II, 'Age and Marital Status for Scheduled Tribes' (unpublished).

Census of India 1971, Series I, India, Part II-A, 'General Population Tables', pp. 56-7.

Appendix II

DISTRICTWISE DISTRIBUTION OF THE SANTALS IN THE STATE OF WEST BENGAL 1971

		Total Population	All Scheduled Tribes	Santals
WEST BENGAL		44,312,011	2,532,969	1,376,980
Jalpaiguri Division		7,418,663	899,824	305,512
Darjeeling	Dist.	781,777	108,586	10,335
Jalpaiguri	,,	1,750,159	428,595	71,539
Cooch Bihar	,,	1,414,183	10,611	2,880
West Dinajpur	,,	1,859,887	221,317	130,473
Malda	,,	1,612,657	130,715	90,285
Presidency Division		19,185,988	213,715	70,886
Murshidabad	Dist.	2,940,204	38,947	28,220
Nadia	,,	2,230,270	31,799	8,523
24 Parganas	,,	8,449,482	137,197	31,447
Howrah	,,	2,417,286	3,364	1,242
Calcutta	,,	3,148,746	2,408	1,454
Burdwan Division		17,707,360	1,419,430	1,000,582
Hooghly	Dist.	2,872,116	100,084	75,132
Burdwan	,,	3,916,174	228,605	180,280

		Total Population	*All Scheduled Tribes*	*Santals*
Birbhum	Dist.	1,775,909	125,250	104,722
Bankura	,,	2,031,039	208,735	157,806
Midnapore	,,	5,509,247	442,963	286,010
Purulia	,,	1,602,875	313,793	196,632

Source: *Census of India 1971*, Series 22, West Bengal, Part V, ST-II, 'Age and Marital Status for Scheduled Tribes' (unpublished).

Census of India 1971, Series I, India, Part II-A, 'General Population Tables', p. 70.

Select Bibliography

Archer, W.G., *The Hill of Flutes: Life, Love and Poetry in Tribal India. A Portrait of the Santals*, London: George Allen & Unwin, 1974.

Berger, Peter L., *The Sacred Canopy: Elements of a Sociological Theory of Religion*, New York: Doubleday & Company Inc., 1969.

Bodding, Paul Olaf, 'The Santals and Disease', *Memoirs of the Asiatic Society of Bengal*, Calcutta, 10 (1), 1925, pp. 1-132.

———*A Santal Dictionary*, Vol. 1, 1932; Vol. 2, 1934; Vol. 3, 1935a; Vol. 4, 1935b; Vol. 5, 1936; Oslo: A.W. Broggers Boktrykheri.

———*Traditions and Institutions of the Santals*, Oslo: A.W. Broggers Boktrykheri, 1942.

Campbell, A., 'Superstitions of the Santals', *Journal of the Bihar and Orissa Research Society*, Patna, 1(2), June 1915, pp. 213-38.

Crooke, William, *Religion and Folklore of Northern India*, Delhi: S. Chand & Co. Pvt. Ltd., 1925.

Culshaw, W.J., 'Some Notes on Bongaism', *Journal of the Asiatic Society of Bengal (Letters)*, Calcutta, 5, 1939, pp.427-31.

———*Tribal Heritage: A Study of the Santals*, London: Lutterworth Press, 1949.

Datta-Majumder, Nabendu, *The Santal: A Study in Culture-Change*, Calcutta: Manager of Publications, Govt. of India Press, 1956.

Datta, Kalikinkar, *The Santal Insurrection of 1855-1857*, Calcutta: University of Calcutta, 1940.

Douglas, Mary, *Purity and Danger—An Analysis of Concepts of Pollution and Taboo*, Harmondsworth, Middlesex: Penguin Books, 1966.

Dubre, Wilhelm, *Religion in Primitive Cultures*, The Hague: Mouton & Co., 1975.

Durkheim, Emile, *The Elementary Forms of the Religious Life*, New York: Free Press, 1967.

Elwin, Verrier, *Religion of an Indian Tribe*, Bombay: Oxford University Press, 1955.

Evans-Pritchard, E.E., *Nuer Religion*, Oxford: Clarendon Press, 1956.

———*Theories of Primitive Religion*, Oxford: Clarendon Press, 1965.

———(ed.), *The Institutions of Primitive Society*, Oxford: Basil Blackwell, 1954.

Fuchs, Stephen, *Rebellious Prophets*, Calcutta: Asia Publishing House, 1965.

———*Origin of Religion*, Kerala: Pontifical Institute of Theology and Philosophy, 1975.

Furer-Haimendorf, Christoph von, 'The After Life in Indian Tribal Belief', *Journal of the Royal Anthropological Society*, London, 83(1), January-June 1953, pp. 37-49.

Gausdal, Johannes, *The Santal Khuts*, Oslo: H. Aschchoug & Co., 1960.

Gennep, Arnold van, *The Rites of Passage*, trans. by M.B. Veyedom & G.L. Chafee, London: Routledge, 1960.

Gluckman, Max, (ed.), *Essays on the Ritual of Social Relations*, Manchester: University Press, 1962.

Goode, William J., *Religion among the Primitives*, London: The Free Press of Glencoe, Collier-Macmillan Ltd., 1964.

Harper, E.B., (ed.), *Religion in South Asia*, Seattle: University of Washington Press, 1964.

Hubert, Henri, and Marcel, Mauss, *Sacrifice: Its Nature and Function*, Chicago: University of Chicago Press, 1964.

Hunter, W.W., *The Annals of Rural Bengal*, (reprint), Delhi: Cosmo Publications, 1975.

Kalia, S.L., 'Sanskritisation and Tribalisation', in T.B., Naik, (ed.), *Changing Tribe*, Chindwara: Tribal Research Institute, 1961.

Kochar, V.K., 'Family Spirits and Deities among the Santals and Associated Rituals', *Journal of the Asiatic Society of Bengal*, Calcutta, 5(3-4), 1963, pp. 59-71.

Levi-Strauss, Claude, *The Savage Mind*, Chicago: Chicago University Press, 1968.

Lienhardt, Godfrey, *Divinity and Experience: The Religion of the Dinka*, Oxford: Clarendon Press, 1961.

Majumdar, Dhirendra Nath, *A Tribe in Transition: A Study in Culture Pattern*, London: Longmans Green & Co., 1937.

Malinowski, Bronislaw, *Magic, Science and Religion and other Essays*, New York: Doubleday Anchor Books, 1954.

———*Coral Gardens and their Magic*, 2 vols., Bloomington: Indiana University Press, 1965.

Man, E.G., *Sonthalia and the Sonthals*, Calcutta: Geo Wyman & Co., 1867.

Marwick, Marvin G., (ed.), *Witchcraft and Sorcery*, Harmondsworth, Middlesex: Penguin Books, 1970.

Moore, O.K., 'Divination: A New Perspective', *American Anthropologist*, Wisconsin, 59(1), February 1957, pp. 69-74.

Mukherjea, Charulal, *The Santals*, Calcutta: A. Mukherjee & Co. Pvt.

Ltd., 2nd revised edition, 1962.

Mukhopadhyay, Sankarananda, *The Austrics of India*, Calcutta: K.P. Bagchi & Co., 1975.

O' Dea, Thomas F., *The Sociology of Religion*, New Delhi:. Prentice Hall of India Pvt. Ltd., 1969.

O' Malley, L.S.S., *Bengal District Gazetteers, Vol. 22, Santal Parganas*, Calcutta: Bengal Secretariat Book Depot, 1910.

Orans, Martin, *The Santal A Tribe in Search of a Great Tradition*, Detroit: Wayne State University Press, 1965.

Park, G.K., 'Divination and Its Social Context', *Journal of the Royal Anthropological Institute*, London, 93(2), 1963, pp. 195-209.

Presler, Henry H., *Primitive Religions in India*, Bangalore: Christian Literature Society Press, 1971.

Radcliffe-Brown, A.R., *Structure and Function in Primitive Society*, London: Cohen & West Ltd., 1959.

———*The Andaman Islanders*, New York: The Free Press, 1964.

Roy, Sarat Chandra, *The Mundas and Their Country*, (reprint), Bombay: Asia Publishing House, 1970.

———*Oraon Religion and Customs*, (reprint), Calcutta: Editions Indian, 1972.

Roy, Sarat Chandra, and R.C., Roy, *The Kharias*, 2 vols., Ranchi: Man in India Office, 1937.

Roy Chaudhury, P.C. *Bihar District Gazetteers. Santal Parganas*, Patna: The Superintendent, Secretariat Press, 1965.

Sachchidananda, *The Tribal Village in Bihar*, Delhi: Oriental Publishers, 1968.

Scharf, Betty R., *The Sociological Study of Religion*, London: Hutchinson & Co. (Publishers) Ltd , 1973.

Schmidt, W., *The Origin and Growth of Religion: Facts and Theories*, London: Methuen, 1931

Skrefsrud, Lars Olsen, *Horkoren Mare Hapramko Reak Katha*, (7th edition), Benagaria: Santal Mission Press, 1968.

Srinivas, M.N., *Religion and Society among the Coorgs of South India*, Bombay: Asia Publishing House, 1952.

Swanson, Guy E., *The Birth of the Gods, the Origin of Primitive Beliefs*, Ann Arbor: The University of Michigan Press, 1960.

Troisi, J., *The Santals: A Classified and Annotated Bibliography*, Delhi: Manohar, 1976.

Turner, Bryan S., 'Belief, Ritual and Experience: The case of Methodism', *Social Compass*, Louvain, 18(2), 1971, pp. 187-201.

Turner, Victor W., 'Ritual, Tribal and Catholic', *Worship*, Minnesota, 50(6), November 1976, pp 504-26.

Vidyarthi, L.P., (ed.), *Aspects of Religion in Indian Society*, Meerut: Kedar Nath Ram Nath, 1961.

———and Binay Kumar, Rai, *The Tribal Culture of India*, Delhi: Concept Publishing Company, 1977.

Wach, J., *Sociology of Religion*, Chicago: University of Chicago Press, Phoenix Edition, 1962.

Author Index

Subject Index